PROJECTIVE
AND INTROJECTIVE
IDENTIFICATION
AND THE USE OF
THE THERAPIST'S SELF

COMMENTARY

"Most welcome of all for the reader is Dr. Scharff's ability to write with both liveliness and clarity. Her admirably scholarly review of relevant literature is distilled for the reader in readily understandable terms, as she enables us to follow the development of her authentically original views concerning projective and introjective identification—views based in part on the contributions of earlier writers, but in larger part on her own clinical experiences with patients in diverse treatment settings. Dr. Jill Scharff is an immensely creative clinician and a writer who will, I am sure, illuminate other readers' lives and work as she has illuminated, for me, my own life and work."   **—Harold Searles, M.D.**

"Jill Scharff provides ample and detailed descriptions of her use of countertransference experience in the understanding of therapeutic interaction and the formulation of interpretations and other therapeutic interventions. It is only in the rare instance that there are countertransference data of the sort provided by Scharff that it is possible to portray and analyze the moment-to-moment experience of being with a patient. I consider this book to be a major contribution to the analytic understanding of the therapeutic process and feel that it is essential reading for clinicians engaged in analytic work with individuals, couples, families, and groups."
—Thomas Ogden, M.D.

"A master therapist, Dr. Scharff is also a writer who brings the consulting room alive. Her descriptions, both of her patients as she works with them moment to moment and of her own immediate reactions, creates an in-depth picture of therapy in action that is as rare as it is valuable. By demonstrating how she uses the concepts of projective and introjective identification in her own work, Dr. Scharff has enlarged our vision and has enriched our understanding of the therapeutic process. A scholarly text, a teaching guide, a casebook for practitioners, this is a unique work that should be read by students and experienced therapists alike."
—Theodore Jacobs, M.D.

PROJECTIVE AND INTROJECTIVE IDENTIFICATION AND THE USE OF THE THERAPIST'S SELF

Jill Savege Scharff, M.D.

JASON ARONSON INC.
Northvale, New Jersey
London

Production and interior design: *Gloria L. Jordan*
Editorial Director: *Muriel Jorgensen*

This book was set in 11/14 Goudy
by Alpha Graphics of New Hampshire
and printed and bound by Haddon Craftsmen
of Pennsylvania

Library of Congress Cataloging-in-Publication Data

Scharff, Jill Savege.
    Projective and introjective identification and the use of the
therapist's self / Jill Savege Scharff.
        p.   cm.
    Includes bibliographical references and index.
    ISBN 0-87668-530-0
    1. Countertransference (Psychology)   2. Projection (Psychology)
3. Introjection.   I. Title.
    [DNLM: 1. Countertransference (Psychology)   2. Identification
(Psychology)   3. Projection.   4. Regression (Psychology)   5. Self
Disclosure.   WM 460.5.I4 S311p]
RC489.C68S33   1991
616.89'14—dc20
DNLM/DLC
for Library of Congress   91-26070

Manufactured in the United States of America. Jason Aronson Inc. offers books and cassettes. For information and catalog write to Jason Aronson Inc., 230 Livingston Street, Northvale, New Jersey 07647.

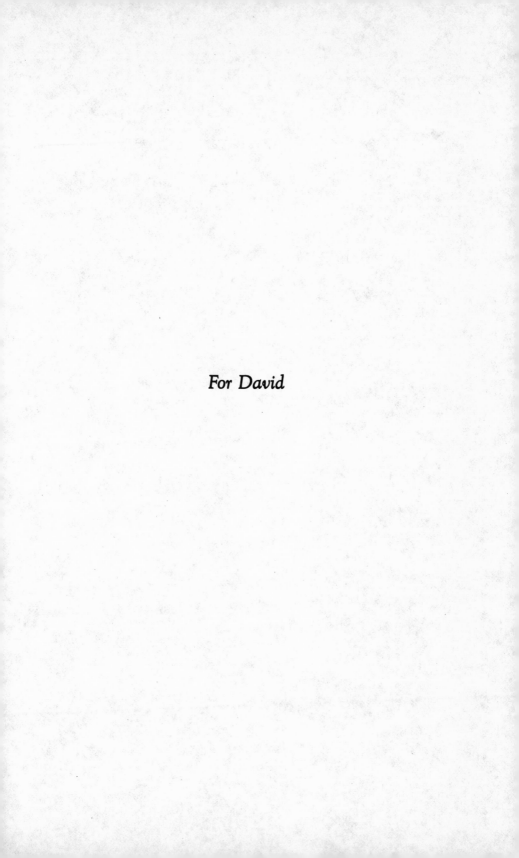

For David

Contents

Part II

PROJECTIVE AND INTROJECTIVE
IDENTIFICATION IN THE DEVELOPMENT
OF THE INDIVIDUAL, THE COUPLE,
AND THE FAMILY

Part III

PROJECTIVE AND INTROJECTIVE
IDENTIFICATION IN CULTURE

Part IV

THE USE OF THE THERAPIST'S SELF THROUGH PROJECTIVE AND INTROJECTIVE IDENTIFICATION

Illustrations

Permissions

Preface and Acknowledgments

Projective identification. We know that concept introduced by Klein and elaborated by Segal. We find it useful clinically because it gives us a way of thinking about unconscious interpersonal communication and the patient's effect on the therapist. It gives us a shorthand way of talking with our colleagues about therapeutic processes. But are we all talking about the same thing? Not in my experience. To check on my purely personal impression that we are not necessarily speaking at all about the same thing, I turned to the literature to explore the meaning of the term *projective identification*. I was drawn into a quagmire of debates and differing opinions, one more interesting than the next, until I no longer knew what I thought. The more I read, the less I knew. The more I wrote, the more I became aware of the inherent ambiguity of the term *projective identification*, spanning as it does the realms of ego and object in the intrapsychic dimension, and self and other in the interpersonal field. I was lost, bewildered, bothered—and bewitched—without even a live body as the object of fascination. In fact, my husband, well aware of the competition, regarded this piece of research as a sink into which I was pouring my best energies. Soon it became obvious that what was to have been one chapter in our co-authored book *Object Relations Couple Therapy* was turning into its own book, whether I liked it or not. I was in the grip of the topic, projective identification. I was quite thoroughly identified with, controlled by, and possessed by this object, a mere theory. There was no way out. I had no choice other than to succumb, learn, write, and hope to separate successfully from the project at the end. But the end was nowhere in sight.

Now, introjective identification. Who ever bothers to argue about that? Deep into the interpersonal aspects of projective identification, I was searching for ways to account for the object's identification with the projection. I was squeezing help out of Wilfred Bion's concept of valency and Christopher Bollas's extractive introjection. One fortuitous day, I heard Isabel Menzies-Lyth read her unpublished paper pointing out that introjective identification had been ignored in the literature. I realized that I had overextended my application of valency and extractive introjection because, like everyone else, I had been minimizing the importance of Klein's concept of introjective identification.

Now with a broader focus, I returned to my manuscript. I found myself drawn toward considering the interaction of introjective and projective processes, an orientation close to that of W. W. Meissner, whose call to abandon the term *projective identification* I had once firmly rejected. This type of about-face is par for the course. Clinically, when I deal with projective and introjective processes, I can find myself twisted this way and that. In fact, I often feel turned on my head. So it should not be a surprise that the same happens when I write a book about the topic.

Working with projective and introjective identificatory processes has given me a theory for understanding my countertransference. In focusing on this topic, I do not mean to suggest that this is the only thing going on in the therapeutic situation. A cake cannot be made only of currants, as Strachey once remarked. Many other aspects of intervention are important and contribute to the therapeutic effort. But in my experience, work with the countertransference is especially effective in enabling change. For me, introjective and projective processes in the countertransference provide the organizing principle of therapy. My reason for focusing on countertransference is to operationalize empathy and demystify the art of intuition so as to elaborate a theory that can be applied systematically to the clinical situation. The resulting clinical practice can then be taught. I hope in this way to contribute to advances in clinical technique and the practice of teaching psychoanalysis and psychotherapy.

An afterthought. Having finished this book, I have resolved some of my confusion. I have established my own position in the dialogue about projective identification. I have contributed to a wider perspective by enlarging the topic of introjective identification. Through intellectual work, I have even improved my own resolution of issues concerning the boundary between self and other. But do not think for a moment that I am free of the topic. My views continue to shift. I cannot imagine what I will think years from now, because I do not know now what I will know then. I do know that I will not know then exactly what I know now. My views on introjective and projective identification will develop in directions that this book, as I separate from it, dares not predict.

My thanks go to Susan Stein of the European Paintings Department of the Metropolitan Museum of Art who helped me to locate and approach owners for permission to reproduce the paintings here. I am also grateful to Katherine Fleet of the Impressionist and Modern Paintings and Sculpture Department of Christie, Man-

son, and Woods for lending a Van Gogh transparency on behalf of
an anonymous private collection, and to Mrs. John Hay Whitney
who donated for reproduction a glossy print of the Van Gogh
portrait. Sandy Gullikson enthusiastically and graciously provided
her pictorial and verbal images. The museums of Solothurn and
d'Orsay responded promptly to my requests for permission to
reproduce their Van Gogh paintings. Crossroads Continuum Pub-
lishing gave permission to reprint from Elias Canetti's autobiography *The Tongue Set Free*. Random House and author Maggie Scarf
gave permission to reprint from *Intimate Partners*. Melanie Fine set
the licensing fee for "Opposites Attract" at an affordable amount. I
thank all these creative artists, generous owners, helpful adminis-
trators, and publishers for enabling me to put my ideas into a wider
cultural context.

I should like to thank senior colleagues at the Washington
Psychoanalytic Institute and the American Psychoanalytic Association who contributed to my clinical formulations: Dexter Bullard,
Gunther Perdigao, David Raphling, Arthur Rosenblatt, Sidney
Salus, and especially Harold Searles who showed me how to use my
own vulnerability in my work with countertransference. I also want
to thank those who generously responded to early drafts, including
Marc Fried and Jackie Zilbach, and especially John Zinner whose
differences of opinion with me are friendly and fruitful. Thanks are
due also to L. David Levi for his enthusiasm and careful suggestions, especially those on how to make the chapter on countertransference more agreeable to the ego psychologist. Revisions and
elaborations of my ideas were inspired by visiting lecturers at the
Washington (DC) School of Psychiatry—British Independent
Group analysts Christopher Bollas, Nina Coltart, Denis Duncan,
Earl Hopper, and the late Jock Sutherland, and Kleinians Anton
Obholzer, Hanna Segal, Elizabeth Bott Spillius, John Steiner, Ar-

thur Hyatt Williams, and especially Isabel Menzies-Lyth whose comments on Chapter 3 and lecture on the forgotten concept of introjective identification transformed this book. I am grateful to Chairman David Scharff and former co-chairman Robert Winer of the WSP Object Relations Theory and Therapy Training Program for inviting me to join their excellent group of faculty colleagues in their intensive work with outstanding advanced psychotherapy students who came from widespread locations in the United States and beyond. That program's current steering committee on which I sit with Martha Chesheir, Sharon Williams Dennet, Macario Giraldo, Joyce Lowenstein, Charles McCormack, and Kent Ravenscroft, and its students and visiting lecturers provide an invaluable teaching and learning situation that, because it values content and process, encourages creative thinking and writing. I am fortunate to have such a wonderfully inspiring and encouraging professional context.

I also want to thank the patients who have chosen to work with me and in so doing have contributed to my understanding of projective and introjective processes. Those from whose material I have drawn may recognize their words but can be assured that their right to anonymity has been carefully protected. I hope that they can tolerate the revelation of my feelings and fantasies, experienced but not revealed during their treatment, knowing that I do this for a scholarly purpose. To them I owe special thanks.

Josephine Parker, my office manager and secretary, kept things under control so that I was free to write. She typed with speed and accuracy when my own developing secretarial skills became too frustrating. Pearl Green, as ever, managed the house joyfully, and drove the children to their activities when I could not tear myself away from the computer. I am grateful to have such wonderful help. Last, but by no means least, I want to thank my husband and colleague and sometime co-author David Scharff for his confidence in my autonomous work, his critical reading of the first draft, his loving support of me and our family, and his commitment to my continued professional development.

1

The Therapist's Use of Self

It is Monday morning, May 13. I am in my office ready for my first patients, a widowed mother and her two children who have trouble getting to their 7:40 A.M. appointment on time. I look at my schedule for the week and note an open hour this morning, a new couple diagnostic scheduled for 8:30 A.M., and a new psychotherapy case starting on Wednesday. I'll have to remember that the children have three dental or eye-doctor appointments and that my husband is traveling on Thursday and Friday. Thursday, I see, is the 16th, my late father's birthday. Yesterday was Mother's Day and I was missing my own mother who lives far away. At the same time, I was being celebrated as the mother in my own family and giving brunch for my motherless sister-in-law and her family. I had to face disappointment when I realized that she might not join me in a project to which I had been looking forward. Nevertheless, the day

1

went well, the sun shone, and the cousins swam and teased the afternoon away.

Now it is Monday. I have had a relaxing weekend with the usual ups and downs of family life. I like my new green-and-black blouse, my hair looks all right today, but I wish I had found time to renew my manicure. I am angry at my husband who reacted unnecessarily negatively to my comment that his clothes did not match. I am upset that he did not reach his mother on Mother's Day. I am worried about my housekeeper's health and my friend's colonoscopy scheduled for later today. The office is cool and I'm all set for the work week. My mind clears and in come the sleepy Silvers.

The children start right in to draw at the play table. For months they used to squeeze onto the couch on either side of their mother and take turns coming forward to complain about or support her. They reminded me of a Swiss weather predictor in which either a glum little person emerges and a happy one retreats, or vice versa, according to the barometric pressure. The family configuration now is quite different and I enjoy seeing them sitting in chairs at the table doing their work. Liz and Ruth talk sadly of how they miss their mother when she works late. She explains that she had to put in extra time at the office so that she could take time off for a trip to Georgia with the children for a cousin's bar mitzvah. They had a good time, but the cousins got together and excluded Liz. Now Liz is hurt and can't understand what is wrong with her. My mind floats over the events of my yesterday, with the cousins teasing each other and threatening to exclude the youngest, as usual. There's nothing wrong with him, except that he is the youngest. I can well imagine the scene at their bar mitzvah. The discussion leads usefully to Mrs. Silver's feelings of exclusion by her family. She was picked on and ostracized for being too smart for her own good and too likely to see the flaws in her parents' facade. She had paid for her own schooling in the Northeast. Her self-sufficiency, which stood her in good stead when her husband became ill and died was seen in her youth as a rejection of southern values. Her interest in therapy was perceived as a criticism of her parents' life-style.

I find myself resonating with all this at two levels. As the oldest girl in my family, I was my parents' first confrontation with a different point of view. My career choice of medicine was fine with them, but psychiatry was regarded with distaste in Scotland. Superstition was standard, but interest in the unconscious smacked of witchery. On May 12th I was not with my mother on Mother's Day, but at least on May 13th I am not worrying about spilling salt, walking under ladders, seeing black cats, or wearing green. I *am* worried about people dying, but not because it's May 13th. And as the mother of an oldest daughter, I too feel the pain of my highly valued firstborn who lost her place in the sun and had to create another spot for herself. She too thinks differently than I do. In her opinion, my way of constructing reality is psychobabble. What career will she choose? Where will she live?

But something *is* bothering me. I can't imagine why Mrs. Silver's family would actually exclude this bright, personable woman. Momentarily, I can't understand why my family is hurt that I am here and they are there. Of course, it's because Mrs. Silver and I make our families feel bad; we have rejected their values, their location, and their wishes for closeness. Perhaps I do not want to feel hurt or accused by her, as my family is hurt by me and my choices. How can I allow myself to feel what her parents or her siblings felt about her at the bar mitzvah?

As often happens, the children's play helps us along. Liz has drawn a remarkable witch with long fingernails. Her sister helps color them red and messes up the ends so that the nails look ragged and sharp like talons. Liz's drawing is signed and entitled "Good Which" (Figure 1-1). I get a noncommittal response when I ask about her drawing. Her mother and sister just go on talking. I feel pushed over. Are they unwilling to hear what I may say? Should I continue or let it go? Pondering this, I look down at my hands and see the old manicure. The nails are too long and the old red polish

Figure 1-1. Good Which.

is fraying at the edges. I feel sure that their experience of me is captured in Liz's drawing—if only I could reach it.

I say, "I am interested in the title of the drawing. It seems to me to ask which witch is this?"

Liz does not know that she has misspelled witch. "I was drawing this lady, see, and then I thought that she looked like a witch, so I called it 'which.'"

"Liz," says Mrs. Silver. "You've misspelled witch." You've put which but it should be witch."

"No I haven't," Liz retorts.

"Yes you have," says Ruth gently. "You've put w-h-i-c-h, but it should be w-i-t-c-h."

"So what? It's still a witch," Liz shoots back, correcting the spelling nonetheless.

"Well, it seems funny, because you are an excellent speller," explains Mrs. Silver. "So I think maybe Dr. Scharff is right. What do you mean, Dr. Scharff?" Her southern phrasing emphasizes the "what" so that I hear her question as What—do you mean Dr. Scharff?

"Yes, I do mean Dr. Scharff," I answer, echoing the hidden meaning of her words. "I am thinking that I'm this lady that you come to see, but maybe you are wondering if I am some kind of witch."

"No, Dr. Scharff," Liz shakes her head and looks at me as if I were hopelessly paranoid. She speaks slowly and carefully to be sure I get it. "You are not a witch. I know you are just a lady."

"I know you know that, and I know that too," I reply. "But you might think there are witchy things about me, mean things you don't like."

"Why on earth would you think that?" demands Liz.

"Okay," I say. "Here is where I got the idea. I looked at your witch's hands and then I looked at my hands with the red polish on the nails that are too long and raggedy today. So I thought which witch are we talking about, her or me?"

"No, no," protests Ruth. "I was the one who did the nails. I helped her. So she couldn't have been thinking that."

Now I connect the red nails to blood. Ruth was upset with me the week before for discussing the important event of her first period, personal information that mother had agreed to keep private from Liz.

I say, "I don't mean that this drawing is proof that Liz thinks of me as a witch. I think that her drawing of the 'which' and what you have all said about the 'which' raises the question: Are there ways in which all of you feel me to be a mean woman?"

Summoning all her spunk that so annoyed her family of origin, Mrs. Silver says, "Y'all have been saying you didn't want to come here. You say it's just that the time is too early, but . . . "

Before she can continue, Ruth asks if they could leave early today because she has a test.

But Mrs. Silver is not to be interrupted. She is just getting around to me. She leans forward in her seat, her body tense as if she is about to spring. Ruth looks anxious. Mrs. Silver looks me straight in the eye and declares venomously, "I think you *are* mean to us. You know we don't have a lot of money, but when we missed the appointment during spring break, you still charged us. I know what your policy is but I don't like it. I always pay your bill and we gave you two months' warning and you should have filled our time and not charged us. So yes, I think you are mean spirited."

I find myself withering and recoiling in the face of her compelling accusatory power. Perhaps this is what her parents wished to avoid. There is something about her tone of voice that implies this whole thing is my fault and demands that I do something about it. I consider letting her off the charge, because I feel a little guilty about taking her hard-earned money. But the family accepted my policy when they chose to work with me. I do not feel like making an exception to appease Mrs. Silver. I know that the anger felt toward me in the transference is of an intensity that goes way beyond the meaning of money. I also think of their anger at being left since

Mr. Silver's death without their previous level of financial support and without a man. That would be hard for me, as it is for my mother. "I know that my policy is hard for you," I acknowledged. "And I know it takes a lot to come here. It also takes a lot to tell me how angry you are about it."

"I am angry. I wouldn't have said that, but Liz's drawing really pulled me into realizing it." Mrs. Silver smiles and relaxes. She hasn't required me to do anything after all. She just wants to be taken seriously and not avoided. "Your drawing really helped me, so thank you, Liz."

Liz beamed for the first time. Often it was her role in the family to whine and echo her mother's complaint about things being unfair. Here she was doing something that enabled her mother to speak for herself.

"I think that Ruth may be angry at me too," I continue. "You were upset with me for talking about your period openly instead of keeping it a secret from your sister."

"That's true," Ruth admits. "Some things are private. You're a psychiatrist. You should know that."

My own children have said the same thing to me exactly, and for the same reason. As a family, they are worried that angry feelings, anxieties, and questions about maturing sexually cannot be addressed respectfully within the family.

"Well, I just want to say," announces Liz, from her new position of esteem. "I did not tell a single soul."

"Good, Liz, you understand when family members' feelings and experiences are private," I say. "And today your drawing asked your question and paved the way for Mom and Ruth to share their feelings. It's time to finish."

Off they go. I have a few minutes for reflection. This session has gone well. The family whose anger usually circles around them, defeating their family goals and lowering their self-esteem, has been able to express some rage directly in its transference to me as the working woman who goes after money and as the absent father from whom they were separated by death. I feel that I was resonating with their issues; my own vulnerabilities on this day did not get in the way. I was able to introjectively identify with the family's projective identification of me as a cruel object. No woman enjoys being seen as a witch, especially one with the sexual affectation of long, red nails in a state of disrepair. But we have to face it. My way of facing it will help Mrs. Silver and the children to face the witch they see in each other and in themselves. So there I am as the phallic mother at 8 A.M. What next?

The new couple arrives. A nice-looking woman with a lovely smile, and a quietly handsome man. They explain that they want to work out a therapy schedule of once-a-month visits. I say that I usually see couples once a week, but if they tell me what they want to work on, we can think together about a schedule that makes sense. Mr. Walters sits quietly and attentively. He has an attractive, self-effacing, solicitous manner that speaks of great concern for his wife. I, myself, feel somehow protected and cared for by him. Mrs. Walters does all the talking about how she feels she is making him miserable with all her complaints and unmet expectations, while he looks depressed. He strikes me as passive-aggressive. She describes how stubborn he is about insisting on his right to two drinks a night, even though it makes him sleepy. She loves it that he sticks up for himself and his rights, and she knows that he isn't an alcoholic, but, as the child of an alcoholic father, she hates the smell and the effect of drinking.

I am listening to their story of unhappiness, but I am not feeling unhappy in their presence. I have to admit I am off in a fantasy world. This is the kind of man I could have fallen in love with, I am thinking, and have an affair with. Ridiculous, he is far too passive to cope with me and I wouldn't want a sleepy partner either. My fantasies just won't fit the facts. Ah, I must still be mad at my husband! That's why I am unable to tune in to this couple. Insight to the contrary, my sexual fantasies persist.

Mrs. Walters is telling how they both want things their way. She decorated the house according to her taste and he just went along with it. She has no idea if he likes it or not, but she doesn't care because she likes it. Now she wants to decorate their bedroom in cut velvet. She wants a four-poster bed with a canopy and a lace coverlet, a sensuous room, but he doesn't, and so they have their same old bed and gray room.

"And that symbolizes our sexual relationship. It's not what we want. It can be pleasant, even great, but it's just so infrequent. If it's good, we withdraw from each other afterwards," said Mr. Walters.

Mrs. Walters concurred. "Then it's hard to try again. We can talk about sex openly; we were instrumental in introducing sex education to the youth program at our church, but our own sexual relationship is totally separate from our liberated attitudes."

"As teenagers, we were experimental but controlled," Mr. Walters explained. "We went four years without sleeping together. I had too much respect for her to force her."

"Even though I wanted it," Mrs. Walters added. "We both felt guilty and retreated after every step forward. We're still doing that now. We've loved each other since we were 14 years old, but we can't enjoy sex together, and neither of us wants to try with anyone else. We want each other."

They are talking about a committed, loving but frustrating, and frequently unfulfilling sexual relationship. Yet, I am still enjoying a fantasy about Mr. Walters. Accustomed to passing fantasies of one sort or another, I am surprised by the persistence of this one and I begin to feel totally out of order. I am puzzled. To my great relief Mrs. Walters addresses the theme.

"Even though I wanted it, Fred would never force me. And he was young then. Can you imagine the control he has over his impulses? It's a good thing too. All my friends love him. One of our friends wants to have an affair with him. She wouldn't do it, but she admits she wants to. My college roommate told me she had sexual fantasies about him. An airline hostess tried to pick him up on the Boston shuttle. Everyone wants to go to bed with Fred."

At last. I am in touch after all. I note my fantasies have now disappeared. "What do you think accounts for this powerful effect?" I ask, quite convinced of how remarkable it is.

"I just love touching people," Mr. Walters replies. "I was
always close to my mother. I like listening to them. Women feel
comfortable with me. They know I am fond of them."

"If you were more in touch with the urgency of your sexual
feelings," I suggest apparently empathically, but with a touch of
vengeance on behalf of all the excited women, "you would lose that
familiar ease with women."

"Yes," says Mr. Walters ruefully. "That would be a lot to give
up."

I hint that they are struggling with a shared guilt about having a
fully sexual, intimate relationship and that I would like to work
with them in couple therapy and could start next week. They
remind me of their preference for once-a-month meetings. I say
that they are planning to deal with therapy as they do with sex,
namely to have it infrequently and to put the longing for more of it
into someone else. They agree to meet weekly. Off they go.

Another few minutes for reflection. Love for each other is
evident between them and although they repress it, I am well aware
of the force of their sexual desire, because of the impact of the
massive projective identification in me of the couple's excitement. I
guess that this projective identification is with a repressed aspect
of the couple's self system and may also reflect their individual
involvements with incestuous objects. Mrs. Walter's alcoholic father may have been a sexually and aggressively exciting object for
her. Mr. Walters, by massive projection of excitement into the
other woman, might be trying to keep his incestuous object comfortably platonic. Who knows? It will be interesting to learn what
they feel so guilty about. Who's next?

An analytic patient in the third year of his analysis. He walks in
briskly and lies down on the couch. A dense silence ensues. My
mind drifts over missing my mother yesterday, and maybe a little
today, now that I think about it. My father's birthday is on the 16th
but he is dead. My mind returns to the patient, silent as death. His
legs are bent uncomfortably on the couch. I think of how his
perfectly normal feet move when he walks into the office, but when

he lies on the couch, his ankles curl inward in an unusual way and his lower torso flattens. He reminds me of a baby born with congenital dislocation of the hip. I long to reach out to him, but I know that he finds my words intrusive. For the same reason, he does not want me to have his phone number. Now he is crying in a quiet, hidden way. I think of him as a baby left alone in a crib. There always seem to be bars between him and me. Am I projecting my own fantasies about a lonely, damaged baby or are they being elicited by his fantasies in unconscious communication with me through projective identification? Am I being used as his object trying to respond to his withdrawn self, or am I identified with his self reaching for a depressed object?

"I hurt like hell today," he says quietly, as if not to upset me. "I pulled a muscle in my calf playing tennis. I'm off the team for three weeks. I can't work out. I don't know what I'm going to do. I have to have exercise. My sisters tease me about that, say it's always been that way. When I was 2 years old, they say, I had to have some kind of splint on my legs, I don't know why, but I would lie in the crib with this thing on, not able to move and screaming for someone to get me out of there, and trying to tear the thing off. No one ever came to let me out. I have to be able to move. It's my greatest pleasure. I just go crazy without it. I'm like my father, I suppose. It's his birthday today. And I hurt. I wish he was here so I could tell him how angry I am that he left town after the divorce, and so he could see how much I hurt because of it."

Now I am glad I didn't speak. Perhaps I was being useful to him as a silent participant in his state of withdrawal and hurt, different from the taunting sister who laughed at his efforts at freeing himself, or the parents who seemed not to be there. When he talked of his father, I realized for the first time that missing my mother yesterday was a cover for the rage I feel at my father for not being alive—yesterday on Mother's Day, or on his birthday this week, or any day. I don't need to say anything to this patient today. He's getting there on his own, and helping me.

Three sessions from a therapist's morning, and so the week

will go on. On another day nothing much might happen. Yet again a certain hour might stand out as especially good. If you were the therapist, the whole experience would be different, because you would have your own valency for interacting with each patient. Each of us has our individual intrapsychic structure with its conscious and unconscious domains, its strong and weak points for connecting and resonating with others.

My self is what I have to offer. I am both myself and the person the patients need me to be. Because I am there, they can experience and remodel their own selves in individual, couple, or family therapy. In each modality I aim at gaining access to the unconscious. In interaction with me, patients re-create the early experience that has shaped their psychic structures. Metabolizing my own experience of the expression of their internal structures, I arrive at understanding, which I communicate in the form of interpretations that ultimately have the explanatory power to modify intrapsychic and interpersonal dynamics.

The therapist's self is the therapeutic instrument. She becomes a necessary object of use to the patient. How she is used determines her understanding of the patient's psychodynamics. How she is used in contrast to her own concept of herself yields the material for her interpretations. In the gap between what she is and how the patient perceives her and needs her to be lies therapeutic leverage, room for interpretation of the burden of fantasy upon reality. At the same time the therapist may come to perceive aspects of herself hidden from her until brought to light by the patient's fantasy. Each patient calls forth our higher reach. As they improve, our patients succeed in making us better, too.

Of course, there are many elements in therapy. Simply being there as an object is not enough. First we provide a holding environment, a therapeutic space free of impulsivity, narcissistic concerns, and retaliation. Our technique includes listening to the unconscious communication coming from the patient in words, silence, and gesture, and in feelings evoked in us. We follow the affect, analyze dreams and fantasies, and point out the compulsive repetition of unhealthy behavior due to unresolved conflict. We stress the mutative importance of interpretation of defense and anxiety and working through. We employ theory to make a formulation of the patient's distress, to comprehend the expression of the patient's conflict in the transference, and to make a reconstruction of the present situation in the light of past experience. We observe, we perceive, we think, we respond, we move, and we feel. We compare our experience with a new patient with our previous clinical experience and with cases that we have read about. We take difficult problems to a consultant or to peer supervision. We undertake our own analysis to prepare ourself as a well-calibrated analytic instrument and we maintain it with constant self-analysis.

As Duncan (1991) observed, the well-functioning therapeutic process has been described as a swan gliding effortlessly on a lake. He then reminded us that a graceful swan is basically a big duck paddling like mad under the water. As the metaphor suggests, when the process is working well, it is hard to see how it is happening. When it gets stuck or slowed down, we get a chance to examine the nature of the work that goes into keeping the whole process afloat.

The subject of the analytic process has interested a number of writers who have been dismayed at a narrow technical, drive-oriented focus. Sandler addressed the topic through consideration of the transference. Departing from a classical view of transference as the repetition of drives displaced in a new edition onto the analyst, he said that transference, like life itself, is the disguised repetition of early object relationships (Sandler 1976). Transference, the patient's projection of some aspect of a figure from the past onto the analyst or therapist, includes attempts to push the analyst into responding in a particular way. The patient attempts to create in the here-and-now of the therapeutic relationship a role relationship like the internal object relationship. The analyst is not the only person to be subjected to this coercion. Any figures of importance in the patient's life are required to enact the internal object relationship set. In fact, life partners are chosen on the basis of their capacity to enact these role relationships. The fit achieved by the patient with friend, boss, spouse, or analyst depends on the other person's capacity for role responsiveness (Sandler 1976, Sandler et al. 1973). Jacobs (1991) addresses the use of the therapist's self through the transference and countertransference. He gives many outstanding descriptions of the collaboration between the unconscious of patient and analyst and proves by his example that self-analysis is essential to the therapeutic task. Recent publications are taking us beyond the study of countertransference to intersubjectivity (Duncan 1981, Natterson 1991, Stolorow et al. 1983). We share an interest in that swan gliding down the river of life. This book results from my study of the paddling needed for therapeutic action.

In my view, the power of therapeutic action derives from the mental mechanisms of projective and introjective identification. I take up this topic by reviewing and illustrating the concepts of projective and introjective identification. I show that projective and introjective identificatory mechanisms determine individual, couple, and family development and that they are found at work in groups and communities and in our arts and media. Building on this theory base, I move on to illustrate the use of the therapist's self, conceptualized in terms of the processes of projective and introjective identification detected in the countertransference in individual psychoanalysis and psychotherapy and in couple and family therapy. Models consistent with the clinical use of countertransference are given for teaching about these processes in supervision and in large-group teaching settings. The ideas sketched in this introduction are developed through the course of the book and culminate in a fully developed view of the therapeutic action of projective and introjective identification.

PART I

THE THEORY
OF PROJECTIVE
AND INTROJECTIVE
IDENTIFICATION

2

The Development
of the Concept
# of Projective Identification

The concept of projective identification (Klein 1946) is used clinically by non-Kleinian as well as Kleinian analysts and psychotherapists. It is useful for communicating experiences of clinical phenomena and providing explanations for them. But I have often observed that many clinicians and writers wrongly assume that the term *projective identification* has a universally accepted meaning and frequently introduce it without definition. This has led to such looseness of terminology and theoretical imprecision that the integrity of the concept is in danger. To illustrate this contention I offer two observation samples, the first from my teaching experience and the second from psychoanalytic research literature:

Sample 1. At a symposium where I was presenting object relations family therapy, a questioner asked me and my closest colleagues to define projective identification. Each of us, to our astonishment, replied quite differently. For years we had been using the term in shared discussions and in teaching but we had not realized that some of us think of projective identification as an intrapsychic or *one-body phenomenon* and others as an interpersonal situation or *two-body phenomenon* (Meissner 1987), even though all of us study projective identifications in analysis and in the interpersonal context of the family.

Sample 2. Dicks (1967) studied the personalities of pairs of spouses in concurrent individual psychoanalytic psychotherapy. Each marital partner saw a separate but collaborating therapist. Each individual spouse's personality was conceptualized according to Fairbairn's theory of endopsychic structure (1944, 1952, 1954, 1963) as consisting of conscious and unconscious object relations. Dicks noted a degree of fit between the unconscious object relations of spouses early in their marriage such that perceptions of the spouse occur "*as if* the other were part of oneself. The partner is then treated according to how this aspect of oneself was valued: spoilt and cherished, or denigrated and persecuted" (p. 69). As the marriage progressed, this unconscious fit persisted along with a blurring of boundaries between self and other to the point where the couple developed a "marital joint personality." "This joint personality or integrate enabled each half to rediscover lost aspects of their primary object relations, which they had split off or repressed, and which they were, in their involvement with the spouse, reexperiencing by projective identification" (p. 69).

To account for his findings, Dicks invoked Klein's (1946) concept of projective identification. Although he referred to it frequently and gave many theoretical descriptions and clinical examples of its occurrence, he did not formally define the concept himself. Like Klein, he tended to demonstrate it in action—in his case, in application to marriage—and to assume that his readers already knew about the basic concept.

Dicks's personal use of the concept is a prototype for what has happened since then to projective identification. Those of us with a working familiarity of the term tend to think we have got the hang of it, without realizing that some of us are talking about an intra-psychic, one-body concept and others are thinking of an interpersonal, two-body phenomenon. Nevertheless, we use the term to communicate our understanding to other therapists. This seems to work quite well, so well, in fact, that it masks an underlying confusion about what is meant.

On the one hand these two samples point to the remarkable flexibility and applicability of the concept; on the other, they demonstrate a lack of conceptual clarity which I suggest originated with Klein's discursive writing style.

KLEIN'S CONCEPT OF PROJECTIVE IDENTIFICATION

In her paper on schizoid states (1946) Klein introduces the concept of projective identification through an illustration of its occurrence in the paranoid–schizoid position during the first months of life. However, she gives no quotable definition. The concept seems to sneak up on us when Klein mentions projective identification as the mechanism for dealing with object relations when the infant is struggling with hatred due to anxiety in its earliest relation to the mother and her breast. Thus in hatred, the anxious infant seeks to rid itself of destructive parts of the self by spitting or vomiting them out, or excreting them in fantasy in its urine or explosive feces and projecting them in a hostile stream into the object residing in the mother's body. Then the infant feels attacked by the mother. "When the projection is mainly derived from the infant's impulse to harm or control the mother, he feels her to be a persecutor" (p. 8). The infant identifies with this persecutory object which further fuels the paranoid schizoid position.

Klein then qualifies her discussion of projective identification by reminding us that the good parts of the self may also be projected. By identifying with the projected good parts of itself the infant personality can experience good object relations; this is important for integration of the ego. She goes on to say that projective identification occurs in love as well as hate under the influence of the life instinct as well as the death instinct. Klein (1946) convincingly makes the case that "processes of splitting off parts of the self and projecting them into objects are thus of vital importance for normal development as well as for abnormal object relations" (p. 9). Klein preferred "projecting into" rather than "projecting onto." She carefully points this out in a sentence that is, however, relegated to a footnote. "I am using the expression 'to project *into* another person' because this seems to me the only way of conveying the unconscious process I am trying to describe" (p. 8, fn. 1).

From this footnote it is clear that Klein is referring to *projection* in the *interpersonal* situation where one person (the infant) splits off and expels unwanted parts of the self into the other person (the mother). It is also clear that this expulsion can be expressed in oral, anal, or urethral modes. But what remains unclear is how the *identification* takes place. At times, it seems to refer in Freud's classical sense to a process where the ego assimilates itself to what it finds in the object (Freud 1900, p. 151). At other times it seems to imply what might more accurately be referred to as "internalization of object relations" (Laplanche and Pontalis 1973). Splitting, a concept borrowed from Fairbairn (1944), projection, projective identification, and introjection are bunched together in Klein's work as part-and-parcel of projective and introjective processes characteristic of object relations in the paranoid–schizoid position normally achieved during the early months of life.

It fell to Klein's expositors to attempt a nuts-and-bolts outline of the processes and to distinguish more precisely between the component parts (Grotstein 1982, Malin and Grotstein 1966, Meissner 1980, Ogden 1982, Segal 1964). Later revisions, while offering necessary conceptual clarification, have, however, tended to dilute Klein's vivid distinctions among types of projective processes based on the developmentally dominant instinctual modes of expression affecting the object relations. They lack the vividness of Klein's descriptions of oral, anal, or urethral modes of expelling the object in fantasy and attacking it or seeking gratification from it inside the mother's body where it is unconsciously imagined to be.

Segal (1964), who has given the clearest exposition of Klein, wrote in her glossary that *projective identification* "is the result of the projection of parts of the self into an object. It may result in the object being perceived as having acquired the characteristics of the projected part of the self, but it can also result in the self becoming identified with the object of its projection" (p. 126). In this succinct definition, Segal precisely describes the unconscious communication between self and object while elegantly conveying the ambiguity of the process. This effect rests on a duality of meaning. I understand Segal to be saying that the *object is misperceived* as if it were like the self and that the *self may also become like the misperceived object*. In the first meaning, the self is *identifying in the sense of perceiving* or recognizing (albeit incorrectly) a part of the self in the object. In the second meaning, the self is *identifying in the sense of assimilating to* and being transformed by the resulting object into which it has projected a part of the self. Thus, identification following projection appears to refer to both naming and assimilating, two different meanings of identification pointed out by Lalande (1951) and referred to by Laplanche and Pontalis (1973).

Segal's glossary definition does not address the effect of the process upon the external object: it is confined to the intrapsychic arena of the projecting infant. But earlier in her text Segal does address the effect on the other person: "In projective identification, parts of the self and internal objects are split off and projected into the external object, which then becomes possessed by, controlled and identified with the projected parts" (p. 14). Unlike the glossary definition, this is a description of a two-body phenomenon. The link between the two is provided by the concept of introjective identification which refers to "the result when the object is introjected into the ego which then identifies with some or all of its characteristics" (p. 105).

Projective identification follows projection only under the influence of anxiety in the paranoid–schizoid position. Segal writes: "In normal development . . . the projected parts are relatively unaltered in the process of projection, and when subsequent re-introjection takes place, they can be re- integrated into the ego" (p. 42). I assume that this statement refers specifically to projection as stated and differentiates introjection and integration occurring in projection from identification occurring in projective identification.

Steiner, a Kleinian colleague of Segal, in a recent lecture (1989) defined projective identification as a primitive mechanism in which part of the self is projected off into the object. According to Steiner, the aim is (1) to get rid of that part of the self, (2) to attack the object, or (3) to be in primitive communication with object. The results are (1) lack of separation between self and object, (2) change in how the object is perceived, and (3) depletion of the self by loss of the projected part. Steiner stated that the external object is somehow affected by the projections into it. Thus, his view of projective identification, like that of Segal, includes awareness of interpersonal effect.

After his exposition of projective identification, Steiner declared, "The only thing in its favor is people don't understand it. The phrase 'narcissistic projection' is much better." Here Steiner shows conviction and clarity about the concept of projective identification with both pleasure in its confusion-generating properties and dissatisfaction with the term. He emphasizes the intrapsychic without excluding the interpersonal, but paradoxically he then provides an alternative that denudes the term of the identificatory part of the process. When dealing with the concept of projective identification, we often find such contradiction.

Another Kleinian, Williams, reminds us (1981) of the distinction between projection and projective identification. "I must emphasize that projective identification is not the same as projection.

In projection a state of mind of the self is ascribed to someone else, not actually evoked in him" (p. 112). Thus, for Williams both are interpersonal events, but only in projective identification is a state of mind of the self evoked in someone else.

Spillius (1991) declared that there is little to be said for the argument over distinguishing between projection and projective identification. She seems resigned to the literature being in a hopeless muddle. In discussion following her paper she contributed the following distinction: "Projection is the mental mechanism. Projective identification is the state of mind."

FURTHER CONTRIBUTIONS: JAFFE, MALIN, AND GROTSTEIN

From his review of writings on projection and projective identification, Jaffe (1968), a Freudian analyst, concludes that projection under the influence of ambivalence is an archaic defensive process that on the one hand "seeks to effect a split from the object and on the other, it seeks to preserve a tie with the object" (p. 662). Noting that many authors tend to use the term projection as synonymous with projective identification, Jaffe suggests that both terms lie on a continuum of ambivalence in dealing with object relationships, their positions determined by "the extent to which the annihilation is carried out psychically, i.e., the degree to which the splitting is completed" (p. 666). He suggests that in projection "the annihilation of the object is predominant" while at the projective identification end of the continuum "identification with and preservation of the object is paramount" (p. 666).

Malin and Grotstein (1966), the latter a Kleinian, agreed with Fairbairn's view (1954) of the human personality as a dynamic structure of internalized objects that determine its transactions with others. Like Fairbairn, they could not agree with Freud's (1905) view of the infant as driven by sexual and aggressive instincts, although they did see internal objects as including drive aspects. In keeping with these ideas, they used the term *projection* for dealing only with the displacement of instinctual *drives*. They reserved *projective identification* for referring to the projection of *objects* in the transactional process between infant and environment, or patient and therapist. Malin and Grotstein refer to objects as "parts of the self (or identifications)" that are projected outward. The object now receives the projected unwanted or disclaimed parts of the self "and then this new alloy—external object plus newly arrived projected part—is reintrojected to complete the cycle" (p. 26). For them, projection always includes identification with the object projected into, otherwise the projection would simply be lost. Thus, in their view, projective identification is synonymous with projection.

OBJECTIONS TO USE OF TERMINOLOGY: MEISSNER

Meissner (1980), dissatisfied with the loose use of the concepts of introjection, projection, and projective identification, usefully took issue with various authors. He found that projective identification gave him trouble because it had acquired multiple, sometimes inappropriate meanings and might be used instead of the concept of projection, which he regarded as less mysterious and less confusing. Others have joined Meissner in trying to make sense of the confusion. Their differing interpretations of the concept have led to considerable debate. The argument tends to focus on how to distinguish between projection and projective identification. Narrowing the field to an either/or situation defends us against the strain of complexity that can be temporarily useful, but not if it leads to a rigid polarity. Nevertheless, this focus seems to have been a necessary step toward grappling with the confusion surrounding projective identification. So in this chapter I follow the argument, emphasizing points of difference among authors and then attempting to categorize them. This leads me to a hypothesis as to why these problems exist in definition and terminology.

Meissner (1980) gets us off to a good start. He reviews the development of the concept of projection from Freud to Klein. He quotes Freud (1911), who wrote that in projection "an internal perception is suppressed, and, instead, its content, after undergoing a certain kind of distortion, enters consciousness in the form of an external perception" (p. 66). Unlike Freud who saw projection as a pathological mechanism of symptom formation seen in paranoia, Klein, who was most impressed with projection's "role of dealing with excessive degrees of aggression and anxiety," nevertheless made projection "a necessary process and the originating point of object relations" (Meissner 1980, pp. 47–48). Freud's scientific view of projection as a mechanism for dealing with energy can be contrasted with Klein's emphasis on the process as a fantasy expressed in instinctually derived body language.

Meissner fully justifies his criticism of Klein's easy slippage in terminology between projection and projective identification. He suggests that the process Klein called projective identification should more accurately be called identification by projection. Its complementary process, which Klein named introjective identification, would better be described as identification by introjection. In Klein's theory, projective identification is crucial in the establishment and maintenance of object relations and it drives the development of the personality throughout the life–cycle.

Meissner (1980) distinguishes projection and projective identification thus:

In *projection* "what is projected is experienced as belonging to, coming from, or as an attribute or quality of the object."

In *projective identification* "what is projected is simultaneously identified with and is experienced as part of the self" (p. 55).

Meissner then declares that, since it involves loss of ego boundaries and taking the object as part of the self, *projective identification is inherently a psychotic mechanism.* Here Meissner contradicts Klein's view of projective identification as a normal developmental process that can only become pathological if the degree of anxiety due to the death instinct is too great to bear. He finds that *projection is a normal mechanism* found in mature relationships. Here he contradicts Freud's view of projection as a pathological process found in paranoia. In my view, he replaces Klein's inconsistency with a new confusion that is equally profound and all the more disquieting because it is based upon well-argued criticism of Klein's views.

Meissner similarly objects to Malin and Grotstein's view (1966) that "projection includes identification, and, conversely, all identification includes projection" (1980, p. 61). In Meissner's view, in projection the contact that the self maintains with what is projected is cognitive only and does not imply an identification inside the self, thus qualifying *projection* as a normal mechanism. Malin and Grotstein's point is that identification must be occurring; otherwise we could never be aware of our projections and the projection would simply be lost to the self. Perhaps the use of Knight's (1940) term *partial and temporary identification* (p. 338) could mediate the argument as follows: When the results of the process of identifying are transitory, there can be no structure building. Nevertheless, it seems to me that such temporary identifications during projection of drive material do act upon the self to prepare the soil for permanent identification with part objects and later whole objects, and to prepare the part objects inside the self for modification by new identifications.

Meissner also addresses himself to a "certain vogue" in using the concept in family dynamics. He agrees that complex projective-introjective processes occur, but projective identification does not. He agrees with Zinner and Shapiro (1972) that when "the subject perceives the object *as if* the object contained elements of the subject's personality" (Scharff 1989, p. 114), then the term projective identification truly applies. However, he states that is not often the case except in psychotic interaction. Moreover, he gives no clinical or research evidence to disprove Zinner and Shapiro's conclusion that it does occur in nonpsychotic interaction. Zinner and Shapiro's argument is, however, based on their documented clinical research.

In summary, Meissner suggests first that the term projective identification be restricted to the psychotic process of projection of elements of the self into the object and the experiencing of these self-elements as belonging to the object. He objects to identification being included with projection because identification implies psychic structure formation that does not occur during projection alone. Instead, writes Meissner (1987), psychic structure occurs when "the interplay of introjective and projective mechanisms weaves a pattern of relatedness to the world of objects and provides the fabric out of which the individual fashions his own self-image" (p. 31). Furthermore, he allows that "the quality of the introject, however, is mitigated by the response of the object" (p. 30). Yet, in his view, although there is projection and introjection, there is no such thing as projective identification, a term so confusing that it ought to be abandoned! It is a surprise to reach Meissner's conclusion of hopelessness about the term after such an earnest and thoughtful examination of the vagaries of the meaning of projective identification. Suddenly the contributor becomes the detractor, when the boundaries of creative ambiguity have been broken by unacceptable confusion.

In later writing, Meissner (1987) defends his view: "One would not be satisfied . . . that projective identification has occurred if the patient simply reports material that can be understood as reflecting a fantasy in which he regards some part of himself as embedded in another object. One would want to see concrete data that suggest that indeed that process has taken place" (p. 54).

How concrete can intrapsychic phenomena ever be? Their expressions through interpersonal enactment in family relationships or in the analytic transference–countertransference are compelling but do not provide the hard data of proof. Projective identification is only a concept, not a concretization of experience. Furthermore, like projective identification, many of the most useful psychoanalytic concepts such as transitional object (Winnicott 1951) are blessed with ambiguity. Such ambiguity is central to many an idea including the concept of object relations and identificatory processes throughout life in health and disease.

Meissner's (1980) criticisms regarding confusion due to looseness in terminology have led to fruitful debate and clarification (Sandler 1987) but not to his proposed abandonment of the term. The concept of projective identification is widely used and has communicative value among professionals who know roughly what it means. Like Ogden, I find projective identification essential for understanding transference and countertransference, and, like Zinner and Shapiro, I am convinced of the occurrence of projective identification in family interaction. In my experience, projective identification is present constantly intrapsychically and interpersonally—most noticeably in family life and in therapeutic relationships. In my view, much would be lost by abandoning the term; much can be gained from precision as to when, where, and how projective identification is occurring.

RECENT CONTRIBUTIONS

Ogden

More recently, Ogden (1982) brought some order to the chaos, attempting a definition of projective identification as he experienced it in clinical situations. He, too, makes a distinction between projection and projective identification:

Projection: ". . . the aspect of the self that is expelled is disavowed and attributed to the recipient" (Ogden 1982, p. 34).

Projective Identification: "The projector subjectively experiences a feeling of oneness with the recipient with regard to the expelled feeling, idea, or self-representation" (Ogden 1982, p. 34).

Here Ogden elaborates upon identification as a feeling of oneness. He also specifies what is projected. It is not just a part of the self; it may also be a feeling or an idea. Later in his text, he concludes that he views projective identification as "a group of fantasies and accompanying object relations" (p. 36) in the intrapsychic dimension. These operate in interpersonal interaction in three phases outlined by Ogden (1982) and derived from his reading of Malin and Grotstein (1966). These are:

(1) getting rid of part of the self into someone else where it takes hold, (2) pressuring the other person to experience it, and (3) getting it back from the other person.

This model of projection, coercion, and reclaiming brings out the interactive sequence. From the intrapsychic perspective of the projector (the one who is doing the projecting), Ogden goes further to ask why the projector goes through all these stages. What are the intrapsychic and interpersonal benefits of projective identification? He comes up with four purposes for projective identification, which we can summarize as follows:

(1) Defense: to distance oneself from the unwanted part or to keep it alive in someone else, (2) Communication: to make oneself understood by pressing the recipient to experience a set of feelings like one's own, (3) Object-relatedness: to interact with a recipient separate enough to receive the projection yet undifferentiated enough to allow some misperception to occur to foster the sense of oneness, and (4) Pathway for psychological change: to be transformed by reintrojecting the projection after its modification by the recipient, as occurs in the mother–infant relationship, in marriage, or the patient–therapist relationship.

Consider Ogden's opening statement on projective identification:

> The concept integrates statements about unconscious fantasy, interpersonal pressure, and the response of a separate personality system to a set of engendered feelings. Projective identification is in part a statement about an interpersonal interaction (the pressure of one person on another to comply with a projective fantasy) and in part a statement about individual mental activity (projective fantasies, introjective fantasies, psychological processing). Most fundamentally, however, it is a statement about the dynamic interplay of the two, the intrapsychic and the interpersonal. [Ogden 1982, p. 3]

In later writing, Ogden (1986) is concerned with explaining the change in the quality of the infant's experience after a projection has been metabolized by the mother and returned to the infant in a more useful or manageable form. Ogden suggests that an actual alteration occurs in the infant, because the "simultaneous oneness and twoness (unity and separateness of mother and infant) involved in projective identification creates a potential for a form of experience more generative than the sum of the individual psychological states contributing to it" (p. 36). In his view, both infant and mother, patient and therapist, projector and projectee, contribute actively to the process and the infant/patient is changed by it. By including the therapist's elaboration of what has been projected, Ogden explores the two-body projective identificatory system.

I welcome his expansion, and so does Goldstein (1991) who based his broad model of projective identification on Ogden's work, but others do not; for instance, Kernberg (1987) finds the degree of broadening of the concept to be unwarranted (p. 93).

Ogden goes beyond Klein to emphasize the interpersonal aspects of projective identification and the importance of the environment that were only implied in her work, but like Klein, he emphasizes the infant's experience. Drawing on Bion (1962), he deliberates upon the effect on the contained infant, (or the "mother–infant" as he prefers to call the infant in the mother–infant dyad), and the containing function of the mother rather than upon the formation of altered psychic structure in the mother. Thus, he points us back to the intrapsychic dimension of the interpersonal process of projective identification.

Sandler

Sandler (1987) recognizes that projective identification shifts its meaning according to context, according to its use by Kleinians or nonKleinians, and because "its collective and necessarily elastic nature must render any precise definition implausible" (p. 14). He describes stages in the development of the concept determined by the effect of the projector's fantasy upon the object.

First stage: The real object is not affected by the fantasy. This corresponds to the early Kleinian description of an intrapsychic process that occurs in fantasy. Sandler views it as a mechanism for regulating, defining, and sorting experience, for controlling the object and for establishing a self-object boundary (Sandler and Joffe, 1967).

Second stage: The object is affected by the fantasy. Evidence quoted for this stage is Heimann's (1950) contribution on the analyst's countertransference that she described as "the patient's *creation*, it is part of the patient's personality" (p. 83). Through projective identification, the analyst as the object of the patient's fantasies has been affected, so that a corresponding state of countertransference exists. Sandler also refers to Racker's (1968) elaboration of countertransference as the analyst's identification with the self-representation or object-representation in the patient's fantasy, leading respectively to a concordant or complementary countertransference. Sandler, who has experienced the actualization of fantasy self-object role relationships in the analytic relationship, accepts this as a form of projective identification.

Third stage: The object affects the fantasy. In this stage of development of the concept, the projected parts are modified by the thought or "reverie" (Bion 1967) of the containing mother. Sandler criticizes this idea, which sounds to him like a "concrete putting into the object." Instead, he sees the analyst's containing role as a neutral one of tolerating the patient's distress while the unconscious becomes conscious and the patient can change the fantasy. Yet, he recognizes the analyst's countertransference experience as a response to the patient's wishful fantasy. Nevertheless, he disputes that the patient–therapist healing relationship is based on a projective identification model.

When we compare the stages in development of the concept of projective identification, identified by Sandler, with the phases of the interactive sequence in the process of projective identification described by Ogden and summarized earlier in this text, we find a remarkable correspondence.

Kernberg

Kernberg (1987) describes projective identification as a primitive but not psychotic defensive operation, which, however, is most evident in psychosis and borderline conditions. Except in the most severe, temporary, neurotic regressions, Kernberg finds that projective identification is relatively unimportant in the neuroses where projection predominates. This leads him to propose "that a developmental line leads from projective identification, which is based on an ego structure centered on splitting (primitive dissociation) as its essential defense, to projection, which is based on an ego structure centered on repression as a basic defense" (p. 94). This evolves from Kernberg's view that splitting and repression are quite separate mechanisms occurring at different developmental levels: splitting characterizes borderline conditions and repression characterizes neurotic conditions. This view is in sharp contrast to Fairbairn's whose point was that splitting and repression occur simultaneously.

Kernberg (1987) gives his clear, succinct definition of projection and projective identification:

Projective Identification

Clinical experience has led me to define projective identification as a primitive defense mechanism consisting of (a) projecting intolerable aspects of intrapsychic experience onto an object, (b) maintaining empathy with what is projected, (c) attempting to control the object as a continuation of the defensive efforts against the intolerable intrapsychic experience, and (d) unconsciously inducing in the object what is projected in the actual interaction with the object. [p. 94]

Projection

Projective identification so defined differs from projection, which is a more mature type of defense mechanism. Projection consists of (a) repression of an unacceptable intrapsychic experience, (b) projection of that experience onto an object, (c) lack of empathy with what is projected, and (d) distancing or estrangement from the object as an effective completion of the defensive effort. There is neither empathy with what is projected nor induction in the object of a corresponding intrapsychic experience. [p. 94]

Here Kernberg agrees with Meissner's view of projective identification as abnormal and projection as normal defense mechanisms and, like Meissner, contradicts Freud's view of projection as a primitive pathological process. Kernberg's concept fits Sandler's description of second stage projective identification. Kernberg discusses his countertransference in two contrasting clinical examples of work with young women, one with a neurotic and the other with a borderline condition. In the latter, Kernberg describes a complementary identification within a complicated countertransference experience. This one is a convincing example of the massive use of projective identification. In the former, Kernberg describes responding to the patient's sexual fantasies with sexual fantasies about her. But because he did not feel controlled by her and did not feel she wanted rid of such fantasies of her own, he thought that neither projection nor projective identification were occurring.

In my view, projective identification occurred in the neurotic case as well. I suggest that there was a concordant countertransference in which the analyst identified with the patient's sexual longings and, therefore, with her self-representation projected into him. I think that a complementary countertransference also occurred to her transference toward him as the loving, excited, oedipal father object. When Kernberg remained silent, the patient perceived him as teasing and seductive like her father. At the least, she had projected this rejecting father object onto him and had identified him with that part of her. Kernberg felt that this behavior had not been induced in him but that his silence had been interpreted by her in an idiosyncratic way. In that case, I would agree no change in the object had actually occurred, but one had been misidentified. This still qualifies as projective identification of the first stage described by Sandler. But in Kernberg's view that stage is projection and does not qualify for description as projective identification. Here Kernberg is close to Williams's view that only in projective identification is there evocation of a feeling state in the external object. Since Kernberg does not recognize his sexual fantasy in response to the woman as a feeling state evoked in him by her, then no projective identification could be acknowledged.

Kernberg's choice of projection as the appropriate term was made on the evidence of lack of induction of the object. From reading these and other examples, it seems to me that Kernberg's use of projection or projective identification depends on how subtle or massive the process's impact is on the external object. To put it another way, Kernberg infers that the process's place on the projection–projective identification continuum is determined by how much the analyst suffers. To me, the degree of suffering in the countertransference is determined not only by the massiveness of the patient's projective identification, but also by its correspondence to my vulnerable areas. But lack of suffering does not preclude projective identification. Kernberg, who is committed to an interpersonal view of therapy, rejects Meissner's use of the one-body, two-body categorization to distinguish between projection and projective identification. Kernberg says that in projection what might appear to be a one-body phenomenon is still a two-body phenomenon in which an advanced neurotic defense of projection simply leads to estrangement from the object. Yet, in his examples, Kernberg seems to me to be reserving the term *projection* for a one-body phenomenon and projective identification for a two-body phenomenon.

CONTRIBUTIONS FROM FAMILY RESEARCH: ZINNER AND SHAPIRO

Zinner and Shapiro (1972) applied their understanding of the intrapsychic process of projective identification to interpersonal situations in family life. Zinner (1976), having read Dicks (1967), brought the concept to bear in marital therapy in the United States. He emphasized that projective identification is an *unconscious* process with defensive and restorative functions. His emphasis on the unconscious is helpful; other writers describe projective identification in such tangible terms that it may seem conscious and sometimes even willful. Zinner writes: "Projective identification is an activity of the ego that modifies perception of the object and, in a reciprocal fashion, alters the image of the self." He adds, "Again through projective identification, the individual may locate the object not inside the self, but as if it were inside the other partner in a relationship" (Zinner 1976, p. 156).

For Zinner, projective identification is an unconscious intrapsychic process through which conflict can be contained inside the self or projected out into a relationship. He noted, as Dicks had, that this happens in marriage and that the process not only alters how the self perceives the object, but actually evokes a collusive response in the object. This fits with Ogden's idea of interpersonal pressuring of the object. But Zinner, like Dicks, goes further to point out that both spouses are involved in processes of projective identification. In modern terms, both are simultaneously projectors and projectees. Thus, Zinner (1976) describes a marriage as a mutually gratifying collusive system (p. 156). Here is projective identification as a mutual process. The goal of marital therapy in Zinner's view is to help each spouse re-internalize these projected conflicts.

Zinner usefully views projective identification as a process that is both healthy and unhealthy. Depending on the extent of the use of projective identification, the nature of the marriage relationship may fall anywhere on a continuum from normally empathic to frankly delusional:

The location of a particular relationship along this continuum is determined by the quality and developmental level of internalized nuclear object relations, by the capacity of the spouses to experience each other as separate, differentiated individuals, and by the intensity of the need for defense. To the extent that a spouse uses projective modes less as a way of externalizing conflict and more as an instrument for approximating shared experience, the marital relationship approaches the healthy end of the continuum. [Zinner 1976, p. 159]

Ravenscroft (1991) uses Zinner's continuum to track the progress of a couple as they take back their projections in the course of treatment. By observing their fantasies and behavior, he assesses the couple's typical projective identificatory system and notes its original position on the adaptive–pathological continuum. As therapy proceeds, the couple's interaction goes in cycles: progressing to the next developmental level, then regressing to a more primitive level. At one time the couple is operating with a style of projective identification more typical of the paranoid–schizoid position, the next time the style is that found in the depressive position. Ravenscroft describes how the couple goes through what he calls this "Kleinian positional cycling," gradually advancing to a more sustained higher level. Then he finds that the couple's style of projective identification approaches the less pathological end of the continuum. At times of stress and trauma, especially commonly that of separation and loss, a regressive cycle through the depressive to the paranoid–schizoid position is to be expected. A couple's shared projective identificatory system can be located along this adaptive–pathological continuum, moving toward the adaptive end as therapy successfully achieves the re-owning of projections by each spouse and the modification of the couple's transference to the therapist.

Based on its application to marital and family therapy, projective identification as a concept can now be seen to have the power to offer a conceptual bridge between individual and interpersonal psychology. We have seen that marital choice is motivated by the wish for an object to complement and reinforce unconscious fantasies (Dicks 1967). Thus, adult development continues to be strongly affected by projective identification. Family studies by Zinner and Shapiro (1972) go further to show its influence on individual development. They write: "Projective identification leads to authentic and lasting structural change in the *recipient* of the projections. A prime example of this phenomenon is the effect of family interaction on the developing personality of the child" (Zinner and Shapiro 1972, p. 110).

In a recent lecture reviewing his use of the concept, Zinner (1989) said that he regards projective identification as entirely an intrapsychic process occurring between parts of self and internal objects inside the projector. For Zinner, it is a one-body phenomenon. Similar intrapsychic processes occur in significant others, but Zinner says that the idea of projecting into another person or vice versa is too mystical for him to accept. So, if projective identification is entirely an intrapsychic process, how does he account for mutual projective identification, which he has described and to which he still subscribes? How does he explain the effect on the object? For Zinner, the missing link is behavior. Zinner states that the wife's intrapsychic operation of projective identification that affects her perception of the spouse leads to changes in her behavior toward him. The husband then responds with his own intrapsychic processes of projective identification and corresponding relevant behaviors. Although in his writing he had emphasized the interpersonal context, in his teaching Zinner focuses on the intrapsychic dimension, on what happens in the individual. Zinner does not regard his statement as a shift in view but rather as a clarification of where projective identification occurs.

Integrating these contributions from family therapy research with my clinical experience as a family therapist, I conclude that, in the family context, multiple individual processes governed by shared unconscious assumptions about family life eventually lead to the identification of parts of family experience inside individual personalities. At the same time, the intrapsychic situation is projected onto the intrafamily group unconscious. An individual is selected as host for, or object for projection of, the unwanted or disavowed parts of the central self of the family. In healthy families the host role rotates among the members, but when projective identification focuses and fixes on one member, a pathological situation has arisen, with an index patient standing for a family group problem in metabolizing unwanted parts of the family group unconscious.

CONTRIBUTIONS FROM PSYCHOSOMATIC AND SEX THERAPY RESEARCH

In projective identification, the projection of a disclaimed thought, feeling, idea, part of ego, or part of object powerfully induces the external object to feel or think as if possessed by the projected part. But the projection may remain inside the internal object and be identified there. In an entirely intrapsychic phase of the process of projective identification, the projector projects not into the other psyche, but into the projector's own soma. This can involve any body part that then becomes identified with the disclaimed projection (Fairbairn 1954). Of particular interest to sex- and marital-therapists is the projection of internal objects into the erotic zones.

In projective identification in the marital dyad, the projection induces a state of mind in the external object. We have tended to think of this happening through the stirring of behavior, thought, or feeling relevant to the received projection. But in the sexual situation, as in infancy, the medium for projection tends to be the body. The projector projects not into the psyche, but into the soma of the projectee, and vice versa in mutual projective identification. Sometimes, in order to protect the other, the projector projects into his or her own body parts. This projection may occur either directly or indirectly after introjective identification with the returned projection. The result of direct and indirect projection into the projector's soma is that the object of projection is now located inside the self. Any body part of self or other can become identified with the disclaimed projection, but the erotic zones are particularly likely targets. Conflicts are projected in condensed form on the body screen of the genitalia (D. Scharff 1982). Penis, vagina, and the woman's breasts become the physical loci of the repressed rejecting and exciting object systems. Then repressed objects return directly through contibuting to or interfering with physical love in the married state.

PROJECTION AND PROJECTIVE IDENTIFICATION: COMMENTS ON THEIR EXTENT

1. *Full and partial projection*: Moses and Halevi (1972) suggested the terms *full* and *partial projection*. In partial projection, the projected material is ascribed to the other person, but is not seen as being turned back. In full projection, it is seen as being turned back. Moses (1987) recognized that in full projection there is continued contact whith the object but he felt it to be insufficient to warrant the term projective identification. *Full projection* gives us a term for a projective process intermediate between projection and projective identification. This is helpful because it suggests a continuum of meaning rather than an absolute difference between projection and projective identification and it leads us to consider a range of projective processes, too.

2. *Projection onto or into*: Tarnopolsky (1987) suggests another distinction: processes of projection of a lower intensity should be referred to as *projections onto*: while those more intense processes "where we lose command, get confused, are flooded with fantasies which we feel are not our own . . . should be referred to as those where the *projection* takes place *into* the analyst, as though the sting of projection has penetrated beneath the skin" (Tarnopolsky 1987, p. 126). Why would it penetrate painfully unless there were receptors under the skin? In other words, the external object had to have

experienced a degree of introjective identification with the projection or it would have been lost upon the external object. In this case the projector would be encouraged by the response to identify the projected part as if it were a property of the object. So, in my view, this "projecting into" would not be a distinct entity but only the first phase of a projective identification.

3. *Contemporary debate on the extent of projection*: Sandler (1987) used three questions to discern an author's view on the process of projection:

    a. Is it reflexive or not, i.e., is there a turning back of the projection?

    b. Is a boundary between self and object a prerequisite or a result?

    c. Is the object influenced or not?

4. *Debate on the extent of projective identification*: Sandler (1987) suggested three stages in the development of the concept that I have already discussed. They are:

Stage 1. The real object is not affected.

Stage 2. The real object is affected.

Stage 3. The object affects the fantasy.

In practice, Sandler noted, projection is not fully differentiated from projective identification.

Lachkar (1989) suggested two degrees of completion: "In single projective identification one does not take in the other person's projection. In dual projective identification, both partners take in the projections of the other." Dual projective identification seems to be her term for mutual projective identification described by Dicks (1967) and Zinner (1976).

SUMMARY OF DEFINITION FINDINGS

I have not been able to reconcile my findings with all the various points of view, but I have found it useful to record my viewing of the different facets of the concept as seen through the lenses of various authors, preliminary to defining the variables used to distinguish between the concepts of projection and projective identification.

Definitions of Projection

Freud: Projection is a defense mechanism for dealing with instinctual energy; an abnormal displacing of an unpleasant, internal perception to the outside world:

Ferenczi: Projection is a process of assigning unpleasant aspects of experience to the outer world.

Klein: Projection is a process whereby the ego expels its own sadistic impulses into the external world through fantasies of physical expulsion, e.g., of poisonous feces into the mother/breast.

Sandler: Projection is the attribution of an unwanted aspect of one's self-representation to a mental representation of another person, that is to an object-representation.

Meissner: In projection, what is projected is experienced as belonging to, coming from, or as an attribute or quality of the object.

Kernberg: Projection is a normal defense mechanism consisting of:

1. repression of an unacceptable intrapsychic experience.

2. projection of that experience onto an object.

3. lack of empathy with what is projected.

4. distancing or estrangement from the object as an effective completion of the defensive effort.

5. not inducing in the object a corresponding intrapsychic experience.

6. is associated with repression not splitting,

7. and is typically seen in neurosis.

Ogden: Projection is the aspect of the self that is expelled—disavowed and attributed to the recipient.

Definitions of Projective Identification

Freud: None found.

Klein: Projective identification is the mechanism for dealing with object relations during the paranoid–schizoid position. In its earliest relation to the breast, the anxious infant seeks to rid itself of aggressive, anxious feelings by spitting, vomiting, or excreting them in fantasy and projecting them into the mother's body. The infant then feels persecuted by the object and identifies with it.

Segal: Projective identification is the result of the projection of parts of the self into an object. It may result in the object being perceived as having acquired the characteristics of the projected part of the self, but it can also result in the self becoming identified with the object of its projection.

Meissner: In projective identification what is projected is simultaneously identified with and is experienced as part of the self. (Prefers to abandon the term. Sees psychic structure as resulting from the interplay of introjective and projective processes.)

Kernberg: Projective identification is a primitive defense mechanism consisting of:

1. projecting intolerable aspects of psychic experience onto an object,

2. maintaining empathy with what is projected,

3. attempting to control the object to maintain the defense, and

4. unconsciously inducing in the object what is projected.

5. It is associated with splitting, not repression, and

6. is found in psychoses and borderline conditions.

Ogden: In projective identification the projector subjectively experiences a feeling of oneness with the recipient with regard to the expelled feeling, idea, or self-representation. The recipient also contributes to the process and is changed by it.

Zinner: Projective identification is an activity of the ego that modifies perception of the object and, in a reciprocal fashion, alters the image of the self. Through projective identification, the individual may locate the object not inside the self, but as if it were inside the other partner in a relationship.

VARIABLES DISTINGUISHING BETWEEN PROJECTION AND PROJECTIVE IDENTIFICATION

We can now summarize a number of factors used to distinguish between projection and projective identification. These are:

1. Absence or presence of empathy with the projected part (Kernberg).

2. Absence or presence of effect upon the object (Sandler).

3. Degree of annihilation of the object (Jaffe).

4. Presence of repression or splitting (Kernberg).

5. Neurotic or psychotic pathology (Kernberg, Meissner).

6. Degree of suffering in the countertransference (Scharff commenting on Kernberg).

7. One-body or two-body phenomenon (Distinction suggested and refuted by Meissner).

8. Evocation of a feeling state in the external object (Kernberg, Williams).

FURTHER CONTRIBUTING CONCEPTS

Ogden, Steiner, and Zinner hold that in projective identification, the external object is affected by the fantasy projections into it. Steiner (1989), who talked with conviction about this, nevertheless admitted, "How these effects are produced in the other person is poorly understood. I think it has to do with subtly engaging our own personalities, especially those parts which are vulnerable." When asked how the effect upon the object is induced, Zinner maintained that behavior is the essential vehicle. When asked how the containing mother communicates her reception and transformation of a prospective identification to her infant, Segal replied, "I don't know—perhaps through some perceptual thing like tone of voice."

Others have devoted themselves to studying this question thoroughly. Crisp (1986) writes that "an element in the recipient must exist that can receive the projective identification" (p. 66). She explores this by considering factors that influence object choice, but finds little in the literature other than Klein's (1955) suggestion that projective identification occurs on the basis of the similarity or difference between projector and projectee. Crisp offers diagrams showing a number of possibilities that could account for the occurrence of a projective identification interaction. These factors are:

1. permeable ego boundaries between projector and projectee in general

2. permeable ego boundaries in a specific area only

3. permeable ego boundaries in general with concentration in a specific area

4. similarity between projector and projectee in one or more specific areas

5. complementarity between projector and projectee in one or more specific areas.

Crisp does not amplify on her concepts of similarity or complementarity. I would suggest that similarity refers to concordance between projected parts of the ego of the projector and parts of the ego of the projectee, while complementarity refers to concordance between projected parts of the ego of the projector with parts of the object of the projectee or vice versa.

For further elaboration on aspects of the induction and reception of projective identification, I turn to Bion (1959) and then look to Racker (1968) and Bollas (1987).

Valency

My starting point is Bion's concept of valency. In his study of small groups, Bion (1959) had noted a striking engagement of personalities around unconscious group themes. To account for it, he suggested the concept of valency: the instinctive capacity for instantaneous involuntary combination of one individual personality with another. Bion (1959) simply said that valency was "a spontaneous unconscious function of the gregarious quality in the personality of man" (p. 136). But this does not take us far enough into understanding how it happens, so I turn to the work of Racker.

Concordant and Complementary Identification

Racker (1968) described countertransference as the therapist's reaction to the patient's projections, organized as projective identifications occurring unconsciously in the therapist. These identifications might be of two types:

In *concordant identification*, the therapist identifies with a projected part of the patient's *self*.

In *complementary identification*, the therapist identifies with a projected part of the patient's *object*.

I have applied these ideas to the family therapist's experience of identifying with family group projections (Scharff and Scharff 1987). I also take Racker's formulation out of its therapeutic context and apply it to the marital relationship where it fills out Bion's concept of valency and Dicks's concept of unconscious complementarity. To put it simply, a wife's self (or part thereof) or object may be related to as her husband's object or as part of his self, exclusively, or simultaneously.

The result is an exponential progression involving mutual projection of and identification with parts of self and object in a growing cybernetic system of unconscious object relationships in the couple and the family.

Extractive Introjection

I also find helpful Bollas's (1987) concept of *extractive introjection* "an intersubjective process . . . in which one person invades another person's mind and appropriates certain elements of mental life" leaving the victim "denuded of parts of the self" (p. 163). The mental theft may be of ideas, feelings, mental structure such as superego, and parts of the self. For instance, when a parent introduces a new piece of sexual information to a child who says "I know that!" the parent is robbed of the information, of the feeling of sharing, and of the part of the self that longs to parent liberally. When a wife fails an exam for reasons that seem unfair and finds her husband more upset than she is, she is robbed of her right to outrage. When a parent is too harsh in punishing a guilty child, the child's capacity for taking responsibility and for feeling an appropriately corrective amount of guilt may be impoverished. In extreme cases, extraction may be "followed by vaporization of the psychic structure" (p. 164). In other cases, Bollas continues, "as a person takes from another person's psyche, he leaves a gap, or a vacuum, in its place. There he deposits despair or emptiness in exchange for what he has stolen." Thus, "each extractive identification is accompanied by some corresponding projective identification" (p. 164).

Now I am in a position to add a fourth stage to Sandler's (1987) three stages in the development of the concept of projective identification. They were: (1) the real object is not affected; (2) the real object is affected; (3) the object affects the fantasy.

To which I add: (4) the object attracts the fantasy.

To account for the attraction exerted by the object upon the projective identification, I had to invoke concepts of valency and extractive introjective identification. To understand the simpler phenomenon of how the object was affected by the fantasy, I needed but did not have access to the concept of introjective identification. Like many others, I rather devalued it. Before completing the development of my own description of projective identification, based on my synthesis of the various points of view that I have presented, I need to devote the next chapter to the topic of introjective identification.

CONCLUSION

The argument has focused on whether or not projective identification is a one-body or a two-body phenomenon. At least most writers agree that projection is a one-body phenomenon but disagree over whether it is always a psychotic process. In the case of projective identification, all are aware of its interpersonal context, but Zinner—even though exquisitely aware of mutual projective identification—conceptualizes the process as entirely intrapsychic; Ogden emphasizes that it is both intrapsychic and interpersonal but he does not develop ideas of mutuality of projective identification; and Bollas takes us beyond projective identification to its polar opposite, "extractive introjection." Between projective identification and extractive introjection lies the comparatively forgotten concept of introjective identification, an independently useful concept in its own right as well as a subphase of projective identification. Introjective identification is the bridging concept that allows us to see projective identification as both a one-body and a two-body process.

In summary, I conclude that the confusion about projective

identification has been to some extent an inevitable consequence of the ambiguity of the process. We have been confused by un-acknowledged differences in meaning of the term *identification* in the writings of various authors, following one and ignoring the other aspect of the dual meaning introduced by Segal (1964), because of the difficulty of holding complexity and ambiguity in mind. I suggest that problems in agreeing on definitions of projection and projective identification stem from differences in viewing the identificatory phase of the process. Authors differ as to where in the identificatory process they think the identification itself is located, either in self or other, in ego or object, in internal object or in external object. In addition to using the two meanings for the term *identification* (assimilation and naming), some authors emphasize identification by the self with the part projected in the object, some focus on the external object's identification with the projected part, and others include both. In debate about projective identification, our opinions are influenced toward the intrapsychic or interpersonal dimensions by our personal experience of the relationship between self and other in the early months of life, in other words, by our resolution of the phase Klein called the paranoid–schizoid position in which projective identification emerges as the major defense.

My goal has been to minimize confusion and miscommunication on this topic of projective identification, without robbing the concept of its versatility or creating further confusion. When a theoretician clarifies his views, I may feel confused because it appears that he has altered the concept yet again. Instead, I can see that he is relocating his views in a certain position on the continuum of meaning. When different personal emphases are understood as elaborations rather than as confuscations or arguments, then we are in a position to deal with the concept of projective identification in its full complexity. To this end, I will propose in Chapter 4 that we agree on projective identification as an umbrella term, subsuming processes of varying degrees of completeness involving the intrapsychic and interpersonal dimensions.

3

The Forgotten Concept of Introjective Identification

In the clinical setting of psychoanalysis, there has been more discussion of the process of projective identification than of introjective identification. Our understanding of countertransference has been vastly increased by the illuminating application of the process of projective identification between patient and therapist. So, why has introjective identification not been equally helpful? What can introjective identification mean to patient and therapist? Here the repudiated specter of corrective emotional experience (Alexander et al. 1946) rears its ugly head. No therapist wants to be accused of that, and so the possibility of the patient's introjective identification with the analyst or therapist object is not addressed. There is, however, a more deeply repressed reason for ignoring introjective identification, namely to avoid recognizing ways in which the analyst introjectively identifies with her patients. These valencies for introjective identification, if ever detected, might be even more revealing than those lit up in response to a provocative projective identification.

Is the analyst ready to take responsibility for her personality contribution to the treatment process? Is she ready to go beyond the classical use of countertransference into the realm of intersubjectivity? Is she willing to explore her internal object relations, her identifications and the accompanying primitive anxieties, sexual and aggressive feelings, and her psychological and physical vulnerabilities, outside a patient role for herself in her own analysis? I decided that I was willing, but the harder I looked, the less I could see. Gradually appearing out of the mists of worked-over case material came the examples with which I hope to make my point in this chapter and throughout the book. Before sharing those, I need to review some contributing theoretical constructs.

INTROJECTION

Introjection has been called "the most important and mysterious concept in psycho-analysis" (Meltzer 1978, p. 14), yet "introjection and introject have in no way found in the psychoanalytical literature a place comparable to projection and project." (Menzies-Lyth 1983, p. 1). Freud's theories of cannibalistic introjection, selective identification, and the formation of the superego, along with Klein's illuminating descriptions of unconscious fantasy and internal objects provided models for conceptualizing the development of the internal world, but even taken together they hardly describe the process by which the child's experience of the external object is taken in (Meltzer 1978).

In his comprehensive Kleinian concepts dictionary, Hinshelwood (1991) devotes thirty pages to projective identification, but does not include introjective identification in the index. He does deal with introjection, but the whole treatment occupies only three pages. He describes two possibilities for introjection as follows:

"introjection of an external object once external which is identified with (introjection identification)" and "introjection of an object which is not identified with, such as the superego" (p. 332). Note that *introjection identification* appears in parentheses, which to my mind restrict its importance. In his excellent, extensive treatment of internal objects, which he reports are normally identified with by the ego, Hinshelwood again refers to the term introjective identification, but it is once more relegated to the constraint of parentheses. He writes: "This fluid arrangement of identifications (introjective identification) suggests that internal objects *are available for* the ego to identify with and exist as a repertoire of identities, attitudes, roles, etc." (p. 77). (The introjects may also not be identified with, in which case they reside in the ego as alien objects.) My point is that Hinshelwood's dictionary accurately reflects the Kleinian use of the term introjective identification and relative lack of emphasis on the mechanics and expression of the process. Hinshelwood observes, "Surprisingly, for a term that is linked with—and a mirror image of—'projection,' the history and meaning of 'introjection' are very different and much less problematic" (p. 331).

I agree that projection and introjection are different. But introjection is no less problematic except in the sense that the problems have been overlooked. Meissner (1987) also remarks on our "tendency to overlook or underplay the equally important though less apparent role of introjective mechanisms" (p. 28). He quotes Searles (1965) on the importance of projection and introjection in paranoid schizophrenia: "Introjection, while less easily detectable, is hardly less important. The patient lives chronically under the threat, that is, not only of persecutory figures experienced as part of the *outer* world, but also that of *introjects* which he carries about, largely unknown to himself, within him. These are distorted representations of people which belong, properly speaking, to the world outside the confines of his ego, but which he experiences—insofar as he becomes aware of their presence—as having invaded his self." Introjection is even less readily detected in neurotic states.

Menzies-Lyth (1983) notes, "Projection seems to have stolen the limelight; it somehow turns out to be more exciting, more innovative, more illuminating, to our understanding of normal and pathological development" (p. 3). She goes on to suggest that the introjective process has been ignored because of interference from the effects of selective introjection by the patient on the analyst's narcissism—to which I might add that the analyst's narcissism may affect what the patient finds available for introjection. In other words the analyst is censoring the introjective process before and after it occurs, because it is gratifying inside the self. The dynamic introjective phase of the introjective–projective sequence in the analytic process tends to remain unconscious and therefore has not often been the object of study. Further consideration of the reasons for this will be explored in Chapter 12.

IDENTIFICATION

Before I attempt to explore introjection, I need to take a step back and consider the concept of identification. In psychoanalysis, identification is the psychological process whereby the subject assimilates an aspect, property, or attribute of the other and is transformed wholly or partially, in accord with the model the other provides (Laplanche and Pontalis 1973). In other words, the subject is tending toward becoming identical with the other in some important respects. Laplanche and Pontalis (1973) classify identification into two types: In *heteropathic, centripetal* identification the subject identifies his own self with the other, and in *idiopathic centrifugal* identification the subject identifies the other with himself. There is a clear correspondence here between the features used to distinguish between the two types suggested by Laplanche and Pontalis and those that Heimann (1951) uses to differentiate introjective from projective identification: "In *introjective identification* the subject's ego becomes like that of the object; *projective identification* renders the object's ego like that of the subject" (p. 166).

Identification made its first appearance in Freud's writing when he invoked the imitative factor to account for the contagion of hysterical symptoms. He realized, however, that it was not a simple imitation, but rather an assimilation by the subject's ego of the object on the basis of a shared similarity in their unconscious phantasies.

INCORPORATION AND INTROJECTION

From his study of the primal horde, Freud (1912) concluded that the sons devour the father and so accomplish their identification with him. Later, when studying mourning and melancholia, Freud (1917a) noted that the subject identified with the lost object in a psychological mode characteristic of the oral stage of development. In the 1912 and 1917 papers Freud described the taking in of the object for the purpose of identification in terms of an oral incorporative or cannibalistic expression of libido. He did not use the term *introjection*, although he used it in 1915 and acknowledged that it was Ferenczi who brought the term into currency. Describing introjection as a neurotic process, Ferenczi (1909) wrote: "The neurotic helps himself by taking into the ego as large as possible a part of the outer world, making it the object of unconscious phantasies. . . . One might give to this process, in contrast to projection, the name *Introjection*" (p. 47). Ferenczi thus defined introjection as the process in which the ego forms a relationship with an object and so includes that object within the ego. Incidentally, Laplanche and Pontalis (1973) criticized Ferenczi's lack of precision about introjection, his broadening it to encompass the transference, and his confusing it with what they would have called *projection*. Hinshelwood (1991) credits the same paper with clarifying the connection between introjection and oral impulses, and the linking of anal impulses with projection.

Freud (1915) described introjection by the ego as: "Insofar as the objects which are presented to it are sources of pleasure, it takes them into itself, "introjects" them (to use Ferenczi's [1909] term)." On the subject of projection, Freud (1915) added "and, on the other hand, it expels whatever within itself becomes a cause of unpleasure" (p. 136).

Freud remained somewhat unsatisfied with the body of work on identification (1933, p. 63), which had not progressed much beyond the succinct summary of his views given in 1921: "First, identification is the original form of the emotional tie with an object; secondly, in a regressive way it becomes a substitute for a libidinal object-tie, as it were, by means of introjection of the object into the ego; and thirdly, it may arise with any new perception of a common quality shared with some other person who is not an object of the sexual instinct" (pp. 107–108). What he is saying is that identification, or being like a parental object, is (1) a way of being in a relationship to that loved, feared, admired, or rivaled object; (2) a substitute for the object once it has been lost or given up; and (3) a way of relating to new nonincestuous objects. It always seems to me that when Freud wrote these ideas in his paper on group psychology, he was on the brink of developing an object relations theory. However, he turned firmly in the direction of structural theory that brought great technical advances in the treatment of unconscious conflict, but in my view curtailed the possibility for further enrichment of his ideas on identification.

By 1921, Freud was more commonly using the term *introject* rather than *incorporate* to express his earlier discovery that when an object is renounced or lost, the ego may find a substitute for the lost object by identifying with and introjecting the lost object. The lost object may be either the parent who is loved or the rival parent. More normally, instead of introjecting the whole of one of the parental objects, the child unconsciously selects parts of both objects and identifies with various admired or rejected parental traits. In an object relations point of view, the accretion of a myriad of such partial identities in dynamic relation constitutes the final total identity of the personality. Freud's point, however, was simply that the ego makes a partial alteration in itself after the model of the lost object that has been given up. "In this way," states Freud (1921) returning to the concept of introjection, "the ego has enriched itself with the properties of the object, it has 'introjected' the object into itself, as Ferenczi [1909] expresses it" (p. 113). However, the ego is not always enriched but rather impoverished when the introjected object is overvalued at the expense of the ego. This leads Freud to question *"whether the object is put in place of the ego or the ego ideal"* (p. 114).

This takes us from the role of introjection in ego development to its contribution to the formation of the superego. Introjection is also the means of setting up parental ideals, prohibitions, and demands in the mind of the child as the superego, formed at the end of the oedipal stage in resolution of the oedipal complex (Freud 1924). Even so, the superego is not derived simply from an introjection of parental qualities and values, alone. Freud emphasized that it includes reaction formation against those qualities and so the character of the superego is not at all a carbon copy of the actual demands put upon the child. Instead, it takes a unique form based on the individual's creative resolution of the oedipal complex and the introjection of accepted parental prohibitions *and* reaction formations against them. Introjection is therefore also an essential mechanism for superego development. The degree of completeness of introjection and identification varies with the age of the child. For the toddler the mother has to be present before the child remembers what she may not do. The latency child remembers in the absence of the mother what her mom has forbidden, and the teenager knows for herself whether or not she ought to give in to her own wishes. Introjective identification with parental prohibitions becomes progressively more secure until it is completely unconscious.

In object relations theory, introjection is similarly accorded an important place in superego development, but it is thought that the superego function of the personality begins to develop in the preoedipal period. The infant certainly has to cope with parental demands in the form of requirements about feeding habits, sleeping- and waking-patterns, and toilet training. So object relations theory holds that the infant begins to introject aspects of the experience with the demanding and controlling parent as early as the oral phase. The superego begins to form as the infant develops the capacity for ambivalence and concern for the loved mother and her nurturing breast that is also the object of its attacks. The infant experiences anxiety and depression about the strength of its aggression. The superego in formation has a less modified character than that achieved in the oedipal period because it is introjected under the dominant influence of the oral sadistic impulses that hold sway at that time. Analogous to Freud's caveat that introjection of parental demands is qualified by the introjection of reaction formations against them, object relations theory stresses the crucial role of projection of and nonidentification with aspects of the parental objects. The harsh early superego needed to counter the sadistic oral attack on the breast is modified in the oedipal period by the introjective identification with the parents' ideals and view of their child and by further projection of aspects of the parents that will not be identified with. Introjection and projection operate together to shape the final precipitate of selectively introjected parental aspects that comprise the personality after creative resolution of the oedipal complex.

Fairbairn (1952, 1954) maintains that introjection, fueled by inevitable frustration that occurs even with good mothering, underlies all psychic organization. Heimann (1973), stating the Kleinian point of view, holds that introjection and projection are "the roots of the ego, the instruments for its very formation" (p. 126). Klein (1946) and Menzies-Lyth (1985) clearly state that introjection and introjective identification with present objects—and not just lost objects as Freud suggested—are the basis for the development of the ego, a fact that Heimann (1973) notes is less accepted than that introjection leads to the formation of the superego.

Under the dominance of oral primacy, the infant's perception of the world is that all sensations are attributable to the feeding mother. Beginning with sucking on and swallowing from the breast, the infant introjects the breast and then by taking every new object into its mouth proceeds to introject all other objects. Heimann takes the infant's imitative behavior not as evidence of an imitative instinct, but as proof of prior introjection of the object as a model for the present imitative behavior.

Sandler (1987, p. 10) advises us to distinguish three meanings in the use of introjection: (1) the perceptual taking in of the outer world; (2) the construction of an important object in the child's fantasy world; and (3) the construction of the superego (Sandler 1960) in which the parental objects (modified by projections and other fantasy distortions) are "set up" in the mind of the child as his superego.

In ego psychological terms, Sandler (1987) defines introjection generally as "the setting up of unconscious, internal 'phantom' companions, felt to be part of one's internal world, yet external to one's self-representation." He allows for the possibility of modification of the self-representation through its identification with the introject (pp. 10–11).

Fairbairn (1954), on the other hand, regards introjection specifically as a defense, the first defense of the ego. Introjection occurs when experience with the external object is too painful to be borne. The external object is introjected as a rejected internal object that is then directly repressed. Introjection is a way of dealing with an object that feels bad, by taking it inside and controlling it there by pushing it out of consciousness. This mechanism leaves good aspects of the object uncontaminated by the more troublesome exciting and rejecting aspects. Fairbairn, committed to the point of view that introjection as a defense against frustration and helplessness is central to the formation of ego structure, is less vivid in his description of introjection of the good aspects of early relationships, and I have regarded his theory as flawed in this respect (Scharff and Scharff 1987). But after further reading and discussion with D. Scharff, who believes that satisfying experiences are also introjected because the infant is pre-wired to build psychic structure by introjecting all aspects of experience, I have revised my views. I now read Fairbairn as holding that good object experience is secondarily introjected to modify the intrapsychic void. Fairbairn's main expositor, Sutherland (1963, 1980, 1989, 1990), says that the good experience is taken in by the central ego and not repressed. It remains active in consciousness as the ideal ego. In his own teaching, Sutherland emphasized the infant's taking in the good experience by drinking in the mother's devoted expression with the eyes while nursing at her breast. Thus the building of an internal world results.

Menzies-Lyth (1983) agrees that introjection results in the formation of an internal world, but she does not believe that introjection has that aim. In her view the purpose has to do with "meaning, safety, security and with defense against anxiety" (p. 3). This aim can be studied during the process of psychoanalysis when we can observe under what conditions we are perceived as objects that give rise to the need for introjection. In gratifying the aim, the infant introjects, projects what is not wanted and reintrojects a modified version of the object, as a result of which the character forms. In discussion, Menzies-Lyth points out that there are some babies who face the dilemma of what to take in when a bad object is offered. Should they choose starvation or poison? Those who survive to lie on the analyst's couch have usually taken the poison option. Introjective identification is not just a defense against the bad object that paradoxically fills the self. It is also a way of having the object, which is seen as better than nothing. At least there is something there upon which to build psychic structure.

In therapy we encounter patients who deal with introjective identification in various ways that fall along a continuum of experience at the poles of which we find the following categories:

1. inhibition in introjective identification with the analyst or the analytic experience and

2. desperate and indiscriminate introjective identification of the analyst or the analytic experience

Inhibitions of introjection are associated with

1. fear of re-entry of that which has been projected into the analyst and

2. fear of the analyst–object's projections into the patient (Menzies-Lyth 1983).

INDISCRIMINATE INTROJECTIVE IDENTIFICATION

Patients who deal with the therapist or analyst through indiscriminate introjective identification are unusually willing to relate and take in what is being offered. At the same time they often curtail the analytic work by nailing the analyst down in the form of introjective identifications that do violence to the healing potential of the ambiguity of the analyst's identity, the reality of which the analyst subordinates to the use the patient must make of it. Offered as an object of nebulous potential, the analyst remains an unknown in relation to which aspects of self and other can be discovered. This unknown creates anxiety and stimulates growth and learning, but some patients cannot stand the ambiguity. They use indiscriminate introjective identification to create the illusion of knowing and feeling at one with the analytic object. In this way the patient deals with the anxiety of not knowing the analyst and with not knowing the internal objects that may appear as they are projected in the analytic space (De Varela 1990).

Introjective Identification with the Ideal Object

Mrs. Findlay had been in therapy for some years for suicidal ideation, poor self-esteem, rages at her children, and immobilizing depression. She recovered deeply repressed memories of physical and sexual abuse that persisted throughout her childhood. Her abuser was her mother, a seriously suicidal, promiscuous, alcoholic woman who had the additional stress of sustaining the deaths of her brother, husband, and son. From her father's death when she was 10, until she left home at 18 years of age, Mrs. Findlay shared a room with her mother. Mrs. Findlay had adored her father, but discovered unsuspected rage at him for failing to protect her from her mother. Mrs. Findlay had loving mothering from her maternal grandmother, a woman who had a strong religious faith and adored the patient.

My demeanor as an analyst hardly made me a likely candidate for the grandmother transference. Yet Mrs. Findlay experienced me mainly as a benign object, even when, through painful and embarrassing abdominal symptoms, she was reliving the abuse she had suffered (in the form of her mother's intense interest in subjecting the patient to enemas and douches). I expected Mrs. Findlay to experience my interpretations as intrusive and perverted. That did happen on a couple of important occasions, but mainly she kept me free from the transference that my work would appear destined to stimulate.

Instead of drawing me away from my neutral position toward enactment of abusive projections, she actively maintained me in a position of neutrality, while she described such enactments involving other people at home or work. Aggressive identification with her mother was present to a mild degree, but although this dynamic pushed her to yell at her children, it did not lead to similar rages at me. A victimized identification with herself as an abused child persisted but she rarely felt victimized by me. Her transference was analyzed mainly in its displacement to current relationships.

Her transference neurosis took the form of preventing a repetition of abuse from parental objects in her relationship with me, while transferring to me her once-idealizing transference toward her maternal grandmother. At the same time, she was creating me in the form of her idealized fantasy of the mother she did not have. She protected me to maintain me as this fantasy object. By far her strongest identification was with her beloved grandmother. Mrs. Findlay's capacity for introjective identification with the ideal object promoted a degree of ego strength that militated against the inevitability of a borderline personality structure. Her introjective identification with me as such an ideal object as her grandmother functioned as an effective and necessary defense against the re-entry of the projective identification of me as a harmful mother object that had been split off in analysis as it had been in childhood.

Mrs. Findlay's defense was so successful that after three years of therapy she had accomplished all her goals and wanted to finish treatment. No longer shy, depressed, and unsuccessful, she was doing well at her volunteer jobs, getting excellent grades in college, and had been cast in a play. I had to marvel at the progress she had made and I could recall good analytic work that I had helped her through. But I always had the feeling there was more work to do, mainly because I had not felt used, or perhaps more accurately I had not felt abused, in the transference. I felt that my therapeutic usefulness and ambition were being blocked. Yet I did not want to be the judge of what her goals should be, or want to make her fit my view of a complete analysis. I waited with interest for further developments that would throw light upon the issue of possible termination. Mrs. Findlay told me that she received praise and encouragement from her husband about being ready to finish. She talked optimistically of terminating her analysis in the near future.

The next day she was "blindsided" by a vicious neighbor who complained to others about her youngest daughter's behavior and inferred that Mrs. Findlay was not supervising her child adequately. Because of the neighbor's previous similar behavior, Mrs. Findlay avoided her; her anxiety about this neighbor reaching phobic proportions at times. By repeated actions, this neighbor had earned comparison to Mrs. Findlay's irrationally aggressive mother. When they heard the whole story, other neighbors discredited the complaining one and supported Mrs. Findlay. But unable to brush it off, Mrs. Findlay felt persecuted by this assault on her integrity as a mother. She became deeply depressed, withdrawn, and actively suicidal. When she called her husband for help, he reassured her, but did not come home. She was furious at him for ignoring her. But she did not call me. Would she not have felt equally angry with me? She was protecting me, as she always had, from the rageful transference stimulated by the neighbor who resembled her mother by displacing it onto her husband, whom she felt to be neglectful like her mother.

Sublimated Introjective Identification in the Arts

Mrs. Findlay volunteered her time at the Jewish senior citizens community center. She took a part in a play about a mother who lived and worked with her own mother in a family business. Usually a shy person, Mrs. Findlay suddenly was enjoying the limelight. But there was one problem. At three points in the play, Mrs. Findlay was interrupted by a recurrent cough.

"I play this woman who really loves her mother," she said, "as I did. But the difference is this mother loves her back and really respects this woman. And it's so different for me. To be in a loving, honest relationship with my mother—it's a wonderful chance for me. Of course, to create it, I can't draw on my relationship with my own mother, as the director suggested. I have to call on memories of being with my grandmother. It really feels great. But I think in some way it's too much for me. I start coughing all over the place, and we even had to devise a system of placing glasses of water for me around the set. In one scene we have to go through a small suitcase of lace collars. It's a very sweet scene and it reminds me of being with my grandmother, because she wore lace. It's when we look for the lace that I start coughing."

Mrs. Findlay was gratefully introjecting the new relationship with her stage mother. At last, the relationship she had with her grandmother could be integrated with her relationship to her mother, but because it seemed too good, she had to eject it in the form of a cough, a symptom that was characteristic of her own chain-smoking mother. The original object was thus allowed to declare itself and to some extent was gotten rid of, so that it did not poison the good introject. But Mrs. Findlay's main experience of the cough was as a threat to her smooth performance, just as the evocation of her mother in the transference would have threatened her smooth introjection of the therapist, held in the grandmother transference.

Introjective Identification and Renunciation

A final note. In the next session, Mrs. Findlay talked animatedly about the opening night of her play.

> *I felt that I would have enjoyed being there. I thought 'Too bad about rules of abstinence. What a pity I had to stay away.'*

Mrs. Findlay went on to say that she was disappointed that her best friend could not come to the show. Using her associations and my countertransference, I asked if she had any feelings about my not seeing her performance. She admitted that she wondered if my curiosity would get me to come, but she had not asked me because she expected that I would not cross that distance in our relationship. Her evidence for this was that I would not tell her if I had seen a movie she was discussing because what movies I went to was private. (This was her distorted perception of what was said. In fact, I had said that I thought that she needed to ask if I knew each movie she talked about in analysis, because she did not believe that her account had its own validity and integrity. I had explained that I preferred not to answer, because I wanted to explore her ideas, not mine.) Using this history of the transference, I pointed out that she wished I had seen the play to know how it had been, as if her account could not convey the experience.

"Of course," she confirmed. "I never feel good enough. And when my mother came to see me perform in school chorus, she always stuck out 'cause she was drunk, while I was buried in the altos. This time I was the lead. But I never see you as my mother. I see you more as a tape that stops and replays."

Here was a rather dehumanizing transference, but I did not feel as shut out by it as I might have, because I am interested in making videotapes and playing them back for study and teaching. I feel grateful to tapes for giving me access to material I would have missed the first time through. Perhaps this helped me see past her contempt to her defense against longing for more access to me.

I said that she had not known how much she wished for me to see her feeling good and competent in her dramatic role, the star of the show, in a relationship with a good mother. She wanted to project into me her wish for me to witness and validate her, so that it became my wish to see her. She then told me that a professional video had been made.

So I, as a tape, was there after all! I imagined getting to see the tape. As a therapist and as an actress myself, I would have liked to see Mrs. Findlay in the play, a feeling I could experience without having to gratify it. I did not burden her with my loss in not seeing the play, or act out my wish to see the play or the video, but used it to get in touch with her longing for me.

This was an example of mutual introjective identification. I was glad to experience this through the medium of theater, hoping that it might provide a rehearsal space for further experiences of introjective and projective identification in the analysis. Until this time, her treatment had been held static by the projection of an idealized transference that blocked the therapeutic opportunity for me to receive the projection of rejecting and exciting aspects of her bad object and identify introjectively with them. This left me with the feeling of there being something missing of her and of me. The countertransference had been in a state of partly blocked introjective identification because of the massiveness of the introjective identification expressed in the transference.

INTROJECTIVE IDENTIFICATION AND FEAR OF RE-ENTRY OF PROJECTIONS

In the next example, the state of introjective identification of the therapist as a good object is achieved as an advance on a prior state of projective identification of the therapist as a bad object. It is then savored and clung to as a defense against the reentry of the former projections into the object.

Introjection of Good Feeling

Mrs. Collins (also mentioned in Chapter 9) had been through a period of intense anger at me. Nothing I said was of any help. Her need to seek consultation about her daughter was perceived as proof of her own failure, and therefore of mine. After the work done at this time, Mrs. Collins became less depressed and her daughter settled down without treatment. Mrs. Collins resumed discussing things in a less pessimistic way, cautiously viewing me as someone who could potentially be helpful. The parents' association of the grade school her eldest child had graduated from asked her to attend a career workshop where she would be one of a number of adults willing to discuss careers with the children. She was assured that it did not matter that she had not worked for ten years while raising her family. Her experience of the work and training for it was what the school children needed to hear about. Mrs. Collins worked hard to prepare an excellent presentation. She read training catalogues, reviewed her notes and worked for two days developing statements of work purpose. She knew she was overfunctioning and overvaluing a minor task as if it were a major presentation. Among other things, I said that I understood her additional effort on the career issue was work on herself, not just work for the presentation.

The next day Mrs. Collins told me how much my comment meant to her, because I helped her to see something positive in her hard work. I had not picked it apart or pointed to the badness in overworking. She knew her anxious preparation did have mixed elements and she was glad I did not point them out. She could so easily have berated herself for being so silly and she preferred not to focus on that this time. She had had a dream: "You and I were sitting facing each other. You held out your hands to me and held them. You looked straight into my eyes. It wasn't an erotic thing. You were just giving me your understanding. And it felt so good."

I realized that this dream showed Mrs. Collins in a state of introjective identification. She, who so often had to push away, destroy, or sexualize what I was giving her, was now able to take it in and hold on to it. The dream confirmed her introjective identification with my positive attitude about her work on the presentation.

As the session went on, it became clear that Mrs. Collins did not want to explore other aspects of her anxious preparation, even though she knew of them. I said to her, "Mrs. Collins, I think you want to savor this experience of feeling good after doing something good and getting something good from me so you have something good to go on from, instead of spoiling it and feeling undermined as often happens."

"That's it!" she exclaimed. "I don't want to do anything else today or the rest of this week. I'm thinking how much I enjoyed the work, giving the presentation and being in that environment, which is so different from being at home. And I'm looking forward to getting out there again somehow. I don't know how yet, but at last those questions about what to do and where to do it are just questions about my work, not questions about me and proof that I'm inadequate."

Mrs. Collins introjected a satisfying aspect of her relationship to me and found within herself a good object she wanted to hold on to and build upon. This good object modified bad object experiences she had experienced with me earlier (see Chapter 9). Mrs. Collins's introjective identification with my attitude reminded me of the child taking in her parents' faith in her and finding the confidence to go on alone.

Fear of the Analyst–Object's Projections

Mrs. Bissinger, a professional woman and divorced mother in her early thirties, had been in four-times-a-week analysis for four years. She had successfully confronted her anorexia and bulimia, and was now a robust-looking, handsome woman, quite different from the long, thin stick I met four years ago. She was now dealing with her separation anxiety in a different modality than the oral route.

"I've mentioned being very churned up around you," she began her last session of the week. "I feel excited when I leave here, especially on Fridays. I feel excited when I leave, and I have to go and masturbate. I worry that my children will find out. And it is very threatening to me. I've been aware of it, and I've been trying not to notice it and not to experience it, while I am here. I don't even know why I'm bringing it up today."

Mrs. Bissinger went on to associate to her primary objects. "My mother was always the most youthful and beautiful woman around, I liked it that other people thought that. I don't remember thinking that about my father who was very handsome. You're very attractive to me. And I'm not sure how come."

Mrs. Bissinger's interest in me as an exciting, sexualized object came about after she saw a notice and photograph advertising a series of public lectures I would be giving in her diocese. She deeply resented my intrusion into her private mail and her religious life. She was envious that people found my views sufficiently interesting to invite me to speak to the lay public. She worried that I expected her to be equally fascinating (which, in a competitive way, she also wished). She resisted her idea that it was her job to entertain me, but she worried that if she said little or bored me with irrelevant details, I would get rid of her.

Having the unconscious meaning to her that other people found me exciting, the notice of my lectures drew the maternal transference to me. But her next comment that she did not know why she found me so exciting let me know that I did not have the physical appeal of her tall, slim, gorgeous mother. In other words, I did not seem exciting, except by association. I felt quite convinced of the difference between this aspect of me and her mother. This response was my introjective identification with a projected part of the patient's self in relation to the maternal object, I thought. A tall, attractive woman herself, she did not, however, present herself as alluring, but instead led with her helpfulness, reliability, and concern for the environment.

"Even now, my mother looks great," she added wistfully. "She dresses with a lot of head-turning appeal. Even going to sleep, she's dressed like a star. And she tries to get me to. She buys me lingerie, even now, and sends them to me. And they are always the perfect size. Beautiful underwear and nightgowns, far more expensive than I would ever buy. I can't take them back. I just put them in the closet and forget about them. Silk pajamas, lace nighties—they're just not me."

Subjectively and objectively, her alluring mother aroused excitement, recreated in the transference to me. Mrs. Bissinger had fallen silent for many minutes. I was not thinking of saying anything nor was I wondering what was stopping her flow of verbal communication.

She said, "I know I'm being silent and I don't want you to talk. I'm aware that I'm not sharing my feelings with you." In a while, she went on to talk about the war in the Persian Gulf. A marine biologist, she was particularly upset when the Iraqis had flooded the waters with oil that was harmful to fish and other sea creatures. "If I speak I'm afraid that a slew of black muck will settle on you," she eventually said.

Comfortable that the embargo against my talking was no longer necessary, I asked, "What are you afraid would happen if it did?"

"The muck might suffocate you. Then I would have to provide all the organization here and I'm afraid I won't be able to. You know what, this whole thing about the gulf is to keep feelings down there, distant and vague."

Her insight gave me the link I needed to interpret: "You've been keeping the feelings about the gulf between us, which you feel especially on the weekends, down there in your genital area where you can organize it as a physical feeling needing release, because this seems preferable to telling me of your feelings."

"Yes," she concurred quietly, "Because I can comfort the physical feeling." She moved away from the physical feeling to tell me about her need for me. "I wish I could be in analysis five times a week so as to see you more often, not to get more work done, but because I take a fair amount from you, and I need that, and I find the interruptions painful, and I lose ground."

I now understood that the opportunity for unconscious introjective identification was far more important than I had realized. She could not tell me of it, perhaps because she could not tell her working single mother how much she had needed her. Equally likely, she could not tell me of her need, because, like her mother, I was unaware how much I mattered to this very independent, well-functioning woman. Her way of obliterating the separation gulf was to transform grief into its opposite, excitement, in a manic defense that held me to her. In object relations terminology, I would say that she was projecting into me an exciting object that defended against her view of me as a rejecting object. Then she felt a manageable, satisfiable sexual longing rather than an unmanageable rage at the abandoning object. For my part, I had to ask myself, was I using theory to defend myself against the discomfort of the erotic transference? No doubt. But the usefulness of theory is that it gives us the distance necessary to experience a feeling state fully and intensely without becoming totally taken over by it.

The dynamic of substituting excitement for hurt and rejection originated with the loss of her father by divorce when Mrs. Bissinger was 7 years old. She exchanged her hurt at losing him for feelings about her mother as cold and unavailable, while unresolved oedipal sexual feelings for her father were simultaneously transferred to her mother who, as a phallic and exciting-looking woman had a valency to receive them. Reading about me as an invited speaker aroused her fear that I would present myself as the need-exciting object and that I might have the fantasy that she should be exciting to me, as her mother was to others and probably to her. In other words, she was afraid of being overwhelmed by my projections into her, as she had been afraid of the projections of the maternal object into her.

In a later session, following a period of anxious silence, Mrs. Bissinger made a joke about her progress in relating to her mother. I laughed along with her. I then learned of a more deeply repressed anxiety to which mention of the oily muck might have alerted me.

"I know I am not talking because I'm worried that if I tell you what's on my mind I will have to terminate with you. What I have to say could contaminate this relationship, could contaminate you."

"You are worried about the harmful effect that this could have, spoiling things, like the dark mess of oil from the Gulf. I feel that you want me to know about your dark and messy parts, but you want to protect me from them," I said.

"What I've been avoiding for so long is telling you about touching my anus," she replied. "I do find it very exciting but mainly I do it because it gives me a feeling of control. The anus seems a much more bounded space than the vagina, no—not the vagina—just the opening. It helps me to avoid anxiety about the vaginal opening and where it leads to. I had the sense the other day when I was masturbating my anus that it was as if someone else was there masturbating me. As if it was being done to me rather than me doing it. Talking about this messes up the environment and I feel I can't stay. I'm deeply anxious about this. If I discuss it more fully how could we continue to work together? I think that what's associated with it is very foul and rank. And it's very exciting to me and must involve a fantasy of wanting to mess you up and therefore having to part. Oh! Maybe the someone else in the fantasy was you! I have also had the idea of controlling you, keeping you near me so you don't leave me."

Until now I had thought of anal masturbation in association to the concept of projective identification, a connection pointed out by Meltzer (1966). He described idealization of the anus through which the patient could project destructive feelings. This formulation applied to Mrs. Bissinger. In order to escape my identification with her projected destructive feelings and my expected retaliation against them, she felt that she must leave me. I also detected Mrs. Bissinger's experience of me as an object that might stimulate or penetrate her anus. What was harder to grasp was her wish to have me close to her in the area of the anus.

I said to her, "You are wanting to send a stream of destructive feelings from your anus to mess me up, a situation which you assume you and I will then want to get away from, but you are also thinking of your anus as a place I might want to get to and a place where you could keep me safe so I don't leave you."

In addition to its role in projective identification, anal masturbation supports introjective identification with the object. In this modality, the anus is viewed as the site of receiving the feared projections of the object and also the place to hold the loved aspect of the object. In the countertransference, I experienced the projection of the fecal stream as something against which I would retaliate, as much closer to consciousness than the urge to project into the patient's anus. Working on these themes however, I found that if I could tolerate the idea of being inside the patient's anus— not just a masturbating finger but my entire person—it seemed to help her talk about this anxiety-provoking subject. In other words, the therapist's introjective identification with the patient's fantasy is essential to therapeutic progress. But this type of introjective identification is threatening to one's reaction formations. It is much easier to deal with the therapeutic process in terms of one's reactions to the other person's projections. I think this is a major reason for the ignoring of the concept of introjective identification.

After a series of dreams illuminating her sense of endangering me and of my retaliating against her, Mrs. Bissinger became silent. She hinted that she had things to say but was not saying them.

"You'll think I'm being withholding," she accused me. Giving me to feel it was my fault that she had thought of it, she continued, "Being withholding reminds me of anal masturbation." She went on to talk of sending and receiving letters from her mother. Her mother's letters were always neatly typed on decorative stationery, whereas hers were always a mess, about which her mother complained. "I don't get upset when my kids do untidy work," she went on. "My mother just gets too aroused about mess. Am I like that? Only with my body, I am fastidious. I don't want her body near me ever. I remember how she used to bathe me and stick a washcloth in my ear with her finger and it hurt. That's connected to anal masturbation when there's a sense of it being done to me by someone else. I've only done it in the bath or shower where I can easily rid myself of it. Hearing you laugh at my joke the other day is what made it easier to talk today. I'm relieved that you can laugh. Much different than my mother. I don't know if I ever heard her laugh."

My laugh represented an introjective identification with the patient's self in relation to the object outside us both, namely the mother who usually did not find things funny. My independence from the object of projection was regarded as facilitating. But in the next session, the patient reproached me for laughing and said that she had found it intrusive. My laugh now represented an identification of me with the intrusive aspect of the maternal object.

THE FUNCTIONS OF INTROJECTION: DEFENSE AND STRUCTURE BUILDING

Meissner (1987) also emphasizes the defensive aspects of introjection. He writes:

> Introjection preserves the relationship to the object within the ego, but in doing so it creates an internalized presence that is subject to primary process influences and preserves its derivative character. . . . The defensive operation of introjection, therefore, attains some self-preservative compromise, but it interferes with the ego's capac-

ity to integrate itself less in drive derivative terms and more in terms of mature object-relatedness . . . Introjection . . . in its defensive aspects tends to fix processes of internal structural formation in drive-derivative primary process types of organization, and thus it prevents the emergence of more autonomous secondary process of ego integration. [p. 34]

Like Fairbairn, Meissner tends to a pathological view of introjection.

In Kleinian object relations theory, the infant experiences the object through sensory experience which is felt as either all good or all bad. From its base in sensory experience, object relations are similarly experienced as all good or all bad until maturation of the drives and the ego permit more sophisticated discrimination. Whether the experience falls in the good or the bad category is determined mainly by the infant's needs, impulses, and fantasies. (Object-relations theorists of the Independent Group traditionally are viewed as more likely to include the crucial contributing factor of the actual mothering, but Bion (1967) and Menzies-Lyth (1985) of the Kleinian group certainly gave due attention to mothering.) If the experience is good it is introjected in a psychological mode equivalent to sucking and swallowing. If it is bad it is projected outside into the object in a psychological mode equivalent to spitting out. These alternating modes create potential categories of good/bad, inside/outside and me/not me. The infant tends to usurp the object's pleasurable qualities and claim them as part of the self and to disown painful qualities and attribute those to the object. In Heimann's words (1973), "There is a tendency to introject what is pleasurable and to split off and project what is painful" (p. 143).

At first the infant is so helpless and dependent on the object for supplies that he defends against this awesome predicament by the omnipotent phantasy that his objects exist only for his satisfaction. As Heimann (1973) put it, "they belong to him, are part of him, live only through and for him" (p. 142). Even when something has been spat out, it got there by the infant's spitting and it still relates to the infant's body, and so the outside is still perceived as belonging to the inside. Furthermore, the outside object of the breast is also incorporated in phantasy so that the good breast can be possessed inside the infant's self and recalled by the stimulation of sucking on part of his own body, for instance the thumb. Following its introjection, "the good object has such strong psychic reality that for the time being the need for the feeding breast can be stifled, overpowered, successfully denied and projected outside, whilst the sucked part of his body is identified with the introjected breast, the desired object" (p. 147).

According to Bion (1967), the infant introjects and identifies with both (1) the mother as the object that contains his anxieties, and (2) the process of containment through which she accomplishes this. She functions as a container by using her capacity for reverie in which she is able to hold in her mind her infant's unorganized expressions of need and distress and return them to the infant in a modified, detoxified form. Thus she contains her infant's anxieties and the infant identifies with her as the container. It bears repeating that the container is not a can full of baby anxiety contents, but is a containing function, operating in dynamic equilibrium between mother and baby.

Bion operationalized a particular feature of reverie that he called the mother's *alpha function*. Alpha function refers to the process that occurs when the mother takes in her infant's unorganized signals of unthinkable distress, need, loving, and hateful impulses—which Bion called *beta elements*—transforms them into tolerable and thinkable experiences—which Bion called *alpha elements*—and returns them to her infant as manageable states of being. The infant introjects and identifies with the alpha function of the containing mother in her state of reverie and can then take in and detoxify experience for himself. This enables the infant to store experience instead of having to evacuate it by projection. Specifically, alpha function converts the more primitive data of sensory impressions into alpha elements of dream, fantasy, or waking thoughts.

In some cases the container is faulty. The infant introjects it nevertheless. The infant is then identified with and hampered by an inadequate capacity for alpha function. The infant still has to deal with its own unmetabolized projections that are experienced in relation to the mother and with her projections into the baby. When her alpha function is not too wholesome, we can assume that her projections are not well modulated either. So in this case the infant is introjecting damage and distortion. One might think that the infant should deal with the situation by keeping things out. Some infants do just that, but such an autistic solution has serious consequences for future relatedness. The less drastic defense is the more common: introjection in order to gain control over the bad experience and to hold on to the pleasure of the good experience.

So, according to Bion, introjection is important in creating the thought process. Meltzer (1978) makes a similar point when he says that the stimulus for introjection is the need for food for thought. Meltzer points out that satisfaction by good or bad experience is the precondition for introjection. The cycle occurs something like this: The infant feels sensations of hunger. The mother recognizes this and nurses her infant. The infant feels gratified. The next time the infant is hungry, his preconception of the needed breast propels him toward it. When this is followed by the actual realization of either the feeding breast, accompanied by the quieting of his sensation, or the unavailable breast, with the aggravation of his sensation, the connecting thought in the state of satisfaction or frustration respectively comes into being and the apparatus for thinking develops. Thinking creates a bridge between the moment of seeking the desired object and its realization. The role of introjection that Bion ascribes to thinking as a process that creates a bridge between the moment of seeking the desired object and its rediscovery, clearly has echoes of Freud's view of introjection as the mechanism for the recreation inside the self of the lost object.

Introjection rarely occurs alone, because what is introjected is then subject to other mental mechanisms including projection. For instance, Segal (1990) described a patient's relationship to her introjected object and showed how this determined two of the patient's reactions, the first to Segal's face as if it were a bottom and the second one of contempt for Segal's interpretations. Having gotten something inside, this patient became forgetful and neglectful of it, or pushed it back at Segal contemptuously. Her motivation for forgetting what she had, was to keep it inside so she did not lose it to the outside world (leading to symptoms of constipation and inhibition in writing), and so that she did not have to look at it, in which case she would discover that it was fecal, a possibility she expressed and avoided by projecting contempt onto the analyst. This patient had the capacity to introject, but because of her need to devalue what she was given, she turned it inside herself into simultaneously overvalued and hated shit of her own making. In summary, what she had introjected was a destroyed yet idealized fecal object. Related but different dynamics are illustrated in the next example from my own practice.

Introjection of a Faulty Container

Andy, a tall, handsome but wasted 26-year-old man, with a somewhat asexual but not gay manner, consulted me for anxiety and depression. He was embarrassed to be living at home with his mother and stepfather, but he could not afford his own place because his ability to earn a living as a musician was compromised by his ill health. He could not stand the strain of playing and driving to late-night gigs. His anxiety took the form of knots in the stomach that prevented his eating and triggered allergies to many foods. This eating problem first emerged when he was 9 years old, following the unexpected death of his workaholic father by cardiac arrest on a business trip. After this he became overly concerned about his grieving mother and even more tied to her as his primary object than he had been. When he left for college, she met and married her present husband with whom she had what Andy described as a committed but emotionally distant marriage. Andy's depression affected his self-image so that he appeared gross-looking to himself, especially because, in his view, his face was disfigured with acne scars from pimples that he had squeezed compulsively to get rid of bad stuff. He was acting out his worries about interpersonal interaction at the skin and mucosal boundary of the self. Andy dealt with the early anxiety of relating to me across these boundaries through severe physical symptoms, rather than words for his worries about me and analysis. He invoked in me a concern for his upset skin and intestine and his underweight body. I expressed this in comments that aimed at finding word equivalents for his communication to me. I interpreted to him that he was wanting to find in me a mother concerned for and devoted to his body. I said that his body was screaming for me to be there and to know that he felt bad. After this interpretation he was able to re-introject the concern he had projected into me, to get some temporary relief from his physical symptoms, and to turn to verbal exploration of his history and life situation, encompassing themes from all psychosexual stages of development.

As therapy progressed, Andy's emotional investment shifted from the skin to the intestinal mucosa and musculature. No longer concerned with squeezing out badness, he was now worried about taking in good food without its turning bad inside. For him, food was a feared and damaging property that turned to painful diarrhea. I asked if mushy food also caused diarrhea. Andy was appalled at the thought of mushy food because it would already look like diarrhea. Now I learned of many associations to food as fecal productions. Prunes, raisins, chocolate chip cookies, applesauce, chunky soup were all disgusting. Any foods with holes in them, even if well formed, like bagels, Swiss cheese, or pineapple rings, were to be avoided. Andy's difficulties with establishing an integrated body ego were based on the failure to take in food from the feeding mother because her food was smashed up like feces. According to him the problem dated from the death of his father. Perhaps Andy's rage at his mother for being depressed when her husband died and for not keeping him alive for her son, or his envy when she found a new husband, had, as one might say, turned her food to shit. Perhaps his depressed mother felt bad about what she had had to offer. Because of her pathological grief, his mother was unable to stay separate from or to process her child's anxiety and depression.

I continued to feel that the problem must have had its antecedents in earlier times. Perhaps these were sufficiently resolved by maturation during latency so that Andy was not symptomatic as a child. Perhaps without the effect on him and his mother of his father's death, Andy might have gotten through life without gastrointestinal symptoms. Nevertheless, the location of his difficulties in that area suggests problems in his mother's way of dealing with the anxieties of the paranoid–schizoid position when she encountered them in his first year of life. It is likely that her functioning as a responsive, non-anxious mother when Andy was a needy baby was somewhat shaky and further threatened by her feelings of abandonment by her husband, not through his death, but his devotion to business travel. In Bion's terms she did not function well as a container. So the patient had introjected a faulty containing function, its vulnerabilities projected onto the external and internal surfaces of his body. The physical correlate of the inhibition in introjecting nourishment, contaminated by its destruction due to projected rage and envy, found its physical expression in low weight and involuntary malnutrition.

Introjection and projection are not, however, confined to the oral phase or paranoid–schizoid position. Strong oral incorporative and expulsive tendencies persist through the depressive position (and on into the early oedipal period). Nevertheless, as the infant matures in the depressive position, simple defenses of denial, omnipotence, and splitting to protect against frustration and object loss have to be given up, now that the infant is capable of holding the object in the mind over time and across different feeling states of gratification and frustration. The gratifying object is now known to be the same object as the frustrating one, the present breast is continuous with the absent breast. This capacity for ambivalence, characteristic of the depressive position, brings severe anxieties in its wake. The infant is now aware of the possibility of destroying or losing the mother.

As Heimann (1973) says, "To yield to the desire to incorporate the good object is fraught with the danger of taking in its badness, and conversely the expulsion of the bad inner object threatens the loss of its goodness" (p. 161). She warns that problems at this stage in development can lead to inhibition of introjection and projection, which retards development, or to a frantic alternation between taking in and expelling, resulting in instability, moodiness, and failure in developing the capacity for attachment to objects.

At the beginning of the oedipal period, oral, urethral, anal, and genital impulses coexist in chaos, all of them frustrated by the parents who, in the primal scene are imagined by the child to be doing to each other all that the child is prevented from enjoying. The frustrated child wishes to join in or else destroy the frighteningly gratifying pair that excludes him so miserably. But love and need for the individual parent preclude that solution. The child resorts to phantasy to cope with the primal scene. Although the impulses are quite polymorphous, there is still oral primacy and it is to oral incorporative phantasy that the child returns. He imagines that the parents in sexual intercourse are incorporating each other and that this will lead to their death and eventually his own death. He deals with this frightening scenario by oral incorporation, that is, he takes into himself not just the image of each parent individually but together as the combined parental figure whose dangerous activities are now felt to take place inside the child's body. There the child finds the mixed blessing of feeling closer to his loved ones and their pleasure only to find that this does nothing to salve his jealousy about being excluded. Following his introjection of the combined parental figure, he is also closer to their imagined cannibalistic attacks on each other (and therefore on him) but at least he can imagine keeping an eye on his loved ones and controlling their destructiveness.

A further aspect of introjection at this phase focuses on the wish shared by children of both sexes to incorporate the father's penis by sucking on it and swallowing nourishment from it as if it could replace the breast after weaning. Imagining sexual union in line with his own wishes, the child imagines that the mother incorporates the father's penis and keeps it inside her as a source of constant gratification and power. Meanwhile the father possesses the mother's breast. Presumably, it is because she has such a valued object to trade that the powerful father goes along with her request and not with his children's wishes. Phantasies about the self or the object incorporating the penis give the male child a way of keeping the father's penis safe from envious attack and his own penis less likely to deserve retaliatory castration. They give the female child some relief from her feelings of loss and deprivation that she is not the proud possessor of her own or her father's penis and provide a bridge to the possibility of her vaginal receptiveness to the penis that could give her a baby. At first, she is focused on receiving the penis of her father in competition with her mother, and later when she has renounced her hopeless claim, she settles for her own future husband.

Heimann (1973) concludes her review of the functions of introjection and projection in shaping the growth of the ego and superego. She writes:

> In this process of growth, unification and clarification which extends over the first childhood years, introjection and projection make important contributions towards modifying the inner and outer worlds, and lessening both persecution and its counterpart, idealization. The child loses more and more of his helplessness and omnipotence, and the parents of their characters as gods or monsters. This goes together with a change in the child's phantasies about his internal parents. He comes to feel them less and less as physical objects within his own body, and more and more as ideas and principles to guide and warn him in his dealings with the world. Thus from the primitive notions about incorporated parts and persons the system of the super-ego is gradually built up. [p. 167]

SLIPPAGE IN USE OF TERMINOLOGY:
IDENTIFICATION, INTROJECTION,
INCORPORATION, INTERNALIZATION

Throughout my reading on introjection, I notice a slippage in terminologies, much as I described in my review of projective identification. In the Heimann (1973) article, which I found most helpful, she clearly follows the Freudian definition of identification, which refers to a process of assimilation in which the ego becomes like the introjected object. For her, introjection is a mental mechanism of taking in experience in a psychological way based on the dominant physical mode of taking in by the oral route. I noted that she then makes a shift from introjection to incorporation without defining the mechanisms separately. It appears from her writing that she views incorporation as a type of introjection occurring under the influence of cannibalistic phantasies characteristic of the early oedipal phase.

Laplanche and Pontalis (1973) similarly note the interchangeable use of terms and ask that "the term identification should be distinguished from other, kindred terms like 'incorporation,' 'introjection' and 'internalization.'" They go on to explain that "Incorporation and introjection are prototypes of identification—or at any rate of certain modes of identification where the mental process is experienced and symbolized as a bodily one (ingesting, devouring, keeping something inside oneself, etc.)" (p. 207). In fact they do not distinguish between introjection and incorporation directly, but they do provide further elaboration on both concepts separately. From these comments, I have drawn the following conclusions.

At first, incorporation referred to the instinctual aim (and later included the relevant object relationship) characteristic of the oral stage in which the subject has an object penetrate his body and then retains it there for the triple purpose of receiving gratification of the pleasure aim, destroying the object, and appropriating its qualities. The latter appropriation is what qualifies incorporation as a prototype of identification. Laplanche and Pontalis also usefully remind us that although oral in mode, incorporation may be extended to other organs that are imagined to substitute as ingesting, or retentive areas such as the rectum and the vagina and less obviously the skin and the lungs.

Like incorporation, which is closely related to identification, introjection also refers to the transposing of objects from the outside to the various parts of the psychic apparatus on the inside, for instance, into the ego or ego-ideal. The boundaries across which the object is introjected do not have a direct correlation with the actual body boundaries, whereas the incorporation of the object involves the bodily frontier literally. Nevertheless, Laplanche and Pontalis say that incorporation provides the bodily model for introjection. They report that introjection and incorporation are often used interchangeably by Freud and other analytic writers. To my mind, however, a distinction between introjection and incorporation could be made: in introjection the transposition is achieved by receptiveness without the accompanying phantasy of the object's penetration that is characteristic for the process of incorporation. That proposed distinction may not prove crucial in practice.

On the topic of identification versus internalization, Laplanche and Pontalis are more forthcoming with a proposed distinction. They say that the ego *identifies with objects or parts thereof*, whereas it *internalizes intersubjective relations* and transforms them into intrasubjective ones. This clarifies their view of the difference in usage, but it does not help me to distinguish between the mechanisms because, as the authors themselves point out, the trait identified with is inextricably intertwined with the relationship in which it is experienced, the relationship being indistinguishable from the object that embodies it. Laplanche and Pontalis (1973) admit that the elaboration of the psychical apparatus as one consisting of the relics of object relationships is not developed by Freud or any other psychoanalytic writers to the point where there is a systematization of the various modes of identification. Since they fail to give Kleinian references on introjective processes (although they do give projective identification due attention) one cannot be sure whether they overlooked them or discarded them as unsystematic. The validity of their conclusion is also limited by their not commenting on the work of Fairbairn (1954, 1963) who did attempt to present a systematic theory of internal object relations based on introjection and subsequent splitting and repression of introjected objects. Nevertheless, their discussion draws attention to ignored aspects of terminology and points the way to the need for a systematic object relations theory to develop the concept of identification further. Since we now have that, I will present an integrated view of the concepts of introjective identification and projective identification in the next chapter and then illustrate their combined action in development in Chapter 5 and in therapy in Chapter 12.

4

An Integrated View of Projective and Introjective Identification

PROJECTIVE IDENTIFICATION

Theoretical contributions to the topic of projective identification have led to brilliant insight and utter confusion. I suggest that the confusion stems from the following:

1. There is looseness in terminology originating with Klein's discursive style of writing.

2. Segal's clarification of the dual meaning for identification led to accepting one or the other meaning, instead of both.

3. Problems in definition stem from the resulting unacknowledged shifts in meaning of "identification" and whether it is thought to be located either in subject or object, projector or projectee.

4. Confusion arises from ambiguity inherent in the process.

5. Theoreticians' capacities to articulate the process are affected by their own projective identificatory processes in relation to the theoretical material and by their personal solutions to developmental issues of separation and attachment that determine personal tendencies toward and tolerance for projective identification.

INTROJECTIVE IDENTIFICATION

Introjective identification, like projective identification, is a somewhat elusive concept. Argument over its definition, however, has been singularly absent. I think that it has been regarded as falling squarely in the intrapsychic dimension and therefore has not excited anxiety about the boundaries of self and other. So there has been no need for heated debate about whether it is a one- or two-body phenomenon. The specter of interpersonal process has not muddied the analytic waters in which the concept of introjective identification has been virtually sunk, though fortunately not without trace. Perhaps its original association with Freud's (1917a) concept of introjection of the dead, lost object has meant that, once taken in and identified with, the concept represents a way of hanging on to the words of the founder. The lack of debate, which Freud himself regretted, has meant that the concept has not received enough consideration and elaboration.

The concept of introjective identification can only find its true measure of importance if our introjective identification as therapists with instinct and ego-psychology theories can be modified and integrated with the developing trend of interest in object relations theories of Fairbairn (1952), Guntrip (1961, 1969), Kernberg (1975), Winnicott (1958, 1965, 1971), Bollas (1987, 1989), Sutherland (1963, 1980) or self-psychology theories (Kohut 1971, 1977). In his characteristic terminology, Kohut (1982) makes the relevant point that psychoanalysis can move on to reach its potential "only if it can make the decisive developmental step of the full transmuting internalization of the great parental selfobject of its past. . . . It must turn from the study of Freud to the study of man" (p. 405).

In summary, confusion and lack of attention to introjective identification in development and therapeutic process stem from the following:

1. It is associated with Freud's use of introjection and identification in mourning.

2. Our phallocentric culture emphasizes putting out rather than taking in.

3. Projective identification has subsumed it.

4. Analysts' narcissism prevents acknowledgment of introjective identification with or by patients.

Based on my review of the literature in Chapters 2 and 3 and on my clinical experience with patients in psychoanalysis and in psychoanalytic couple- and family-therapy, I present my own description of projective identification as an umbrella concept that subsumes a series of subtypes. It also includes introjective identification as a subphase. Similarly, introjective identification, a process in its own right, is refined by ensuing processes of projective identification. Both processes carry normal structure-building and defensive functions. Both are necessary for normal development and both are exaggerated in pathology. Introjective and projective identification occur along a continuum from health to pathology.

INTROJECTION, INTROJECTIVE IDENTIFICATION, PROJECTION, PROJECTIVE IDENTIFICATION

For simplicity, I refer to the person who is doing the projecting as *the projector*. The person receiving the projection will be called *the projectee*. The person initiating an introjective identification will be called the *introjector*. The person from whom the introjection is selected will be the *introjectee*.

The following steps characterize introjective identification.

1. Introjection

The introjector takes in a feeling, an idea, or a part of the self or object of another person, the introjectee. Introjection may be simply a way of perceiving the outside world or it may be the first step in the construction of an internal object in the realm of the ego or superego. Introjection is classically viewed as occurring by the oral route. I think that it also occurs through the eyes, ears, nose, skin, vagina, and, as I demonstrated in Chapter 3, through the anus.

2. Identification

The introjector now identifies with the introject. The self becomes like the part that has been taken in from the introjectee. In the course of development, the introjectee is most often a parent. The part taken in may be a loved, feared, or rivaled part of the other person. It may be accurate or distorted by feelings about the other person. It will form an amalgam with other introjections to form an internal object with which the self is in close relation and which represents both becoming like and reacting against the external object found in the introjectee. Introjective identification occurs in order to maintain a tie to the introjectee, to re-create a lost relationship, to possess something good that is admired or envied, to protect the other person from something bad, or to displace and become the other person.

3. Psychic Structure Formation

Introjective identification leads to the formation of the ego and the superego. Freud saw the superego as a superimposed censoring structure made up entirely of introjective identifications with the parents and reaction formations against them at the oedipal stage. In Fairbairn's object relations theory, in relation to objects experienced as bad, we see aggressively forbidding parts of the ego splitting off as subformations to preserve the central ego from intolerable aspects of its interaction with the parents. These ego parts are somewhat equivalent to superego structure described by Freud, but they develop long before the oedipal phase. In Kleinian theory, introjective identification contributes to the development of the superego in infancy. When the introjective identification is with a bad object, the self may act aggressively to that internal object and its representatives when it is re-projected in a relationship, or the self may be bombarded by the bad object found in a new relationship. If the introjected part is identified with by the superego and overvalued, the self may actually be denigrated. When the introjected object is a good object, it contributes to the formation of the ego ideal and colors the ego positively.

4. Reprojection and Projective Identification

Now the process ties in to the steps of projective identification.

Projection

In *projection*, a part of the self—either a part of the ego or its internal objects, or a feeling or an idea originally connected to the self or objects split off from them—is expelled from the intrapsychic domain and displaced to an external object during an unconscious mental process. The person doing the projecting (called the projector) has no awareness of the projection onto the other person (the projectee), and so has a feeling of separateness from the external object that possesses the expelled part of the self. The object is believed to be invested with qualities that it does not have. The only identification occurring is that of identifying or misrecognizing a quality in that object. Semantically, one might argue that the term projective identification applies because of the occurrence of identification in a form inherent in Segal's definition of projective identification. But technically it does not qualify as a projective identification because there is no feeling of oneness with the recipient of the projection. The projection does not necessarily fit. It may be a delusion as in paranoia, a misperception as in neurosis, or a normal momentary expulsion followed by reintrojection of an unaltered projection.

Projective Identification

In projective identification, a number of steps follow. The first step is always a projection. Whether it remains a projection or becomes a projective identification depends on whether the second step of identifying the object with the projection occurs. Here I mean the external or the internal object. If the only object affected is the internal object, then the process remains an intrapsychic one. Whether it remains a single projection- or a dual projection-projective identification depends on whether the object of the projection actively contributes to the process or not. When the external object of the projection contributes to the process, either actively by exciting and deserving the projection or passively by not refuting it, then projective identification has entered the interpersonal dimension. Then the object may simultaneously project parts of itself into the subject, thus creating a mutual process of projective identification. If all the steps are completed, the process of projective identification goes beyond description as a one-body or two-body phenomenon to a multi-part-and-object phenomenon, a description that does justice to the recruitment into the process of any number of parts of self and objects of one, two, or more personalities in unconscious communication during interaction in family life.

The following steps characterize *projective identification*.

1. *Projection*. The projector expels a part of the self or its objects into an external object and identifies the external object as if it were imbued with qualities that do not pertain to it; in fact, they pertain to the projector. (This is the original projection. Identification occurs only in the sense of naming or recognizing a quality.)

2. *Object induction*. The projector so convincingly identifies the projected part of the self in the external object that the feeling state corresponding to that part of the self is unconsciously evoked in the projectee.

3. *Introjective identification by the object*. At this point the projectee has identified with the projection of the projector through the process of introjective identification at the unconscious level. This feeling state may persist, affecting attitude and behavior toward the projector. Alternatively, it may be dis-identified with and shaken off as alien. Or the feeling state may be compared against other feeling states experienced in relation to the projector and modified by the discriminating and integrating functions of the projectee's personality in a process of transformation.

4. *Transformation by the object*. Since the projectee has his or her own personality, the projected part of the projector's self with which the projectee identifies is not the same as the part was when still inside the intrapsychic arena of the projector. The part has been transformed by its temporary lodging in another host, its goodness or badness being confirmed, exaggerated or, diminished. This process has been described by Bion as containment of the anxious infant's projective identifications by the mother in her state of reverie.

5. *Types of introjective identification by the object*. The part of the self projected may be a part of the ego (part of the self-representation) or a part of the object. In other words, the introjective

identification of the projectee may be, in Racker's terms, concordant or complementary to the projector's self (Racker 1968).

a. Introjective identification of the *concordant* type. The projectee is induced to embody the projected part of the ego (in shorthand, the self) while the object remains located in the projector.

b. Introjective identification of the *complementary* type. The projectee is induced to embody the projected object in relation to the projector's ego (self).

The introjective identification is determined not only by which part of the self or object is actually projected but also by the projectee's valency (Bion 1959) to respond in identification with the projector's projected part of self or object.

6. *Valency of the object to receive a projection.* When the projectee has a valency for a certain projection, then the projectee will tend to accept that projection and identify with that part of the projector's self. Sometimes this valent part is actively seeking parts of another to identify with to the point of stealing part of another person's mind through "extractive introjection" (Bollas 1989, p. 5).

7. *Reintrojective identification by the self.* The self identifies with or assimilates itself to the reinternalized confirmed or modified part of the self that had been projected. Then psychic structure is "cemented" or slightly altered. Cementing can be a healthy process if accurately received projections are accurately returned by the external object, but it can be unhealthy by not permitting change. Alteration can be healthy if the modification is slight and based on the projectee's unconscious capacity to appreciate the otherness of the other person and to harbor and return the projected part of the projector in a detoxified form that calms anxiety and reduces the likelihood of future distortion because of it. Alteration can be unhealthy when it returns the projection in a totally distorted form which does nothing to modify anxiety, may even aggravate it, or do violence to the integrity of the projector.

8. *Mutual projective identification.* The projector that projects into the projectee is at the same time receiving projections from the projectee. Projector–projectee pairs unconsciously match up based on valencies to identify with each other's projections. Because more than one person is present in a relationship, projective identification becomes a mutual process: for example, husband and wife connect according to unconscious complementarity of object relations, patient and analyst relate through the transference and countertransference. And projective identification is intimately tied to introjective identification.

I find a medical analogy helpful here. I see introjective processes working like osteoblasts, those cells that busily build bone without much thought to the final product. Osteoclasts break down the bone that the osteoblasts have built, but they do so precisely according to an architectural design that shapes the final bone form. Like osteoclasts, projective processes sculpt the final form of the introject. Working in parallel with introjective processes, projective processes also have a proactive role in shaping what is taken in. As the bone is subject to the strains imposed by the stronger pull of more developed muscles and by stimulation from growth hormone, the osteoblasts have to respond with more bone mass and the osteoclasts fine tune the resulting bone formation. So at each developmental level in infancy and adulthood introjective and projective processes shape the growing personality.

PROJECTIVE AND INTROJECTIVE
IDENTIFICATORY PROCESSES IN PARTNERSHIP

The following diagram summarizes the child's projective and introjective identificatory processes in unconscious communication with the parent. Longing to have his needs met, the infant projects that part of himself into the parent and identifies it in the parent. The parent empathically identifies with this part of the needy baby and knows to feed or comfort him. If the parent does not identify

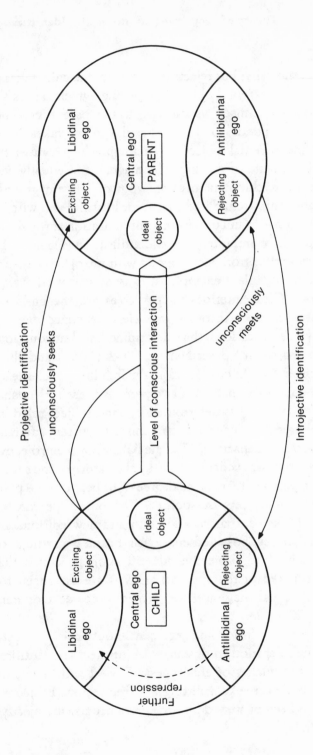

Figure 4-1. An integrated view of introjective and projective identification. Reprinted with permission, Routledge and Kegan Paul. Copyright © David E. Scharff, 1982.

with this part of the baby, but rejects him instead, the child takes in an experience of the parental object as rejecting, which causes the infant to experience himself as rageful. If the parent becomes anxious and overresponds to the infant, the infant takes in an experience of the parental object as exciting, which causes the infant to develop a state of craving. The diagram can equally well represent the endopsychic structures of two people in any growth-promoting relationship—child and parent, or husband and wife, or patient and therapist—in unconscious communication through the processes of projective and introjective identification (Figure 4-1).

Projective identification occurs along with introjective identification and in more violent examples it is associated with extractive introjection. These interlocking processes are the basis for valency. Spouses connect through valencies for concordant or complementary identifications that determine the "unconscious complementariness of fit" described by Dicks (1967) and illustrated by Bannister and Pincus (1965). A match in valencies leads to the instantaneous combination of two personalities in friendship or falling in love. Valency is determined by inner object relationships seeking expression, repetition, or healing in current life relationships (Scharff and Scharff 1987). The balance of the projective and introjective processes is determined by the nature of the object relations of each personality and the degree of fit between the parts of self and internal objects of spouses. The prototype for the balance is found between parent and child and new editions are found between spouses, boss and employee, business partners, or friends. Introjective and projective identification processes that have been overlooked in therapy and analysis are as crucial for therapeutic action as they are for growth and development throughout the life cycle.

Underlying the confusion and argument about projective identification and the relegation to obscurity of introjective identification is their shared quality of elusiveness. To deal with them, we have resorted to a degree of splitting and repression. Projective identification has been projected into the literature and introjective identification has been repressed. We have to remember that these are unconscious processes, a form of primitive communication originating in the early months of life before we had words or thinking as we now know it. Thus the problem is to find words for experience that lives on not as ideas or memories but as psychic structure. That very structure is what we bring to bear on the cognitive task of understanding projective and introjective identification, the processes through which the structure formed is continually being modified. So it is no surprise to find our reading of one person's view may change over time, that the author may move beyond or retreat from his original meaning, that we may collude to suppress introjective identification while emphasizing projective identification, or that inconsistency, ambivalence, confusion, and dismay abound.

Our gratitude to Klein for her inspiration is confounded by our envy of how much there is to be gotten out of projective and introjective identification and by our greed to have more understanding. The concepts are vulnerable to plunder and promiscuous use as well as to stultifying idealization. They are vulnerable to the action of projective identification that identifies the concept as if it were part of what one already knows. Introjective identification can lead us to an encapsulated, inflexible, wholesale adoption of the concepts, or even to a group identification with them. We want to be clear, but we have to guard against nailing down the meaning in a hard and fast way that leads to a concretization of their meaning.

Ambiguity is inevitable and, indeed, intrinsic to projective and introjective identificatory processes. Our struggles to comprehend or clarify the concepts are shrouded in the unconscious process to which they refer. My hypothesis is that one's preference for resonating with the one-body or two-body dimension of the process is probably determined by one's individual resolution of the dilemma of separateness from and attachment to the object.

I recognize that the views I express now may also change with further experience and theoretical advances. I applaud the concepts' resilience and their ability to defy attempts to nail them down.

PROJECTIVE AND INTROJECTIVE IDENTIFICATION IN THE DEVELOPMENT OF THE INDIVIDUAL, THE COUPLE, AND THE FAMILY

5

The Influence on
Individual Development
of Projective and
Introjective Identification
in the Family

Processes of projective and corresponding introjective identification characterize unconscious communication among family members. A complex prototype of characteristic mutual projective identification is developed in interaction between husband and wife before children are born. Then different aspects of the prototype are unconsciously distributed among the various children. Each child derives the building blocks of character in unconscious communication with these projective identificatory processes between the parents and the siblings, each of whom relates especially to an aspect of the parental bond. By the process of introjective identification each child's personality assimilates to aspects of each parent and their couple relationship.

Marriage, a relationship of commitment, of physical intimacy, of meeting each other's needs, and of giving each other identity, echoes the infant–mother relationship. It offers a second chance in adulthood to modify the personality structure as it draws to consciousness the primitive repressed parts of the self that seek expression and resolution. The healthy marriage provides a growth experience for both partners in which individual personality splits can be healed. In the less healthy marriage, splits are confirmed and reinforced. Repressed parts of the wife are projected into the husband, identified there as if they were aspects of the spouse, not the self. The husband, having a valency for doing so, identifies with the projection, thus confirming the repression. Simultaneously, the husband is similarly involved in identifying projected aspects of himself in his wife and she is identifying with these to the extent that she has the valency to do so. The unconscious fit between their unconscious object relations protects each individual's defensive structure with the shared aim of preserving their marital union. Their marriage is characterized by a unique conscious and unconscious object relationship system.

When the couple has a child, unmodified ego and object aspects of the repressed object-relationship system of the marriage are projected into the child in order to maintain the stability of the marriage against the threat of a potential rival, and thus to ensure the viability of the new family. Long before the oedipal stage, the threat comes in the form of primary maternal preoccupation. The anxiety of the infant in the infant–mother relationship leads to defensive projective identificatory processes that the mother tries to contain, is affected by, and may import into the marital relationship. In addition, the mother and father relate to their infant according to fantasies and expectations they have developed about their shared child. These fantasies are the product of their shared unconscious object relations, the resultant of the blending of their personalities into a joint marital personality that reflects their experiences with their families of origin. The child is then viewed as the hated or longed-for part of the spouse or self and resembles a hated or longed-for part of a grandparent. Hate or uncomfortable longing is then felt inside the parent to or from the child, depending on whether it is the repressed ego or object that has been projected (Scharff and Scharff 1987).

The marriage will continue to be challenged by the demands of future developmental stages and by any subsequent children. Their children's individual personalities will derive from the mental structures laid down during the accumulation of interactions with parents and siblings at every developmental stage. The nature of these structures is determined by the child's constitution and valency for identifying with or refuting projections from the parents. As Zinner and Shapiro noted, "Projective identification leads to authentic and lasting structural change in the *recipient* of the projections. A prime example of this phenomenon is the effect of family interaction on the developing personality of the child" (Zinner and Shapiro 1972, p. 110). The following example illustrates how the personality—in adulthood as well as in the formative years—is affected by family interaction, determined by experience in the families of origin.

The Effect of a Couple's Object Relations History on Their Son's Development

A successful tax accountant and his wife, Mr. and Mrs. Morrison consulted me for help in limiting their destructively generous impulses toward their 34-year-old son Mark. Never married, he lived from one woman to the next, from one college to the next, and from job to job. Unlike his settled, married sister with her suburban home and two children, he owned nothing but a Corvette, and that was not paid for. He spent everything he earned (which was not much compared with Mr. Morrison's salary) on women and travel. He walked out of jobs with no idea of where his rent was coming from, they told me. But I soon learned that he knew very well where it would come from—Mr. and Mrs. Morrison. Now they had seen the error of their ways. They were completely together in realizing that they must let him hit bottom before he could have a chance at becoming responsible. But both realized that they were incapable of tolerating the crash. What if he were on the streets? How could they let that happen? He was always so sweet and thoughtful with them, but he just couldn't seem to find a job he liked, make a decent living, or get married. It had always been that way. As a child, he was a joy at home, but Mrs. Morrison would get calls from the school about his behavior and learning habits. As an adolescent, he became a pot-head and skipped school, yet because he was so smart and so charming, all the teachers gave him glowing recommendations for college. Even as a 5-year-old he could twist his mother round his little finger and his father could not stop it.

As they told me about it, I shared their dismay at the long history of their domination by their son. As they began to embellish the story, I noted my own fascination and their relish at his deplorable antics. His perpetual helplessness about his own life and his power over them was somehow exciting. When I pointed this out, they nodded enthusiastically. When I asked how it got to be this way, I was surprised that I had forgotten Mark was not an only child.

Mrs. Morrison leaned forward in her chair. Her eyes lit up, her voice was infused with wonder. "My daughter, Suzanne, was one of those wonderful responsive children who make the world go round. Everyone loved her. She was always the favorite grandchild, all the cousins knew it, but she was everyone's favorite cousin and niece too. She was so sweet. They all loved her so much they didn't mind."

As I looked at her I thought of Mrs. Morrison herself as a most appealing baby. Her cherubic round face and mop of red curls reminded me of Annie, the adorable orphan who wins the heart of Daddy Warbucks—and the rest of America.

Mrs. Morrison's brow darkened as she went on to explain what happened when her son, Mark, was born. "Then *he* was born and everyone hated him." I thought of all the envy and rage at her

daughter being displaced onto the new baby. But Mrs. Morrison
had a different view of it. "They hated him for being in the way of
their relationship to her," she said. So, I thought, Suzanne remained the idealized child and Mark was seen not as a competitor
for family love but an interloper in the idealized dyad of Suzanne
and the collective extended family. Mrs. Morrison continued,
"They wanted to tease him, gang up on him, run away from him,
and even push him over, so they could get Suzanne all to themselves. As soon as this started to happen, and it started the minute
I got home from the hospital, I would look at him, and I saw *me*.
Everything from my childhood was visited on this little boy. Dr.
Scharff, I grabbed him and I held him and I never let anyone hurt
him—including his father. And I'm still doing it. I know I shouldn't.
I have to let go. He's 34 now. But I just can't do it. Dr. Scharff. . . ."

*As she appealed to me again by name, I felt drawn to her and
encircled by her respect and trust. But I started to wonder where was
Mr. Morrison? Was he feeling shut out in the session by me and Mrs.
Morrison, and was this what happened at home with the children and
their mother? He did not look hurt or annoyed. He was leaning toward
her, as captivated as I was by her appealing way of putting things. All
eyes were on her, and he seemed to represent nothingness inside the
self. I started to wonder whether I was being idealized like Suzanne
and, if so, what part of Mrs. Morrison did I represent? But Mrs.
Morrison was thinking of her boy, not Suzanne or me.*

"Dr. Scharff," she continued. "*He* is *me*—no ifs, ands, or buts.
As he's gotten older, he's even started to look like me. And when
he's in pain and calls me at 3:00 A.M., I don't mind. That's what a
mother's for. I always found an excuse to get up when he got
home, just in case he wanted to talk. I felt so close to him. I know
him so well, because he is a part of me."

So Mrs. Morrison had projected into her children two parts of
herself, the idealized self into Suzanne where she could identify
with it as everyone's idealized object, separate from herself, and the
damaged, destroyed part of herself into Mark. She was much more

identified with the part of herself she saw in Mark than in Suzanne. I also noted that the extended family as a representation of her internal object was also split in two: into component adoring and denigrating objects. How did this reflection of her internal object relations reflect her experience with her family of origin?

"How does your relationship with Mark compare with your relationship with your mother?" I asked.

"I was my father's favorite," she replied, not mentioning her mother. "By far the youngest. All my siblings were dazzling intellects, always expected to do well, and now nationally prominent in their fields. I was a Depression baby. I was a mistake. But my father said that during the Depression when people weren't using accountants, he was ready to jump out of a window but didn't because he had me. I was his obsession. He was always saying, 'Come and sit on my knee.' It was obvious to everyone, Dr. Scharff. Aunts and uncles noticed it and they chastised him. Oh, there was no sexual abuse. There *was* far too much fondling, but I loved it. And my brothers especially hated it. They treated me like a toy. Dr. Scharff, they tortured me, teased me, watched me scream. Other than that, they had no time for me. My father's expectations for me were entirely different than for them. I was just supposed to be pretty, have lots of boyfriends and get C's. I never heard a cross word from him."

"And your mother?" I persisted.

"My mother wasn't interested in me," Mrs. Morrison responded curtly. "She was involved with the older children and their school work and activities. I was a mistake."

No "Dr. Scharff" to make me feel included and trusted here. In contrast, I felt rebuffed and warned against hurting her.

I think that I was simultaneously identified with Mrs. Morrison's self as the object of her mother's rejection and with her rejected object representing the mother who could make a mistake and hurt a child. In her dealings with her children, as a mother herself, Mrs. Morrison was heavily defended against being rejected or rejecting by substituting an excited closeness with both children, based on the model of her relationship with her father. Possibly her daughter was less gratifying of Mrs. Morrison's needs for symbiosis. Suzanne's valency for accepting her mother's projective identifications instead appeared to be toward identifying with the ideal object, infused with excitement from the exciting object, and capable of autonomy. So what protected her, I wondered? I guessed that she must have had the benefit of a different projective identification from her father, one that valued self-sufficiency and autonomy. In a healthy family with differentiated individual parents, we find that the other parent's projective identifications may have a mutative effect upon the child's introjective identifications. I wondered specifically what Mr. Morrison's projective identifications might be, based on his family history. So consciously following that line of thought, and unconsciously identifying with Mrs. Morrison's tendency to turn to the male when feeling shut out by the female, I turned to Mr. Morrison. As I did so, I realized that I was also feeling identified with Mr. Morrison as the left-out part of the family. I projected into him my own left-out feeling generated in the interaction with his wife and hoped to take care of it in him by asking about his object relations history.

"What about your family?" I asked him.
    "My mother is still living," he replied. "She should have left my father but she didn't."

I noted silently that this was a very different starting place from Mrs. Morrison's story of her family. Here was an earlier version of a man who should have been let go. Was he too dependent? Was he bad with money?

He went on, "My father was a very complex person. He was lacking in self-confidence, I think, very insecure, and so he compensated with a strong authoritarian personality. He didn't have a single friend. He was tolerated, more than anything. He went into business in Lancaster, Pennsylvania, and was there for a year before we moved to Pittsburgh for better opportunities. He was a good, responsible provider but just terrible to my mother, and he was just nonexistent as a father. He loved infants who had no views. But the minute they disagreed with him, he turned 'em out. I had no discussion with him more personal than about football.

"After my brother was born (he was seven years younger than I), they started to fight. I listened to them night after night. One night my father left and I ended up in their bedroom, with my mother bawling her eyes out, trying to convince her to leave him, but she wouldn't."

Here was an earlier version of the current situation between the Morrisons. Mr. Morrison was trying to convince his wife (and the dependent part of himself lodged in her) to take a stand with their son, just as unsuccessfully as he had tried as a child to persuade his mother to leave his father. As Mr. Morrison went on, it seemed that perhaps he had been successful with his mother in later years.

"One time she really did leave and took us with her to New York where she had lots of support from a big family. We stayed there for some months and I quite liked it. But one night at table, all of a sudden she stood up and said, 'There'll be no one to get his dinner.' And she took us back, right then. He wouldn't speak to her after we came back, but every night she had his food on the table. Here's this woman, he's not saying a word to her, and she's putting his dinner on the table, night after night.

"When I left college, I joined the business, but I couldn't stand the way he dealt with people. When I left the company, he flew into a rage. I was 36, and that was the last time we ever spoke."

Now that his son was in his mid-thirties, no wonder Mr. Morrison was afraid of a repetition of a sudden, painful disruption of the father–son relationship. If he took a stand, his son might experience it as a rejection; if his son became self-sufficient, Mr. Morrison could take that as a rejection by him. To avoid coming to such an impasse, Mr. Morrison had been much closer to his son than his father was to him. Since his son was 5 years old and began to need limits enforced by the father's authority, Mr. Morrison had spared him the pain—and thus had spoiled his son and left him too close to his protective mother. Because of this solution, Mr. and Mrs. Morrison were not in conflict over their child and the harmony of their marriage was preserved: the integrity of their couple relationship was important in healing their shared internal couple. Then Mr. Morrison had the pleasure of seeing his wife and son together without it threatening their marriage, while Mrs. Morrison had the joy of being a much more loving and involved mother to her boy, uninterfered with by the father, than had been the case in her growing-up years.

Mr. Morrison had a view of his father as absent or rejecting while Mrs. Morrison saw her mother that way. Mrs. Morrison was successful in bonding intensely with her father. Perhaps she did so in order to compensate for her mother's lack of interest. Her stealing so much attention that was rightfully her mother's may have led her mother to turn away from her in despair. Mrs. Morrison's mother was unable to break up that pairing just as Mr. Morrison was unable to break up his father and mother, or his wife and son. Mr. and Mrs. Morrison shared a parental internal couple in which one parent is absent and rejecting. They differed in that her defense was to substitute excitement and closeness (characterized by the relationship between her and Daddy then, and between her and Mark now) or excitement and autonomy (shown by her with her many boyfriends then, and her enjoyment of her gregarious, adored Suzanne), whereas his defense was to concentrate on rescuing the rejected self from the rejecting object (seen in his attempts to deliver his mother from his father) and by his repeated efforts to rescue his adult son from trouble.

Mr. Morrison had put his need for a nonrejecting parent–child couple into the relationship between Mrs. Morrison and each of their children. It fit well with Mrs. Morrison's wish to relive her close contact with her father and to undo her rejection by her mother. Mr. Morrison was reinforcing their pairing to gratify his wish through them, and would not perform his fatherly role of aiding their separation or forbidding his son's oedipal longings for his mother. His failure to deliver his son as a child from the clutches of his mother reflects his hopelessness about separating his parents and speaks to a desperate need not to be rejecting of either of them as his own father had been of him and his mother.

In therapy the task of taking back their projections required that the Morrisons share their despair about not being loved by the rejecting parent, which for him had been the father, for her the mother.

Through projective identification a mother's fantasy about a child who has the valency for receiving the projection affects her child-rearing and ultimately shapes the child's personality development. The collaborative effect of the father's fantasy is a critically mutative factor in freeing the mother–infant relationship from the grip of a projective identificatory system. Once the fantasy is made conscious, the other parent has the opportunity to counteract its effect. However, work still is needed on the original inhibition against doing so.

Projective Identification in Childrearing

The following example demonstrates in a couple with two young children the usefulness of sharing a projective identificatory fantasy. I had been seeing them in couple therapy for a few months during which they made rapid progress to change their child-rearing practices, which resulted in the immediate reversal of their baby's sleep disorder and considerable improvement in their 3-year-old's feeding disorder. As parents they felt much happier. As spouses they now felt stuck at the level of their personality differences.

"We're so different," said Becky. "Vince is really interested in people. He can go into a room full of strangers and talk to them about how they fix up their basements and what they think of the Ayatollah. I can't do that. It takes me a long time to make a friend. I care about my family, my two best friends, Vince and the children, and I like my two neighbors. And I'm very good to my employees. Other than that people don't interest me. But Vince, he loves all the guys at softball, the golf club, the checkout person at the Safeway, whoever. But I'm not interested. People aren't that nice. My family really suffered at the hands of strangers." Turning to him, she concluded, "I can't be the way you are."

"I know that," Vince replied. "My family was very cold. So I sought warmth elsewhere. Other relationships were very important for me. Other kids, their fathers, my dog. No point in complaining about what they couldn't do. I saw to it that I got it. But Becky stuck with her family. They were very involved in each other's lives and I understand that. Becky asked me to read books about the Holocaust, which I did, so I know the background."

"What was the Holocaust like for your parents specifically?" I asked Becky.

"They were both in concentration camps," she said quickly. "My mother, she was an only child, she never expected to survive. And my father saw his three brothers shot and then they were incinerated." She spoke like a news reporter getting in all the facts in a short sound byte. I asked whether that was all she had heard at home. "No," she said. "I'm summarizing it for you."

I replied, "This is so horrible, it will take much longer to talk about it, to really work on your feelings about all that happened."

Becky headed me off. "Vince knows about it," she stated. "He's read about it."

"Are you afraid he won't hear it from you?" I asked. Becky's eyes filled with sorrow.

"I never talk about it because I can't without crying," she said through her tears.

I asked, "Do you feel that Vince won't sit with you when you are upset?"

"He will," she nodded. Vince put his hand kindly on her knee.

"But do you want to?" she asked him. And "Why do we have to?" she demanded of me.

I continued, "I think there are a lot of feelings left over from that generation of your family and it will be helpful to understand how it affects your present family."

"Well, it affected my choosing Vince. One of the reasons I wanted to marry him was that he's not passive. He would never just follow a guard to the train and go off to his death. He might die fighting for his life, but he would definitely do something," Becky said confidently. "He would protect us."

"You still think the Nazis could reappear," said Vince. "I don't worry about that. But you are always looking out against that. You can't hold on to that forever."

"But I don't want to forget it. I would never want to get over it. Every time I hold Lara, I remember. Every time I look at my child," Becky protested.

"What?" Vince remonstrated. "What?"

"Of course," said Becky. "I *want* to remember. When Lara was born—and I wanted her to have a Russian name—it was the first thing I thought about."

"She was so petite and so delicate," Becky enthused. "When I held her in my arms I thought of my mother holding me in her arms and all the babies who were held in their mothers' arms and then incinerated. I thought of *Sophie's Choice*: Sophie's in the line to learn whether she'll live or die. She's attractive so she gets to "live," or rather go to the work camp. Just for spite the guard says, 'You can only take one of your children.' She had twins and finally she chose the boy (I think it was the boy because he could look after himself) and, of course, she couldn't live with the choice. She committed suicide. How could you ever live with a choice like that? Well, this is my first daughter and she reminds me of all those babies in the concentration camp. I hold her in my arms and I think Holocaust. She's my Holocaust baby."

"Poor kid," said Vince. "I had no idea all this was going on. So you can't say no to her. You can't because you're thinking the Nazis might come and take her away. And the way you keep making her eat—you're thinking she's going to starve. Oh! This is not right. You have to bury your dead."

"I will never do that," replied Becky defiantly. "My parents never expected to survive, never expected to have a child. To them, I'm a miracle. To me, Lara's a miracle. I wanted a Russian name. I wanted her to have that. Now with Rachel I never think about it. She's so big and so sturdy. I look at her in my arms and it just wouldn't occur to me. But I look at Lara and that's it, that's what she is, she's my Holocaust baby."

In the next couple-therapy session, Vince and Becky reported a terrible week in which Becky had been more anxious and tentative about decision-making than ever. She came to bed late each night. Vince had become enraged by her passive avoidance of him and had pushed her a couple of times to get an answer out of her. Violence had been a feature of discipline in his own family and he did not care to repeat it.

Vince continued, "I feel awful about doing that. It wasn't right. It's never right. I just felt driven to it by her behavior. I couldn't stand it. She was going around cleaning things up, over and over. She criticized the running shoes I bought. She woke up the children to feed them in the night. She went shopping for drapes and obsessed over her choice, and then took them back, and then went and bought the same ones again. I experienced her behavior as disintegrating. I felt that I was living with a crazy person."

Becky justified her actions. "I'm not crazy," she asserted. "I'm just rushed. It's not easy to get the colors right. You want things to look nice and to go well together in the room, and you are so critical. You make me anxious with your fault-finding. I am not crazy."

"You were crazy," he insisted. "Normal people do not do the things you were doing."

"I am not crazy," she replied. "I wouldn't be like that with anyone else. You are driving me crazy."

I asked, "Might these accusations of craziness relate to our discussion of last week?"

"Sure," replied Vince. "I think it is completely crazy to think of our baby as a Holocaust baby."

Becky vowed, "I have not and I will not ever, ever mention it again."

The matter had not been discussed. Vince had been made anxious by the revelation of the fantasy at a time when he had not yet developed skills to work with it. Becky felt traumatized all over again by his repressive reaction. She had changed her child-rearing habits in response to his suggestions but she could not maintain her improvements. Her sudden reversions to the previous overfeeding and underdisciplining of Lara drove Vince wild. With the projective identification of Lara as the Holocaust baby still active, Becky and Vince could not expect her behavior to change, despite good intentions.

I thought that they would require many more weeks of work on this before the projective identification could be taken back. But the couple would not reopen the subject, even in an individual interview for Becky. Vince and Becky simply steered clear of it. They applied what they learned in our sessions to their child-rearing problems, they reduced external stress, and they got along better. But even in sessions they stayed away from discussing their relationship—until Vince got angry again, that is. This time I could understand the projective identificatory system between them by experiencing it in relation to me.

Vince became frustrated with the lack of depth in the couple's work. He confronted me with the full force of his displeasure.

"What do we do here? We talk about how to discipline the children, and I'm not saying we haven't found that useful, but you just are not helping us with our relationship. You sit there and let us ramble on. We need direction. Do you know what you're doing? Because you're not making these sessions productive. You go to a real doctor, you get a diagnosis. Well you gave us that, but a real doctor gives you a prescription. Where's the prescription? Where's the advice?"

> *I felt quite anxious and unappreciated. I had stayed with them at the level of work that they could tolerate. Now I felt on the spot. I wished his anger would go away. I felt belittled. I found myself wondering if what I did was any good after all. A series of silent justifications lined up in my mind and helped me to bear the attack.*

Before I had to discard my defensive thoughts in favor of something worth saying, Becky interrupted.

"Vince is just mad that I was late picking him up, but I was only three minutes late, and we got here on time" she tried to explain.

I thought that Becky was hoping to divert and defuse Vince's anger. She was anxiously making excuses for Vince to protect me the same way she usually did for herself when Vince got mad at her for the way she was raising the children. I was introjectively identified with Becky as the recipient of Vince's rage. And I felt guilty without real reason. Perhaps his anger was meant to provoke a guilty response. Perhaps he was projecting his own guilty incompetence into Becky and now me, so that he did not feel belittled by feeling stuck and helpless.

"Maybe Vince is angry at you too," I replied to Becky. "But right now, he is angry at me."

I was not enjoying Vince's anger and I wished it would go away. I felt anxious that I would not be able to handle it well. I was wanting to make excuses. But I knew that I had to meet his challenge with a strong response.

So I said, "Vince, you are upset about me and the way I do therapy. Tell me more about that."

I immediately felt under attack as Vince leaned toward me and told me all my faults. I hated it, but I had to admire his forthrightness. I supported myself by thinking of Bion's theory of containment. I was filled with two identifications: one produced an angry response of wanting to fight back like Vince, the other a scampering mouse-like response in identification with Becky's anxiety when under attack from Vince. I saw my task as having to contain and metabolize Vince's disappointment and rage, Becky's tendency to run from confrontation, and feelings of helplessness and low self-esteem.

At last Vince finished. He concluded, "It's simple. This is my diagnosis. We need structure and you're not providing it. You're the doctor here, you're supposed to know what to do. You should give us your opinion, tell us how to address the issues, otherwise we might as well stay home in our own living room. So, over to you."

"Well," I said, "you want me to do it your way, same as you want Becky to discipline the children the way you would. You don't want to feel uncertain or helpless. You think that being directive and firm or getting angry will produce the result from her or me that you want. But I haven't found that that works for me or for you. I welcome your initiative in using your anger to change course and confront your relationship with me and with Becky. But your anger at me carries with it contempt for my failings. I'm having to fight against shrinking away from your anger or crumpling up. My reaction helps me to understand why when you get critical and angry with Becky she gets anxious and becomes more likely to mess up and make excuses."

"I know," he replied. "Becky, you try to wriggle out of it, make it nice. I wish you'd take me seriously."

"Vince," said Becky, "I just get so frightened. I don't know what you'll do. I think maybe you'll hit me like your father did you. You get so mad, it's like I'm a rotten child. And I'm not that bad. Dr. Scharff, you are not that bad either. You knew how I felt, but you didn't seem to feel as bad as I would have. It's really been amazing for me to hear you deal with Vince's anger. He gets madder and madder at me the more I try to placate him, but here he has calmed right down."

Vince's experience with his family was of being beaten into shape. Unlike his father, he did not beat his children or his wife, but he did get frighteningly angry. Like his father, apportioning blame was as important to Vince now as accepting it had been when he was growing up. He dealt with it by being almost perfect, beyond blame. He married a woman whose family had every reason to blame the outside world, while regarding children as entirely blameless. She did not identify with his rigid standards, nor did I. Even if Vince was at fault, Becky excused his behavior as a mistake with the same tolerance she showed toward herself.

In their projective identificatory system, Vince projected into Becky the yelled-at, helplessly-at-fault child part of himself and she identified with that in the marriage, even though at work she was a competent executive and manager. He identified with his object, representing the critical, choleric part of his father. Becky accepted the infantile projection from Vince in order to maintain her image of him as strong and willing to fight. While experiencing him as a potential savior and protector, she was simultaneously evoking in him the Nazi-like authoritarian personality, dreaded and hated by her parents with whose opposition to such absolute consistency and obliteration of human failing Becky had identified.

The Projective Identificatory System of a Marriage

The next example provides a further opportunity to study why a particular projective identificatory system forms in a marriage. Even though the children of this marriage showed serious disturbances as a result, their symptomatology did not bring attention to the unconscious underpinnings in the marital relationship. It was not until illness thwarted the projection of strength into the father that the marital projective identificatory system came up for review.

William and Wendy Sheldon, a military couple, came for family therapy with their three beautiful daughters, Sandra age 8, Wilma age 14, and Bobbie, who at 19 was married to a serviceman but lived with her parents while he was at sea. The Sheldons were concerned about Wendy's depression since learning of William's recent diagnosis of scleroderma, a chronic connective tissue disease for which there is no cure. They also mentioned their daughter Wilma's severe school phobia, which began two years earlier when her father first had symptoms and when her elder sister, Bobbie was becoming furtively sexually active. Wilma was currently being treated by a child psychiatrist with anti-anxiety medication and by a psychologist using a desensitization program. The child psychiatrist in charge of the case referred them for family therapy to a military social worker who asked me to work with him in co-therapy. The family agreed to our terms that the treatment be conducted in the TV studio at the military medical center in which they had great faith.

William (also called Will) was a noncommissioned Marine Corps pilot who had been promoted to the highest grade of warrant officer (W 4). As such he was highly respected, but carried the strain of living on the boundary between the commissioned and noncommissioned ranks. At home he was admired by his dependents who appreciated his accomplishments and his status as a pilot and an officer. Unfortunately, he had lost his flight status and the accompanying bonus after a single, freak migraine headache three years before. He had adjusted apparently well to the loss and characteristically denied its impact. A year later he had generalized, vague symptoms of stiffness and tingling in his hands. These complaints remained undiagnosed until he became so stiff that he could hardly walk or use his hands. The diagnosis of scleroderma was then confirmed. Scleroderma runs an unpredictable course, with thickening of skin and stiffening of muscle tissue, variably extending to affect the esophagus, heart, and kidneys, often but not inevitably leading to death within five years. Despite the severity of his fatigue and stiffness (which had improved somewhat by the time I saw him), Will continued in his job as actively as ever, refusing to apply for sick leave or a handicapped driver's permit. Now he was about to retire after twenty years of service, again insisting on the usual retirement procedure instead of applying for retirement on medical grounds, which would have earned him a higher pension. His condition did not deter him from planning to actualize the family dream for a boat trip around the coast of the United States to their place of retirement in the West.

In the first two sessions Will talked about himself and his family. He talked anxiously, covering over his feelings and speaking for everyone else. We could hardly get a word in. My cotherapist Mr. Heulatt pointed this out, and Will told us proudly that he was the captain of the family unit: it was his responsibility to explain the family to us. Despite my intention to demonstrate on tape the group-interpretive approach to the family, I found myself unable to get past the individual.

In my countertransference, I experienced enormous frustration, not just of my goals. Early attempts to analyze the family's need to use Will as their delegate and family boundary led only to further individual explanations from him. I felt exasperated. I felt that Will was holding on to me tightly and giving me no room to be with the group. Struggling for room to relate, I felt dogged and over-cautious in my work with their verbal material and stilted in my attempts to understand Sandra's play. I often felt tense and stiff in sessions, needing to stretch, in identification with the strain on Will. While identified with his position, I felt massively controlled and constrained by the family as if I were stuck inside an inelastic skin like Will's. Based on my experience, comments about the family's use of him to be the boundary against our interventions gradually led to an acknowledgment of a repetitive pattern of reliance on him. I felt compassionate toward him, a competent, physical man robbed of his powers and still under strain. At the same time I felt totally squashed by his manic and counterphobic defenses. How would I ever express my own competence to help him and his family?

This feeling put me in touch with his wife's inability to express herself. She could signal her upset to me, but suppressed it before her tears came, and could not find the words to tell me about herself. Nevertheless, I felt her unspoken appeal to me to help her reach across the helpless, wordless void. I tried to relate to her wordlessness silently so as to make space for her thoughts. I learned that she felt helpless in the face of his illness, frightened and unable to cope. In their intimate life, she was miserable that his hands that had been so sure were now like stones. She felt anxious and driven to keep eating. This left her feeling shapeless and ugly.

Mrs. Sheldon, aware of the visual impact of the family on the screen (see Figure 5-1), sat to the far right of the family group and put her youngest daughter at the play table in front of her so that she could hide her bulk from the watchful eye of the camera. This young child fulfilled Mrs. Sheldon's wish to put up a good front and was attentive to her mother's needs for comfort. On the far left sat the therapists. Mr. Sheldon always sat next to me with his elder or middle daughter on the other side of him. Mrs. Sheldon preferred it that way so that the center of the videotape picture would show the attractive couple of her trim, good-looking husband and one of their cute daughters. She did not look good enough to sit with him, she felt. She preferred to sit between her two youngest daughters, which meant that Wilma was always between her parents.

Mrs. Sheldon was an accomplished watercolorist whose seascapes had earned the admiration of neighbors, but because of her poor self-esteem she felt incompetent and could not believe that they really liked her artwork. So she was unable to sell any of her paintings and had no means of supporting herself. She was entirely dependent on Mr. Sheldon, who had been glad to be her source of reliable support, but now she realized that she would soon have to do things for him. She did not add that she would have to do things for herself as well.

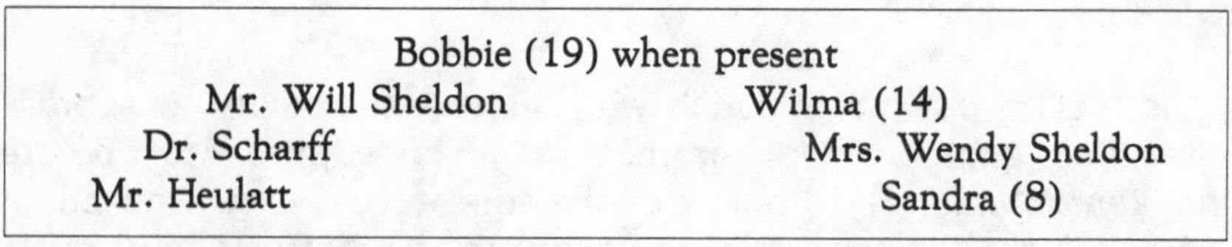

Bobbie (19) when present
Mr. Will Sheldon   Wilma (14)
Dr. Scharff   Mrs. Wendy Sheldon
Mr. Heulatt   Sandra (8)

Figure 5–1. The Sheldons' seating arrangement.

By the third session in therapy, I had seen that this family used substitution as a coping mechanism. The father was used as a substitute for the group. The eldest teenage daughter had been creating a sexual reproductive couple instead of the parents; her attractive appearance next to her father substituted for his wife's being at his side. The latency child's responsiveness and creativity covered for the mother's, and the husband's competence compensated for a lack in his wife. The fantasy here was that the male protects the female, the adolescent child pairs with the grownup and is dangerously sexual, the young child parents her own mother, one strong person is more effective and safe than a whole group, and the family skin embodied in that individual had better cover and hold together what is inside. I did not yet know why it had to be that way. What were they covering for?

Sometimes the eldest daughter was not there, reflecting her status as partially independent of the family. Sometimes the youngest daughter was not there because of school activities. Their absences were regarded as opportunities to say things that might upset them had they been there. For instance, early in the opening phase in the third session when the eldest daughter, Bobbie, was not present, the family spoke about the trauma that occurred when she was 16.

Session 3

Wilma had been describing her panicky feelings. Mrs. Sheldon said that she understood how Wilma felt because she too had experienced panic at the time she was pregnant with Sandra. The couple had thought that their family was complete and they knew that a baby born now could hold them back, particularly delaying their intention to buy a sailboat. They had planned to take sailing trips over the next eight years in preparation for their grand year-long sail. To her dismay, Mrs. Sheldon found herself thinking of terminating the pregnancy. She actually made an appointment for an abortion and ten minutes later canceled. She and her husband felt good about their decision, but Mrs. Sheldon felt unbearably guilty that she had intended to do such a thing, if only for ten minutes. Shortly after that, she had to be hospitalized for depression and panic, which were treated with moderately successful relaxation therapy without any discussion of her conflicts.

I asked whether there was any similar circumstance that led to Wilma's panics. Wilma then described a terrifying incident three years before. suddenly in the middle of the night Bobbie work up covered in blood. Mr. Sheldon was away at sea on a training course and Mrs. Sheldon called her neighbor for help. Her neighbor said that Bobbie must be having a miscarriage. Mrs. Sheldon was stunned: she had no idea that Bobbie was pregnant or even sexually active. How did her neighbor know? Wilma had told the neighbor's daughter about the secret of Bobbie's pregnancy.

Bobbie had wanted to keep the baby so that her boyfriend would marry her. When she told Wilma this, she had sworn her to secrecy. Wilma, who already felt terrible to think of Bobbie being sexually active, now also felt terrible about keeping the secret from her parents, and about revealing the secret to her friend. She had first become aware of Bobbie's sexuality when Bobbie was in a bedroom with her boyfriend at the hotel where the family was housed before returning to the United States after their previous posting. She then felt sure that Bobbie was having sex. Again she said nothing but felt frightened and sick. When she reached 14, an age at which her friends started dating, Wilma was unable to go out with boys even in a group and avoided them by not going to school. Bobbie, however, recovered from the trauma and soon fell in love with her present husband. Her parents had been married in adolescence themselves and quite approved of early marriage. Their only worry was that Bobbie might not be able to have children because her miscarriage had been caused by ovarian cysts for which she must remain on hormone treatment.

As the parents and Wilma recalled these traumatic times, Sandra played with colored blocks. She arranged them in two tight circles one of which had rectangular shapes inside. I deemed her concern with boundaries partly age-appropriate and partly a response to feeling a lack of safety in this family. She explained that she was building a hotel room next to a lake, much like the one where the sexual incident had occurred. Her play was acknowledged but not explored this time. It was sufficient for me to know that her play was in tune with the discussion.

Session 4

As Sandra played the next week in therapy, the family talked about their response to our work. After the last session, all the old feelings had come back—grief, anger, bitterness. Mrs. Sheldon had been worried that she would not get over her feelings, but she and her husband talked a lot about the incident and both of them were relieved to discover that they could re-experience feelings and not be overwhelmed by them. The family colluded, however, to tell Bobbie that what had been discussed was nothing but an old family joke about Sandra, as a baby, throwing up on her lap. I could see that the family was afraid of the power of words to evoke unmanageable feelings and that they experienced the catharsis of reviewing the trauma as a vomiting of bad stuff that had to be laughed off and hidden. They were afraid that sharing knowledge in the group would be destructive to the individual. With good reason they were also afraid that sexual knowledge outside of marriage would be destructive. The eldest girl had proved it, the middle girl was phobically avoiding the possibility, the latency girl was not yet confronted with it personally and so she was doing just fine.

According to our theory of projective identification (Scharff and Scharff 1987), three aspects of the parents' unconscious object relations, expressed in the marital sexual bond, have been projected variously into the three girls. The latency child carries a conflict-free aspect of it (because, not being at the leading edge of her development, sexuality can remain thoroughly repressed), the middle daughter relates in fantasy to a terrifying sexual object that must be rejected, the eldest daughter embodies a sexually exciting object relationship that is longed for despite danger and damage. The symptomatology points to a degree of ambivalence in the parents' sexual bond. At this time in their treatment, I knew only that their sexual relationship was not what it had been because of his muscle and skin condition.

I now had evidence that conflict over sexual issues was experienced by the parent and identified with by the child whose panic resembled her mother's. Layers of sexuality conflict had been revealed, but I still did not know its source or its connection to the projective identificatory system of the marriage in which competence was ascribed to the husband and helplessness to the wife. In the fifth session the couple gave a vivid example of their projective identificatory system so that it was clearly recognized and named. In the sixth meeting they went on to explore its roots in their families of origin.

Session 5

Wendy was glad that Will could now admit to his illness in therapy, but she wished that they could talk about it at home when she became concerned for him. "If I talk about his sickness, then he's fine," she lamented.

"I admit I've got the disease," Will protested. "I don't admit it's as bad as it might be. I've got the symptoms and I admit the prognosis is uncertain, but I don't accept that all those things will happen." Turning to me, he explained, "When she talks about it she gets upset and I try to talk her out of it. Me, I get on the phone talking to *my* folks at home and *I* say everything's fine, but Wendy, when *she* gets on the phone to *her* mother, she'll start crying and I get upset with her." To Wendy he said pointedly, "We've got your family thinking I'm critically ill and my family thinking there's nothing wrong with me. They don't even ask. The way I put it to them, I might as well have a cold. It leans too far on both sides: her family is overconcerned because of her attitude and my family doesn't even know there is anything wrong because of mine. And the families live in different states and they don't talk on the phone to each other."

I said to them, "Your families have two totally different views of the illness because neither of you, Will nor Wendy, can experience both views of the illness inside him- or herself."

When ambivalence and potential loss could not be tolerated, splitting and polarization predominated. These projections of doom and helpless dismay into Wendy and fighting spirit into Will were easily detected because of their amplification by further projection into their families of origin. The projective system was now named and recognized in a few of its varieties, and I was curious to learn what drove it.

Session 6

Bobbie attended this session ostensibly because she did not have to be at her job that week, but Sandra was not present. She had often had to miss school events for therapy, and this time Mr. and Mrs. Sheldon decided to excuse her so that she could go to a balloon launch to benefit her school. As the session began, the parents were talking about their distress over Wilma's continuing school phobia and how it was an additional stress when they were already worried about Will.

Mrs. Sheldon (Wendy) reported a theory she heard from Wilma's psychologist: "He says she's built the school bigger than her Dad. Do you think that's it, Wilma? What are you feeling about Dad and school?"

Wilma could not answer. She confirmed her upset by crying but she did not know how to speak about it. A few minutes went by as she mopped her eyes and tried to say something. "I can never put anything into words," she lamented. I waited quietly, bearing her discomfort. Eventually it was Wendy who helped her out.

"I feel just like Wilma," Wendy concurred. "I'll talk about Will and I'll start crying, but basically I don't know what I'm thinking. Just the word 'Will' sets off something—it's got to be deep. I don't know what I'm thinking and what's upsetting me. So I understand what Wilma's going through. I guess it's just everything. When you say his name, it triggers everything you ever think about and worry about."

Wendy went on to explain that she did not expect Will to die but that she was worried about his becoming unable to do what he had done before. "He might get pretty dependent on us," she continued, "but that's not how we've seen him. We've always seen him as taking care of us. And it scares us to think that we might have to take care of him. We do have to do a lot that he used to and could do."

One of the things that Will used to do was to think for them, as my co-therapist pointed out. It was painfully obvious that when Will was kept quiet, the others found it unfamiliar and hard to find words for themselves. Their inhibition was pleading for Will's rescue.

I could feel Will next to me itching to protest, to speak for her, to make everything all right. I was determined to protect the space so that Wendy could find her voice. But I expected to be foiled by him. How was I going to deal with his anxiety and keep him quiet?

Following on my co-therapist's idea, I added, using my countertransference, "You are struggling to find your own words because you are people for whom Will has usually spoken—and he's ready to start any minute now. If I don't keep talking he'll be in there!"

"He's ready to burst," Wendy agreed. Responding to my countertransference comment she found her voice and continued, "I go to do something and you can feel him ready to take over. I think a lot about things that have happened and why. Maybe if Will had married someone different from me, he might not be so dominant. But he's got a big responsibility with me because . . . I wanted to say this because Sandra is not here, but I've been putting it off. I don't think I can say it," she sobbed.

"We'll wait 'til you're ready," I said, mainly to keep Will from filling in the space. He was able to follow my cue.

After minutes of tense, pregnant silence, Wendy pushed herself forward through her tears, gaining in confidence as she continued, "I think a lot of the problems I've had with Will being sick stem from my past. I don't feel special. Oh, Will has made me feel special, but I was sexually abused by my grandfather for two years beginning when I was 8 years old. I was in second grade and I had emotional problems. I didn't learn well. So when I met Will, I had never told anyone. I told him two days before the wedding and I really thought he wouldn't want to marry me. But he did. So he just basically ran things, and I let him, because he'd make everything better and I felt safe. Because of that, I don't feel I'm good enough so I let him have everything his way to make up. Now that he's sick, I have to change things."

As the family talked with Wendy about their history, Bobbie described how cunningly the whole family prevented outsiders from detecting their mother's learning deficiencies. Wendy admitted her shame that she had never learned to read or write.

Wendy's revelation provided information necessary for understanding her contribution to the couple's projective identificatory system. In her man, she looked for control and structure that she had not had from her parents. She also admired his academic success since this was a part of herself that was lacking. But why did Will want such a traumatized, unrepaired, submissive woman? He had not felt special in his family either, whereas Wendy made him feel extremely special and definitely irreplaceable. In his family he had been ousted by a doted-on younger brother. No one listened to Will's views or valued his intellectual achievement and hard-working attitude. No matter how he tried, he was unable to alter the fact that his parents responded positively only to his brother, the all-star athlete who flunked out of high school. He escaped from feeling unimportant and worthless by an early marriage to an admiring woman and by joining the Marines where his ambition was rewarded. In marriage, he projected his family's sense of his worthlessness and his own helplessness to change things into Wendy who readily identified with the projection. She projected her appreciation of competence into him where it could be safe. She could take pleasure in his work and status while denying her own demonstrated competence as an artist and her potential to learn to read and write as an adult.

At the end of the session, Will told us that Wendy had found out just that week that one of her sisters had also been abused by their grandfather. Unlike Wendy, she had told their mother at the time it happened. The mother, however, did not confront the grandfather, but the family moved away soon after, probably for unrelated reasons. Wendy thought a lot over the years about why she didn't tell and could not come up with an answer. Even now she could not tell her mother.

"It would kill me if she ever found out," Wendy supposed. "I always remember trying to make my mother love me. I worked really hard at it. And she didn't like me much. She was jealous of the relationship between me and my Dad. He never touched me, but I was his favorite. I don't want to tell her what happened with Grandpa, and yet I do want her to know. I want her to give me some of the love and comfort she never gave me," she concluded sadly.

Two aspects of technique facilitated Mrs. Sheldon's revelation. During the long wait at the beginning of the session, my bearing Wilma's affect and anxiety ensured that it did not destroy the family or the therapists. During the next, long and more tense wait, I used my countertransference to speak of the threat to psychological space posed by Mr. Sheldon's anxiety and protectiveness. With trust established over time, he was able to accept my restraint of his defensive impulse. Once I had acknowledged the effect on me of his taking over, Mrs. Sheldon was able to speak of its impact on her. Mr. Sheldon could then contribute to creating the space for Mrs. Sheldon's revelation.

Session 7

In the next session I had a problem. Sandra was present this week, and like Wendy's mother, she had not been told of the abuse. The family talked of other things of interest, but nothing of importance emerged.

> *I felt bored and withdrew, thinking over how to solve this problem. I did not want to push them one way or another, but I myself felt pushed into silence and helplessness. I stopped fighting my boredom. I looked into my own experience and finally found a way to work with it for the family's benefit.*

"The family seems to be in retreat today from the difficult work done last week," I began. "I find myself in retreat, too," I admitted. "I don't want to push you to say something that is on my mind and I can't say what I'm thinking, not knowing what Sandra knows."

"I don't think Sandra knows anything," said Wilma.

"What a confusing spot for her to be in," I suggested. "If it's tying me up in knots, it may be doing the same to her."

Sandra corrected me, "I don't think it makes any difference. I don't have to know what's going on."

Will responded to her by speaking around the point. I had the impression he was working up to telling Sandra what had happened to her mother when she was Sandra's age. Sandra put the furry shark puppet on her mother's body, half nuzzling her, half biting her neck. Wendy diverted the play by asking about Sandra's drawing of the balloon launch she had been to the week before when the family was at the therapy session. There was a family wish to keep Sandra back there with the joyful things of childhood. Her play with the puppet, however, suggested that Sandra was unconsciously relating to a theme of seduction and abuse. Wendy thought that Sandra could not understand her story, but Will found a way to explain it so that Sandra knew what he was talking about.

"Do you know about those programs on TV where they are telling you about bad things happening to children?" he began. Sandra nodded and he continued, "Like when strangers take children and do sexual things with them. Well that happened to Mommy when she was a little girl, about your age, except that it was her granddaddy that did it. And that's why Mommy has always been worried about your and the big girls when you walked through the woods to the bus or went to play with a friend whose father was the only parent in the house."

Sandra nodded gravely and looked over at her mother with concern. Wilma reminded the family that she knew at Sandra's age never to let a friend's father bathe her during a sleepover. Will agreed that Wendy had taught the children to take no chances.

"Wendy is constantly on the lookout against anyone harming her children," Will asserted, almost proudly, "—including myself," he added ruefully. "I have never changed a diaper," he went on. "I have never had anything to do with that part of them. People have called me a chauvinist pig because of it, but I didn't even bathe them when they were 2 or 3 years old. They never sat on my knee with me drying them off. I've not had much of any kind of intimate relationship with them," he ended regretfully.

Wendy said that Will was better than she was at helping the girls with their emotions and she had left that to him. Each of the older girls described fondly an intimate conversation she had had with her Dad who had comforted her when she was crying in her bedroom. But in each case their mother had felt compelled to come in. Wendy explained, "All of a sudden it hits me: 'they're alone.' I have to get in there. And they're just sitting, talking. And I feel ashamed because I would never think that he would do something, but it just comes over me."

It was easy to empathize with Wendy's compulsion. But why was Will resigned to this position of mistrust? Perhaps he was afraid of his own sexual impulses. Perhaps he was familiar with rigid boundaries against incest in his family of origin. Perhaps, like Wendy, but for different reasons, he had not had an experience of the healthy family transitional space for relating in which incestuous wishes can be felt, responded to, and acknowledged without enactment.

Will threw some light on his motivation: "I grew up in a house where the parents' bedroom was sacred. If you went in there you better have a good reason. That door was always closed, locked. You don't go in there. Now that's the way it is with my children's rooms! I don't go in there for just any reason. It's the opposite of how I grew up."

I noticed that his current situation was both the opposite and exactly the same as when he grew up. The bottom line was that he was still excluded from a primal scene.

"So the *children's* rooms are closed to *me*," he continued. "And *I* can't close *my* door."

So that is what he meant by its being the opposite of when he was growing up: he as the grown-up was not entitled to privacy for an adult sexual relationship as his parents had been.

"Our door has got to be open so that she can be listening to be sure that nothing can be happening to her children," he finished.

While Sandra comforted her, Wendy cried, "My grandfather used to come in and shut the door. So I can't have the door shut. If we are going to have sex and he gets up and shuts the door and comes toward me, that's something he can't do."

"You can't be spontaneous. It restricts the times drastically," Will responded regretfully.

"But we knock!" protested Wilma, supporting her parents' right to sexuality, yet reminding them of a child's urgent needs. "We knock like five times."

"I know you do," said Will appreciatively. "And Wendy tries once in a while to shut the door. But most of the time that door cannot be closed."

In his marriage, Will the "powerful captain of the family ship" was not able to be the potent male excluding the children from claims on his wife during sexual relations. Hatred as the excluded child from the parental space was inhibiting Will's expression of his own sexuality as an adult. He feared that sexual assertiveness would damage Wendy and possibly their unguarded children and in fantasy kill off his parents, a murderous wish that found its complement in Wendy's fear that it would kill her to tell her mother about her incestuous involvement with her grandfather.

Session 14

Will's denial of his handicap had lessened. He began to tell the brutal facts of how his deterioration began: "All of a sudden I couldn't use my hands," he began. "I couldn't walk. I'm not that bad now. Now I can work around it. It doesn't bother me to ask Wendy to take a lid off a bottle for me. Then I was always reading textbooks. One of them put me in a state of shock for a week. It said, 'With proper medical care most patients should survive five years.' That means that after five years things are questionable. And to me proper medical care meant replacing kidneys and everything." He went on and on, each sentence more graphic and brutal than the next. He spoke directly and realistically, which I admired, but with such speed and pressure that others could not respond. Now facing the reality of this illness he had reverted to his old way of taking everything on himself.

I found myself squirming. I was tense and sore. My co-therapist was absent and I was missing him terribly, wishing that

I did not have to bear the strain of this session by myself. I was thinking, 'Surely Wendy would miss Will if he were not here. Surely Will must miss Wendy as a partner who could equally share the strain of family life with him.' As Will talked of his sore chest and difficulty breathing, I found myself pressing my tense rib muscles, stretching my side and flexing my finger joints. I was experiencing my countertransference in the form of physical sensation rather than in feeling or fantasy, not surprisingly, because that was how the family unconscious was expressed—through Will's physical condition and its consequences.

In retrospect, I can see that I was experiencing Will's pain through introjective identification. I actually felt like a dying man. I also felt invaded by this dying man, an experience that I thought of as a projective identification into me, one that I wanted to take in so as to understand it, but one that I definitely felt burdened by and wanted to shake off. My countertransference helped me to experience the strain on Will of being the focus of the family unconscious projection. I sensed his tight muscles and skin as a representation of his ego boundary stretched to the limit by the task of containment, just as mine was. But there was more to be gained from this countertransference, when Wendy would provide the necessary information.

My interpretation of Will's blocking his family's response led at first to their all talking at once so that still no one could hear anyone. Then they began to differentiate: Bobbie was mad that she had to hear all these things one after the other with no chance to get used to any of them. Wilma was mad that she had not heard them spoken until now. And Wendy was mad that although Will could address these things in therapy, he could not talk about them at home.

"It's not that I don't want to deal with it," protested Will. "It's just that there's nothing I can do about it."

"Then just let me say 'I'm worried,'" Wendy retorted.

"There's no use in worrying," Will insisted. "We can't dwell on that." Her emotions suppressed, Wendy's eyes filled with tears.

I asked Will how he felt looking at Wendy with her eyes full of tears as she told of being worried. All his defensiveness slipped away.

"I feel helpless," he said simply.

At last Will was able to re-own his projection of helplessness into Wendy. This psychological action created space for Wendy's next contribution.

"Sometimes he says things. And I think things and it's hard," she began. "Sometimes I panic because I have phobias where if I can't move . . . or the thought of not being able to open my mouth. . . . I've always wondered if that stemmed from my grandfather being on top of me. But when I think of how Will can get, maybe not able to move his hands or open his mouth, I panic and think of how will I be able to bear it. I think of it when we go to bed at night and it's hard."

Wendy was thinking of Will as a strong, healthy person overpowered by the hardened body of an aged man. She projected into her sick husband the part of herself in relation to her grandfather, and then to her grief saw him trapped by a body as she had been in childhood. Based on her own experience, Wendy was thinking of how awful it would be for Will to be unable to move and Will was thinking of how awful it would be for her to be helpless. At last they were able to re-own their projections into each other. Instead of projecting strength and weakness into each other, they became able to acknowledge their shared anxiety about being in the position of a weak and helpless child in the face of life events.

In tolerating such weakness separately and together, a couple can find the strength to develop a more adaptable projective identificatory system for the marriage as it moves through the developmental life cycle. A more mature couple is thus made available to modify the split versions of the immature couple that are already variously internalized by the children. The parents' growth through crisis and treatment can be expected to have a positive influence on the developing structures of the children's personalities.

6

Projective and Introjective Identification, Love, and the Internal Couple

THE ROMANTIC COUPLE

Where does romantic love come from, and can we always find it? According to Person (1990), love is not universal in all cultures. In China and Japan where loyalty to the group is esteemed, love has been viewed as a comic or tragic aberration, yet in Western culture where individuality is highly valued, the absence of love is regarded as a disgrace. According to her, love is possible only in cultures that value individuality. In those cultures the accumulation of narratives and myths that organize instinctual or cultural life form a cultural unconscious that fuels individual capacities for creating love.

Person emphasizes that imagination is the key: it colors the effects of early experience and thus shapes the choice of the beloved. Love does not attend the gratification of an instinctual impulse tied to sex alone. Love transcends the physical level of instinctual need through renunciation of the parental objects and the transformation of instinctual need in relation to the beloved, nonincestuous object. As Freud guessed, love is a refinding of a lost object. Regressive and progressive identifications with the mother, the infant, and the parental couple lead to a new integration that changes the sense of self. Person concludes that at its best, love moves beyond the limits of our own consciousness.

How do people fall in love? Bergman (1987, 1990) says that it happens when the beloved is identified as the source of goodness and as such promises union with the lost good mother and the achievement of an ideal state, in which earlier inadequacy in relation to the ideal object will be expunged. He suggests that three conditions must be met, if love is to occur: (1) in the beloved, one must refind the lost love object, (2) the beloved must undo the injury done by the original object, and (3) the beloved must provide what the original object did not.

What is love anyway? Bergman recognizes four factors that characterize love: (1) idealization, (2) tenderness, (3) identification, and (4) play.

What goes against loving? Bergman (1990) usefully suggests six enemies of the capacity for love: (1) insufficient transfer from the original object, (2) too much trauma in childhood love, (3) too much trauma in adult love, (4) jealousy and the wish to possess the beloved, (5) narcissism, and (6) hostility, that is to say, repressed anger that leads to a sense of boredom and a loss of sexual vitality.

Geddiman (1990), addressing the topic of fatal attraction in love relationships, focuses on the commingling of themes of love and death. At one end of the continuum, there is the pull of fantasies of dying together with a loved one with whom there is no hope of being loved. The polar opposite of such a death wish is found when death is feared. When death anxiety is extreme, its deflection may result in sexual love affairs. In this case, compulsive envious possession of the woman as the source and guardian of the life process represents a fantasy of immortality.

According to Bristol (1990), love evolves on a developmental line through nodal points according to Freud's theory of psychosexual development. He has reviewed factors that complicate loving, namely fears of annihilation, loss of the newly found object, loss of love of the object, and fears of bodily hurt including castration by the object of passion.

All of these views give a coherent structure for thinking about the vagaries of normal and pathological love. They have in common a reliance on Freudian theory beyond which they reach for the explanation of passion and love by looking to cultural anthropology, art, and literature. To develop the ideas further, I suggest reaching out to object relations theory. Bergman (1990), aware of Klein's concept of projective identification from his reading of Dicks (1967), points out that we seek in the lover those parts that we have repressed in ourselves. Reverting to a classical Freudian view, however, Bergman concludes that to stay in love, a favorable balance between libido and aggression has to be achieved.

Putting together these two ideas of Bergman, which I regard as disparate, I suggest that what is needed is not a simple balance of power between instinctual forces of libido and aggression, but a healthy balance between conscious and unconscious object relations sets of husband and wife.

Well-versed in the cultural and individual mental contributions to the loving state, Person (1988) nevertheless draws a blank when she asks *how* imagination creates a loving couple. She gets some help from the image of "the lover's shadow" hauntingly described by H. G. Wells (G. P. Wells 1984). In his situation of unrequited love, H. G. Wells fantasizes an elusive couple, his passion for the woman perhaps augmented by its frustration. His adult identity forms in the shadow of the lover, the frustrating lover casts a shadow over his life, and the lover is experienced as more of a shadow than a reality. One might say that the reality of the lover has been killed by yearning so that the shadow is more accurately a shade. In summary, imagination creates a fantasy that drives the search for the beloved. Imagination, I suggest, creates a symbol that stands for the integration of accumulated experience with early objects. This symbol is related to as a fantasy of an ideal object, sought interpersonally in platonic peer relationships, in adolescent masturbation fantasy, and ultimately in sexual love relationships.

Kernberg (1991) says that falling in love "implies the lover's capacity to link idealization with eroticism and, implicitly, the potential for establishing an object relationship in depth" (p. 46). He amplifies the lovers' "capacity not only to link unconsciously eroticism and tenderness, sexuality and the ego ideal, but also to recruit aggression in the service of love" (pp. 46–47). Each partner is freed from inhibition against finding in the lover both a re-creation of the exciting, oedipal parent of the opposite sex and the tender, pre-oedipal mother. "For both man and woman, the love relation represents daring to identify with the oedipal couple and overcoming the oedipal barrier at the same time" (p. 47).

I suggest that to explore further the formation and maintenance of a loving couple, we need the concept of projective identification (Scharff and Scharff 1991).

Kernberg (1991) recognizes that when emotional intimacy develops, specific dynamics between the partners are produced by the compulsion to repeat and repair pathological aspects of past relationships with the parents so that "the partners tend to complement each other's dominant object relation from the past, and this tends to cement the relationship in new, unpredictable ways." (p. 50). "By means of projective identification," he says, "each partner tends to induce in the other the characteristics of the oedipal or preoedipal object with whom they experienced conflicts around aggression" (p. 50). Kernberg also usefully extends the concept of projective identification to account for dynamics operating between the couple and their social context. Their intimate friends or analysts may become ideal objects for absorbing aggression in order to preserve the goodness of the couple relationship. The large group in which the couple lives and works may not, however, be so willing to contain aggression because of envy for the couple for having each other when individuals in the large group may feel lonely and anxious.

Taking a more specifically Fairbairnian object relations view of the dynamics of the couple in love, we can amplify upon the discovery of the pre-oedipal and oedipal maternal and paternal objects in the partner. We may find that in the couple relationship, a wife chooses a partner who does not represent these objects but rather he encourages her own identification with them, in which case her husband becomes identified with her childhood self in relation to her objects. Furthermore, we note the intermingling of conscious and unconscious exciting and rejecting object relationship systems operating within each lover's personality, not necessarily directly correlated with the maternal or paternal object. In other words, these systems that comprise psychic structure are built from the individual's unique adjustment to and creative blending of the experience of the self in relation to both parental objects, each of them being perceived differently at different developmental stages. This occurs because of changes in the modes of relating to the parental objects and changes in their affective and behavioral responses. Experience varies from the orally dominated, lap-baby stage of total dependence on the physically and orally gratifying and sometimes envied mother, father, or child-care helper; to the stage of making a phallic appeal to both parents; to the oedipal period of competition to the death and renunciation of the claim on the incestuous object; and beyond. All these stages are subsumed in the resultant internal object relationship systems, which then seek expression and reworking in relation to the partner in the current loving couple relationship of adulthood. These internal object systems are in a constant state of dynamic equilibrium and tension, the repressed ones always seeking to be reintegrated with the rest of the conscious part of the self.

Falling in love loosens the boundaries between the parts of the self; the established dynamic equilibrium goes into flux. The emotional commitment of marriage, echoing as it does the psychological devotion of parenting, further stimulates the expression of repressed treasured or despised aspects of the self. As in infancy when the emotional commitment was expressed through intense physicality, so in marriage the intensity of the sexual bond encourages the interpenetration not just of body parts but of parts of the self and the other (Scharff and Scharff 1991).

The lover's motivating conscious fantasy of an ideal object includes unconscious phantasy seeking a fit in relation to the loved one's personality. Self or object parts of the unconscious exciting and rejecting object systems are projected into the potential lover who warrants being identified with them, and who may or may not then actually identify with them. My point is that the ideal object choice is colored by the unconscious object systems. This coloration may enhance the ideal object, usefully bringing excitement and passion to the choice. On the other hand, it may substantially reduce the value of the ideal object, often without reducing its appeal. Denial of unacceptable qualities in the spouse supports the idealization necessary for falling in love with a force equal to the original disavowal of similarly unacceptable parts of the self.

In other words, what is needed is a projective identificatory system that cements without petrifying the marital bond and accommodates and modifies projections between the spouses so that the marital system moves toward the healthy end of the continuum. The well-functioning, maturing projective identificatory system enables the person to take back impoverishing projections. It simultaneously enriches the self and maximizes concern for the spouse as a separate person as well as refurbishing the internal object or part of the self to which the spouse corresponds.

THE DEVELOPMENT OF THE INTERNAL COUPLE

Equally important in development of the individual and in the selection of a marital partner is the motivating fantasy of "the internal couple." According to Klein (1952), the infant has a fantasy of the parents in intercourse. At that stage it is a fantasy of union and possession of sexual parts of the father by the mother (and of the mother by the father), through oral, anal, and genital routes, with the oral predominating at first, but the other elements contributing to the picture as early as 4 to 6 months of age, according to Klein. In Klein's view, oral, anal, and genital phantasies coexist and do not conform sequentially to stages of development. She says, "The infant's feelings in relation to both parents seem to run like this: when he is frustrated, father or mother enjoys the desired object of which he is deprived—mother's breast, father's penis—and enjoys it constantly" (p. 219). As Ogden (1986) puts it, the infant relates not only to its mother separately but to the father-in-mother (and to the mother-in-father). In this perception lies the origin of awareness of the integration of male and female elements both in the individual human personality and in its interpersonal expression in the couple relationship.

Integrating Klein's idea of the compelling fantasy of the parents in unending intercourse with Freud's theory of psychosexual stages, I suggest that as the infant grows, the fantasy is given a polymorphous coloring as it becomes more thoroughly infused with derivatives from the anal and phallic stages. The toddler in the anal stage of development may view intercourse in fantasy as a battle for control and domination over the object or a way of holding on instead of letting go. A child in the phallic stage may see intercourse as an opportunity for display of urethral competence as well as physical qualities of muscular strength. This blends into a yearning for possession by penile penetration in a situation of ultimate genital gratification, subsuming oral, anal, and phallic trends.

In addition to psychosexual development, there is a concomitant maturation in the child's ability to perceive and distinguish between ways of relating. Infant research has documented that infants behave differently with their fathers than their mothers. They respond with faster rhythms and wider circling arm movements in a generally more excited way than in the lower-keyed arousal sequences enjoyed with the mother. Traditional analytic theory has presented the father as a shadowy figure of little importance until he looms large out of the pre-oedipal fog as a threatening and forbidding figure in the oedipal stage. That may be a fair picture of the Victorian fathers that Freud encountered, or of some fathers now who cannot relate to their children until they are reading and throwing a ball accurately. But most parents nowadays are involved with their children from birth. Any of them could describe their child's awareness of the parents' relationship. The toddler who sees his parents kiss will get between their knees, not attempting to pry them apart and repossess his mother, but hoping with his arms around their thighs to be included in the loving embrace. For the couple, this recalls when they maneuvered around the wife's pregnant abdomen in the final months before their child was born. For the child, this is the inclusive loving couple.

THE IMPORTANCE OF THE LOVING INTERNAL COUPLE FOR MENTAL HEALTH

The importance of the loving internal couple for good mental health is referred to in passing by Bion (1962), who mentions the mother's relation with her husband while he focuses intently on the mother–infant relationship as one in which the mother, through her capacity for reverie, contains the projections of her infant—whether they are suffused with love or hate—and transforms them so that they can be re-introjected in a more manageable, containable form. He says, "If the feeding mother cannot allow reverie or if the reverie is allowed but is not associated with love for the child *or its father* [my italics], this fact will be communicated to the infant even though incomprehensible to the infant" (p. 36).

As the child grows, this loving couple becomes a source of conflict. In the background the security of it is loved and needed. In the foreground the pleasure of it is hated—originally because the child loses the feeding, soothing breast and mothering person— when the mother moves away from her bodily preoccupation with her child to relate to her husband erotically. Later it is hated because the child, now more aware of the nighttime separation from both parents, who guard their privacy, feels painfully excluded from their relationship. In addition, increased genital sensation in the phallic and oedipal stages drives the wish to enjoy sexual pleasure as the grown-ups do. Accompanying fantasies of sexual possession lead to the fantasy of killing the rival, which provokes guilt about stealing, spoiling, and hurting, and anxiety about losing a loved and needed parent. Now the internal couple is a conflicted internal object.

Spillius (1991) in a paper on clinical illustrations of projective identification gave an example of an interpretation which, as I heard it, dealt with the patient's introjection of the perceived, creative parental couple and the re-creation of it in the analysis. Her patient had had a dream in which a friend got married, which left the patient, a productive career person, feeling left out and unsuccessful. Associations to the dream and work with the analyst on the dream led to the following interpretation. Spillius said that the "friend" part of the patient had come into marriage with the analyst and had created children in the form of productive work. She added that the patient felt left out by this pairing and was unable to enjoy success in work. Not surprisingly, Spillius was not allowed by the patient to enjoy having made this interpretation. Instead of feeling appreciated for her understanding, she felt somewhat despised. On further reflection Spillius realized that the patient had felt humiliated by this and by earlier interpretations, and was responding by diminishing the analyst's work, partly in revenge and partly in an unconscious attempt to communicate what being humiliated by a creative couple felt like. In Spillius's view, the understanding generated by her emotional experience of feeling despised was more important than the other aspects of her intellectual interpretative understanding. In my view, the patient's despised feeling had to be projected into and identified with by the analyst in order to confirm her intellectual understanding of the powerful exclusion of the patient by the internal, creative couple, representing parents that, in the patient's view, loved each other too much and the patient too little.

In the following illustration from the mid-phase of couple therapy, a couple's introjective identification with the therapist was so massive that it remained unintegrated and had no healing effect, until this phenomenon was acknowledged and worked with by the couple. Once each spouse's defense was recognized, then I could demonstrate their shared functioning according to fantasies determined by the unconscious action of their internal couple.

Introjective Identification as a Defense

I had been aware for some time of Mrs. Galloway's idealization of me. She loved my books, my clothes, my accent, and even my interpretations. I knew from her individual therapist that Mrs. Galloway was equally idealizing of him. Although depressed about herself and her life, she was excited about therapy and found it gratifying and inspiring. Despite admitting to envious and aggressive feelings toward both of us, Mrs. Galloway maintained a positively loving attitude to her therapists. Her husband, who was not the recipient of such adoration, often felt excluded by her bonding with me in this way. Nevertheless, he tolerated it in the hope that what she got from me would rub off on him some day. I thought that he might need to deny his own feeling of attachment to me and project it into his wife, identify it there and express it through her, because for some reason he was too frightened to notice his own feelings.

I met them in the waiting room for their next session at noon on a hot day. I carried a cup of water into the office with me. As Mr. Galloway entered the office, Mrs. Galloway noticed my water and took a moment to get some for herself. I realized for the first time that like me she usually had water at hand.

As usual, Mrs. Galloway began. "There's so much I feel about you. I wish I could say it all and get rid of it, but it would take up all the couple session and that wouldn't be fair to Tom."

"You mean the Jill-Pills," Tom ventured.

"Oh yes, I could tell you about that," Meg agreed. "You know I got these antidepressant pills from my therapist. At first he tried me on a lower dose, well it wasn't really low, but I felt it was too low for me. I told him I wasn't taking in enough of the medicine. Sure enough, when he checked my blood levels, although the dose was good the blood level was low. So," Meg said, reaching in her purse to show me, "he prescribed more pills. That's why I have these green ones and these melon colored ones. They are the same as the colors of the paint on the walls inside your house! I saw them the time you rescheduled our appointment to the evening and the lights in the house were on. Bright green and orange. I love those colors and they're not what I would have expected because the outside is so conservative. Bright, vibrant color on the inside. I think of it when I take my pills."

Since I do not myself prescribe drugs, I had a moment's difficulty identifying the antidepressant pills with my home decor. I found myself thinking the colors were not the same at all. When I got past that, I realized what she was saying to me.

"You are taking my inside inside," I said.

"Exactly," she smiled. Then her face clouded over. "It's another example of that taking in I do of you and my therapist. Like you said before, I do this massive taking in, but it doesn't make any difference to the 'me' inside."

I noted that she had taken in that interpretation, had held on to it, and had applied it in this instance. I felt hopeful that her insight about her wholesale introjective identification would pave the way for a less defended, more assimilable introjective identification.

Mr. Galloway surprised me by relating the topic to himself. Until now, it had seemed to be his wife's issue. His response made it clear to me that, indeed, he had been projecting part of himself into his wife and ensuring his own intake from me through her. Now he re-owned his projection.

Tom said, "I had a parallel thought. When I read or listen to music, both of which I will do for hours, I am massively ingesting, absorbing, and attending to the material, but it doesn't have meaning that results in changes. It's a passive or static thing. It wouldn't be that way if I could use the thoughts I have, transform them into a paper or a performance. I think the only meaning my absorption has is not what I take in, but what I keep out. Listening to music, which I associate with my mother, is a way of emotionally distancing myself. Like I was deep into the Brandenburg concertos and Meg asked me to do the laundry, while she ran to catch the last mail collection. She was rushing off and said 'You have to look out for special care instructions on these three things.' I could sense it going in one ear and out the other, so I said 'Write it down.'"

"I was so furious," Meg interjected. "He didn't care enough to remember just three things and I didn't have time to write them down, because *I* was going to mail a letter *for him*."

I said, "Meg, I don't think he couldn't remember them." To Tom I said, "I think you couldn't take them in, because there wasn't room for both Meg and music. Tom, can you tell me more about music and your mother?"

"Well," said Tom sadly, "my mother wanted me to learn to read music and I could never do it. To this day I can't. She hovered over me at the piano and covered my hands and somehow my mind was not free anymore because of her lack of boundaries and her ambition for me to do something. She was just so into the form of things and doing things the right way. But I learned by where the hands are, not by the notes on the page. So I gave up piano. Later, I taught myself to play the saxophone. I play well and I can compose, and I've tried to learn to read music, but I just don't get it."

As a couple, the Galloways shared a problem with introjective identification as a defense mechanism. Mr. Galloway took in music, which he loved, not to make something of it but to keep out the intrusive image of the loved woman that he associated it with, while simultaneously reuniting him with her through her love of music. Mrs. Galloway took in her therapist massively to keep out the image of her intrusive mother.

In Mrs. Galloway's endopsychic structure, we can see her use of the therapeutic relationship to create an internal couple. She took in both her therapists, each equally loved, as a collaborating pair to neutralize her internal couple of viciously quarrelsome parents, who nearly killed each other and were felt to have destroyed her internal psychic structure. Her introjective identification prevented the projection of dead and destructive aspects of herself into either therapist where she might have metabolized them.

Similarly, we can see the operation of Mr. Galloway's internal couple. In earlier sessions, he absented himself and related to me vicariously through his wife. This pattern created a pair from which a man was left out. But in Mr. Galloway's case, the one left out was his father, who seemed to lack the authority to claim his wife. Instead, she formed a close bond with her favorite son, Tom. This left Tom Galloway with an anxious attachment to his mother, who he felt did not love him for himself but only for how well he performed as a substitute. It also left him with an internal couple in which there could be no desire and no identity validation.

In the next couple-therapy session, the internal couple was revealed first in the focused transference of one spouse and then in the contextual transference of the couple to the therapist. Mr. Galloway reported somewhat sheepishly that he had had a sexual feeling about me after the last session. He liked the way I had been dressed that day and thought my legs looked pretty (a comment Mrs. Galloway had made some months before). Mrs. Galloway smiled approvingly. Not at all jealous, she felt glad that she was not alone in having feelings about me. In fact, she felt relieved, because at least his feelings, being heterosexual, were "normal" in her view. I noted that she was identified with what she projected into his feeling about me, and that she was not asking for elaboration. I thought that if she heard more, she might have to face her jealousy and become aware of a competitive threesome. I asked for more information about Mr. Galloway's experience.

"I became aware of your breasts," Tom replied. "There wasn't a fantasy of doing anything, just a wish to see you naked. It had to do with seeing you as an attractive, older woman, successful and independent. And I was pleased to be able to feel desire. I'm not so pleased to have to tell you about it."

"That puts me in the Mommy category," I said, struck by his oedipal longing for me.

Even though I welcomed his comments, I clearly had to defend against seeing myself as alluring.

Tom then spoke about his voluntary suppression of sexual feeling for Meg this week because she had had a urinary tract infection. He did not want to be contaminated but would not use a condom. He would rather deprive himself of sex than be deprived of pleasure in sex. Meg spoke of her fear of pain and her memories of shame when as a child she had painful urination but had no words to explain about that part of her body. Both Tom and Meg had been in a bad mood after seeing a video film about a couple of storekeepers who ate people and were upset because their dog was barking for food all evening.

I pointed out that the theme had spiraled down from the sexual level, to urinary, and now, eating concerns. Perhaps these were contributing anxieties underlying their discomfort at the sexual level, but equally likely, I thought, they represented a defense against continuing the discussion about Tom's sexual desire and its suppression in their couple relationship, and in this session because it involved me.

Tom said, "I felt put down by what you said earlier about the mommy category, like I was an 11-year-old boy, talking about breasts. I guess what I didn't finish saying was that I hoped you might reciprocate."

Meg giggled.

"What?" asked Tom.

"I just thought of us as the couple in the video!" Meg answered, still laughing. "We could be the couple and Dr. Scharff could be one of the people who comes into their store."

"Do you know, a moment before you said that I was thinking of eating Jill's breasts!" said Tom.

"Well!" said Meg. "Well, that's okay, Tom, 'cause you like white meat and I like dark meat . . . "

"So there'd be something for everyone, and no competition," I concluded.

I felt bleak. I had an unpleasant fantasy of myself with most of my breasts bitten off. I wondered if I was substituting an aggressive image for an erotic one, and so I checked with Tom.

"You're not talking about eating, meaning taking sexual pleasure from the breast, are you? You mean eating until the breasts are gone, am I right?"

Tom nodded. "Until they're gone. Eating them up."

I went on, "Talking of sexual desire in the threesome tends to create a fantasy couple with the third person left out, but Meg, you didn't feel that. Instead, thoughts turned to a couple dealing with the threesome by each pairing with me, but in a way that would annihilate me. Although you would both get plenty, there would be none of me left for you to relate to."

"We'd be lost in the woods," agreed Tom. "It's the reverse of Hansel and Gretel, eating up the witch."

"Perhaps that is the point," I suggested. "Reverse the story so that I do not eat you up."

"I know you are right, because when you said that, I got a contracting feeling in my gut," said Meg. "It was a sexual kind of feeling, but I felt it in my gut."

"When you said 'reverse the story,' for a moment, I thought you were going to reciprocate my fantasy and say you have feelings for me too," Tom rejoined. "Like 'hey, we can all have sexual feelings. It's okay!' The more I think of it, the more I realize, I am looking to you in this fantasy for something I didn't get from my parents. Meg didn't get it from her parents either. I want to get a sense of myself from you. I want you to notice my talents, maybe even reciprocate the feeling I had for you. I wanted that from my mother, so I could go out into the world feeling strong. I wanted to be near her, to have feelings, and for that not to be *horrible*—no pun intended."

Intended or not, Tom's pun highlighted his worry that his arousal would turn the woman into a whore. The session was over.

Meg and Tom had come a bit further toward understanding their
desperate need to introject me, as an antidote to their disappointing
parents. They created a substitute babes-in-the-wood couple to
turn against the witch-bad-mother-in-relation-to-father. Based on
experience of the parents' couple relationship, each individual develops an internal couple structure in the psyche. Because of an
unconscious fit that brings the present couple together and maintains their bond, their images of the ideal couple and the feared and
hated couple tend to overlap and coalesce. The Galloways' internal
couples were concordant with each other and created an unmodified shared internal couple that had been killed off for years. In the
course of therapy this internal couple was brought to life. When
excitement could be felt, then the couple ran the risk of rejection
and of annihilating the object by the force of the unleashed hunger.
At this stage of therapy, they could not imagine possession of the
loved object through a sexual mode. As yet, possession was seen
predominantly in the oral terms of introjective identification.

With further maturation, the child learns to resolve the unbearable conflict by renouncing claims on the desired opposite sex
parent, in favor of maintaining the parents as a loving couple. By
this time, the internal couple is more important than any individual
internal object. This stage of development obviously goes much
better if the parents really are a secure couple, able to withstand
their child's assault. If the couple loves each other despite disagree-
ment, then a loving, flexible couple will be internalized, provided
the force of the child's drive for sexual possession has not been too
extreme or has been well metabolized by the couple, leaving no
undue residue of resentment in either parent. If the couple is barely
together, the child may be afraid to express naturally disruptive
oedipal wishes, or if she does may crumple with guilt if her parents
separate. If the couple is securely together but in a sadomasochistic
or fatal attraction, the internalized couple will then be of that type.
If the couple is actually divorced, the child faces an arduous task of

maintaining the fantasy of a potentially loving couple without distorting the reality of the parents' broken marriage. In this case, the internal couple may remain a fractured object or, if it is formed, it is one built on loss and yearning. Again the internal couple undergoes further development as the child builds onto it experience with other couples—the grandparent couple, the uncle and aunt, remarried parents, male–female work couples such as student–teacher or doctor–nurse, and husband–wife relationships portrayed on television and film. Eventually, the internal couple comes up for massive overhaul during the resurgence of the oedipal period in adolescence. Sufficient trial couple relationships with peers are crucial in securing an independently conceived, personally modified internal couple that can guide the young person successfully to a suitable life partner.

THE INTERNAL COUPLE
IN THE MARITAL RELATIONSHIP

The Fragmented Internal Couple

Sue Montgomery called for a marital crisis consultation for herself and her husband, Matthew. They wanted to be seen the next day if possible, but I could not see them until after the weekend, on Monday at 7:35 A.M. But 7:40 A.M. came and went with no sign of the couple. At 7:45 A.M. the Montgomerys arrived with no mention of being upset at the delay. So I asked if they had some feelings about coming to see me, feelings that had made them late. Sue said, "No, I thought you said 7:45. I'm not worried. It's just a mistake." End of discussion. I felt quite dismissed. I asked Matthew for his point of view and he said Sue told him 7:45, so it was just a mistake.

I did not press the issue with them and went on to discuss why they were here. Sue began by describing a twenty-year marriage of which the first ten years had been extremely challenging. "Matt was unwilling to commit himself to a faithful relationship," she said. "But ten years ago he made changes and has been a committed and loving partner for the past ten years. Then he comes home this month," said Sue, "Says he's having an affair and wants a divorce. Our younger daughter is going off to college next year and we've been planning a rosy future with lots of leisure for just the two of us. So this came as a total blow. It's like being stabbed. And Matt, who is not in touch with feelings, has no concept of the depth of the hurt this has done to me. I'm not eating or sleeping well and I'm pretty angry, though I'm trying to work and carry on. But I'm in shock. Things seemed so loving between us."

How could Sue not have known? I wondered. I guessed from her way of dismissing my questions about her feelings about therapy that she had a powerful mechanism of seeing only what she wanted to see and excluding anything that did not fit her view, and that Matthew tended not to challenge her.

Matthew did not look cowed or guilty. He was attentive but clearly yielding the floor to Sue as the injured party. Sue went on. "I took so much crap from him already. You'll find out that Matt was a transvestite those first ten years and had many affairs, and I've got a lotta scar tissue." Sue's accent distorted her vowels so that scar tissue sounded like "skirt issue." It emphasized my assumption that there would be congruence for the transvestite interests at some level in Sue's personality. Sue concluded with a challenge to me, "Someone's got to convince me as to why I should pour more of my soul into this man."

I was very much struck by her way of putting it. She projected her good spirit into Matthew and thought that he had identified with it, confirming her worth in a loving marriage. But now she was asking me to prove to her that he was still a worthy container for her projections.

Now it was Matthew's turn. He did seem out of touch with feelings as he spoke of remarkable insights he had achieved from reading

Intimate Partners (Scarf 1987). He advanced a complex theory of
the causation of his affair. He mentioned as particularly relevant
his and Sue's recent empowerment as individuals and the rele-
vance of their daughter's coming of age.

"So we are at the cusp," Matthew said. "We had a vision of
our post-parenting years, spending lots of time at the beach
house we are having built—a significant fiscal undertaking, symbolic, too, of our love of nature. Our first date was a beach nature
walk. So why did I get involved with another woman? I met someone I fell in love with who seemed to have so many characteristics
I thought I'd never have in this marriage with Sue." He did not
elaborate on the missing characteristics at this time but went on
to say, "Twenty years with Sue is a lot to give up. My younger
daughter says we are the envy of all her friends because we have
such a wonderful family. I thought she should have come here
today, but Sue didn't agree. Anyway, I've been reading about
cross-generational coalitions. I'm not just giving a book report. It
fits with what I find in my family. The dynamic of our wonderful
family has been that I perceive Sue as more powerful than I am, so
I made a coalition with my younger daughter—and now with my
lover."

With this, Matthew insisted on his right to continue with his
lover, while exploring the possibility of rebuilding his marriage.
Sue had thought Matthew would put the affair off while they tried
to rebuild. Nevertheless, although it made her angry, she agreed to
a six-session consultation without putting any conditions on Matthew's fidelity.

Sue said, "I've taken this crap from him before. I've stomached
his affairs in order to keep the marriage and because he had a lotta
trauma in his childhood. Hell, I was a damaged kid too." Sue
viewed Matthew as damaged and had taken great power from
having healed him to be capable of faithful marriage. "I thought we
had pulled it together," she said. "We had a committed relationship
and I've been leaning on that trust. I love Matthew and he says he
still loves me. He's sensitive, gentle, a good Daddy, shares interests, and he pulls his load. He's not a chauvinist. He really cares for
women. That's why I put up with the transvestite stuff. And we fit
well together sexually. At least we have the potential for being
wonderful lovers. But our sexual life has been abbreviated because

of remaining resentments about the damaging effects of the transvestite stuff."

Matthew objected, "That transvestite stuff hasn't been a part of my life for over ten years." Explaining to me, he added, "As soon as I felt powerful as a man at work, the transvestite thing just sort of fell away." Turning to Sue, he complained, "But our sex life isn't so wonderful as you say. In fact I've been completely frustrated with having sex like woman to woman. It's a case of mutual masturbation, do you understand me, Dr. Scharff? No intercourse in ten years."

So when Matt became a powerful man at work and no longer needed transvestite fantasies to make him potent, he nevertheless agreed not to express his phallic power in sex. I wondered if his affair might be a sign of phallic assertion and confidence, but I soon learned, to the contrary, that Matt was most often impotent in the affair. What he enjoyed so much about his lover was that, unlike Sue, she could accept sexual attention and respond to his touch. Because of her valency for accepting sexual pleasure, this other woman provided Matthew with an external object into which he projected the part of himself that was in relation to the exciting object and gratified that part of himself there.

In their marital sexuality, Sue stimulated Matt and became aroused because of his arousal. Through his orgasm, she experienced sufficient tension release for herself or sometimes masturbated. Sue projected the exciting object into Matthew and gratified it there. Sue projected into his penis the sexually responsive part of her and took great pleasure from seeing the response flourish. But in so doing she confirmed his view of her as outstandingly stimulating and powerful, the more so when she took a stand against his affairs and, as he saw it, forbade penetration. In Sue, there was recreated the internal couple in which the father prohibited the sexual expression of oedipal longings and the mother gratified her child without seeking her own pleasure from her husband. In Matthew, there occurred an image of him as greedily and childishly taking, rather than giving, love. Because of their shared projection and identification of each other with rejecting and exciting objects, which must be kept separate, Sue and Matthew shared anxiety and guilt about penetration and were unable to establish a fully mature, co-equal adult couple relationship enhanced by mutual sexual satisfaction.

When I commented on their evidently shared anxiety and guilt about penetration, Matt said that the few times they had had intercourse had been followed by a great deal of pain for Sue.

"Cystitis," she explained, adding "That's nothing to all I caught from him those first ten years of his affairs. Nonspecific urethritis and I could have gotten genital warts, but he kept those to himself, thank God. Now another affair and there's herpes and AIDS out there, nowadays."

I got a picture of intercourse as a highly risky, damaging prospect. I saw a string of couples in multiplying danger. Here the internal couple shared by the Montgomerys was fragmented into many fantasied alternative couples doing harm to each other and to the actual central couple of the marriage. On the other hand, alongside the fragmented, minimized internal loving couple, there coexisted a loyal couple with an enduring bond. How else could the Montgomerys have stayed together for twenty years, weathered many storms, healed a transvestite symptom without therapy, and raised two successful children?

THE INTERNAL COUPLE IN THE INDIVIDUAL AND IN THE TRANSFERENCE

Recreation of the Internal Couple in the Transference

The internal couple is also re-created in the transference between therapist and patient. Andrea, a single young woman in analysis complained of waking at night with her heart pounding so hard that she was afraid of dying. As a child she could remember similar feelings after her parents' parties, where she consumed dessert food and sodas. At first she attributed her symptom to sensitivity to sugar and caffeine. Then she remembered other childhood fears of fire in the basement of their house. She remembered being taken to see a doctor whose house had burned to the ground. And finally she recalled that the reason she had to see the doctor was to have her genitals checked because of her masturbatory activities. Now the picture of an overstimulated, anxious child emerged from the process of association. The reconstruction of this was experienced as helpful and interesting.

In the transference, however, a different picture emerged. The woman experienced me as unhelpful, intrusive, and tormenting, picking away at her skin, trying to see what horrors lay underneath. She picked away at me, complaining that I was a punishing and withholding figure who worsened her depression and panic.

> *My countertransference was a guilty, anxious one. I could hardly bear to have my sadism and schizoid aspects so in focus. The atmosphere was usually tense. I felt hyper-alert and worried about doing or saying something when I should not. I felt too in tune with the affect that the patient transmitted. I did not have as good boundaries protecting my neutrality as I am used to.*

At first I interpreted her transference to me as the enactment in the therapeutic relationship of her relationship with her mother, whose interest and devotion to her daughter covered over a deep depression. Later I interpreted her re-creation in the transference of her father as a critical and abandoning object, who left her to her depressed mother when he went on lengthy business trips.

An intense experience in the waiting room led us to another interpretation of her dynamics and shed light on my countertransference experience of having weakened boundaries. A couple in an adjoining room were talking heatedly and unrestrainedly about their disagreements. They were so loud and shrill that Andrea felt included in their argument, even though she could not hear the words. Her heart began to pound and she realized without a shadow of a doubt that as a child she had often been sleeping in her parents' bed to allay her fears, and had experienced their intercourse, which she now thought must have caused her childhood fears and their re-creation in her present symptom of panic.

Andrea's sadomasochistic relationship to me could now be seen as the re-creation of the primal scene, viewed through the eyes of an overstimulated, uncomprehending, and jealous child, who interpreted her experience in the light of the aggression she directed toward the couple that excluded her and impinged upon her sense of safety and the boundary of her skin. I now understood my countertransference as arising from my introjective identification with the projected part of her self, the frightened wakeful child being bombarded with affect that she could not understand or keep out of her space. The offending object, namely the parental couple in sadomasochistic intercourse, was projected into and enacted in the relationship between us. Andrea felt raw, overwhelmed, and panicky. She described herself as a nonperson, uncared for by me. The internal couple in this case was threatening to her sense of self and led to fears of annihilation.

The internal couple can also be detected in the history of the transference. As it happens, the young woman that I have just mentioned was previously in analysis with a male therapist with whom she got along splendidly. She found him quite helpful, but she did not actually confide in him. He referred her to another therapist for reduced-fee treatment when she could not afford to increase her sessions with him. She found the new therapist to be an unbearably cold woman who did not care for her and could not understand her. She quit after many months of total silence that was uninterrupted by the therapist. In her therapy history, we find a couple of therapists, the man quite understanding but abandoning because of the need to make money, and the woman a remote, cold fish. Fortunately for the outcome of her treatment with me, the split between her parental objects was contained within the transference this time and the full impact of their coming together as the exciting, rejecting, and fundamentally annihilating internal couple could be experienced and recovered from.

In the case I have just described, the tense atmosphere was a feature of the primal scene projected into the transitional space provided by the therapeutic relationship. Duncan (1990) has also addressed the issue of the atmosphere as a separate concept worthy of study in therapy. Thinking of his own experience with his patient Mr. F., Duncan (1990) asks:

> Is the atmosphere in Mr. F.'s session to be thought of as belonging with him (i.e., he brought it with his material) or me (I identified it and he didn't), or only with us both as a couple? Without our merged intersubjectivity it is inconceivable. . . . Self and other, inside and outside, conscious and unconscious, subject and object, never stay still, never submit to simple objective questioning. They merge, alternate, hide, and peep. They dance in mockery of the cold stare of our objectivity! [p. 8]

To me, his description of the atmosphere suggests the affective activity of the internal couple at work in—and just out of reach of—the therapist–patient couple.

The internal couple appears rather obviously in the situation of remarriage. The remarried partners carry with them a marital history. The new marriage may be a repetition of the previous unsuccessful object choice, its polar opposite, or a developmentally higher or lower version of it, depending on whether the person has addressed problems of ambivalence and has grown or regressed in the course of the previous marriage. Because of the wish to suppress the memory of the broken ideal of the first marriage, the version of the internal couple represented there is often deeply repressed, but then emerges in enactments with the former spouse or child of the former marriage. Sometimes the stability of a new marriage depends on the defensive projective identification of the former marriage as the only one subject to the problems of the troublesome internal couple. In couple therapy, the repressed former version of the internal couple has to be integrated with the present internal couple if the partners are to achieve a flexible stability rather than a brittle one that rests on massive projection of badness into the rejected internal couple.

As Dicks (1967) noted, marital choice is ultimately determined by unconscious factors, and the long-term quality of the marriage is a result of unconscious complementariness of fit. To these important points, I add the quality of the internal couple. Unconscious factors include not just the repressed, exciting, and rejecting object systems in dynamic interaction as I have described, but also the internal couple. The internal couple is a psychic structure based on the child's experience of the parents as a couple. In health, it promotes a guiding interpersonal fantasy of the conscious central ego and its ideal object in successful relation to repressed exciting and rejecting object systems within the context of an enduring, healing, and growth-promoting marital relationship that has the generative capacity to create and interact with future object systems in various personalities as children are added to the family system.

PART III

PROJECTIVE AND INTROJECTIVE IDENTIFICATION IN CULTURE

7

Projective and Introjective Identification in Groups and Communities

With the bridging concept of projective identification, the object relations approach to understanding the individual in the life group readily transfers to understanding groups and their relation to surrounding groups. I had the opportunity to study this in two illustrative settings: in the laboratory of the group relations conference, where a sample institution of teaching and learning and a microcosm of society was created (Scharff and Scharff 1979) and in the real life working of a community (Savege 1973).

IN THE SAMPLE INSTITUTION

The sample institution was created in a conference designed by David Scharff and me (Scharff and Scharff 1979). The design

161

evolved from our previous experience with schools' consultation research (Savege 1974a, D. Scharff 1975, D. Scharff and Hill 1976) and with traditional group relations conferences, based on systems theory and Bion small group theory, and offered by the Tavistock Institute in Great Britain and the A. K. Rice Institute in the United States (Bion 1959, Rice 1965, Rioch 1970). The conference task was to study the relationship between experiential and cognitive learning and the interdigitation of the personal processes of teaching and learning occurring in individuals and groups. David Scharff and I were invited as consultants to this study task by a number of interested teaching institutions. The examples that are quoted come from our experience in two of those settings.

Our conference focused on the personal and group factors that inhibit and facilitate teaching and learning. The conference design provided varied sizes of groups and different formats ranging from lecture, large group discussion, small group discussion, psychodrama, and videotape events. These provided contrasting modes of experience to generate the data upon which to base the study of the processes of teaching and learning. As consultants, he and I behaved in various styles, tailored to the format, so we might be interpretive, interactive, or positively directive in different roles. In these ways, we presented ourselves as different types of objects for use by the membership, all of them available for study. Teaching was defined as the attempt to facilitate the learning of others. Learning was defined as the attempt to experience the various events cognitively and emotionally and to subject them to process and review. So teaching was seen initially as a projective process while learning was a predominantly introjective one. As soon as dialogue and interaction between the roles of teacher and learner developed in the interpersonal situation (and corresponding communication in the intrapsychic dimension occurred among parts of the self identified with both roles), introjective and projective identificatory processes combined to shape the teaching and learning in both roles. Since the "lesson" was unstructured (like life itself), the membership was pulled toward complexity, integration, and tolerance for not knowing.

As consultants we found that the membership attempted to defend themselves from the anxiety inherent in the ambiguities of the complex study task by expecting us to be the kind of "teachers" who "knew the answers." We might then be revered for our secret knowledge or vilified for not passing it on. Here projective identification was operating so that the conference membership tended to split off their own competence and project it into the consultants. There they identified it as a characteristic of the consultants, even though the consultants could not possibly know or predict the members' experience of the various events. This use of polarization also operated between conference members designated as students and teachers in the teaching institution where they usually worked and studied. (I will refer to this as the original institution to distinguish it from the conference institution.)

This defense was employed in one small group to which I was consulting. When I avoided identifying with the group's projection into me of knowing what each person should be learning, substitute leaders were found to meet the thwarted dependency needs. Two group members, themselves teachers in the original institution began to tell others who were students in that institution what they would learn in the conference institution. The "students" assumed the position of ignorance and of expressing confusion on behalf of everyone, while the teachers undertook to know, in keeping with their previous roles. This splitting of ignorance and knowledge and their projection into the self and the other, functioned as a group defense against both its members' frustrated dependency wishes that were not met by the consultant, and their anxieties about exploring their roles as both teachers and learners in a new temporary institution of teaching and learning. This defense kept the group from the collective anxiety of not knowing what the current experience held in store and of sharing that unknown and thinking about it together.

In another event, a large group with a psychodrama format (Moreno 1946), a conference member who identified herself as an undergraduate student named Anne presented her psychodrama concerning a conflict that had confronted her in a small group seminar at the original institution. In that setting, another student had shown a painting of a small child and asked others what they thought of it. Anne had wanted to say "That's terrible. The colors are not good." Instead, she said, "Gee, that's nice." Anne said that she was afraid of her capacity to hurt someone with her bluntness. She herself would be offended if a teacher said that her work was terrible. This led to her conflict over honesty—a conflict that she had experienced in an earlier small group in the conference.

In the ensuing psychodrama, Anne exchanged roles with the other student and experienced herself as that student being protected from criticism. Other conference members who had been present either at the seminar Anne was describing, at similar events, or at Anne's small group in the conference where the issue had come up, took turns taking on roles as Anne and as the other student, each being protected and then being criticized, and so gave their impressions from various perspectives of identification with Anne's self or object. From their feedback and from the graphic representation of the conflict that Anne created, she learned in action how her own fears of vulnerability had kept her from developing her capacity to teach through the tactful use of criticism. She had projected her own hurt into the other student and had identified her with it and then tried to undo the hurt by covering over her criticism.

Another event was designed to explore the effect of art media on teaching and learning. Both small groups that we had consulted to were asked to paint their experience as groups in the conference. At the end of half an hour, the two small groups assembled as a large group to describe their paintings, the process by which they made them, and to elaborate on their themes.

The processes by which the two groups arrived at their pictures were different. The small group to which David Scharff had consulted, painted as a group working together. In my small group, individuals took turns drawing. Despite the apparent difference in approach, the production from my group was an integrated group effort, an image of a large and a small rhinoceros (see Figure 7-1), whereas his group members had individually painted circles arranged in group formation (see Figure 7-2). Amid much hilarity, my group, upon completion of their organized painting, had created a second production, a messy inchoate finger painting (see Figure 7-3).

For the purposes of this chapter, I will focus mainly on my own group (Figure 7-1). They described how they had first wanted to draw two unicorns, but felt that this idea somehow did not fit. They moved on to drawing two rhinos, each with wings—and both pregnant with twin unicorns. The large rhino stood on firm grass, the other slipped on the mud. The sky was blue with a black cloud on which a smiling sun had been drawn and from which lightning emerged. The group offered little about the finger painting (Figure 7-3) except to giggle and react with hostility to any attempts at putting into words its meaning.

The circle of circles painted by the other group represented a flower, we were told. Each petal represented one individual's experience in the small group (Figure 7-2). The flower's center, which depicted the small group, did so by a series of individual summary symbols that they called "signatures." The flower also looked like a bomb to some people.

Discussion of associations to the images before us led to the emergence of themes and fantasies. The rhinos represented two horny, fantasy beasts that could stand up to critical comments while protecting the inner unicorns, unborn and full of creative promise, possibly with sharp horns (critical comments), but with valued mythical magic for the uninitiated. The large rhino on solid ground and the small rhino in the mud were thought to represent the aggrandizement of the teacher and the belittlement and insecurity of the student, respectively. The twin unicorns stood for the hope of equality and creative pairing between teacher and student.

Figure 7-1. Large and small pregnant rhinoceroses by J.S. group.

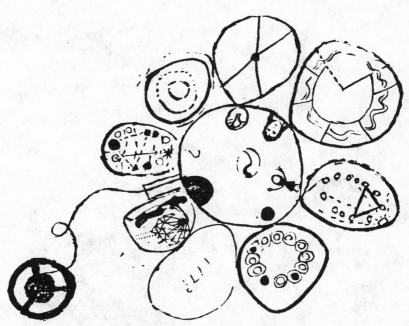

Figure 7–2. Flower of circles by D.S. group.

Figure 7-3. Finger painting by J.S. group.

There was some recognition and envy of the creative work pairing of the consultants. Fantasies about the consultants' life partnership were denied by fantasies about the rhinos' immaculate conception by a bolt of lightning or exposure to a unicorn.

The messy painting could not be commented upon. It seemed to represent preverbal needs for mess, pleasure, and body contact. These had been split off from the task and became a defense against it, rather than being used to enrich the original production. Pleasures of body play had been repressed and were not available for learning. My group guarded their playful expression from what they perceived as criticism from the other group. The other group's production was seen by my group as an explosive, intricate flower that represented intellectualization to achieve autonomy as a defense against the wish to fuse and be taken care of. A hostile, repressive attitude to dependent needs was then projected by my group into the other group, and to some extent the other group identified with the projection and became increasingly hostile, the more their attempts to relate verbally to the material were thwarted.

The conference ended with application groups in which participants discussed how their learning might help them in the original institution. As a consultant, teacher, and student myself I learned that the dynamic of projective identification and the resulting polarization of knowledge and ignorance powerfully inhibit both teacher and learner. I also determined to apply this knowledge in my own efforts at teaching, curriculum planning, and program design.

A major application of principles of teaching and learning confirmed by this conference has been the design and implementation of an innovative object relations training program at the Washington School of Psychiatry. Since my husband and I are both on the faculty, our relationship is inevitably a feature of the learning environment. The effect of this representation of the internal couple (see Chapter 6) is always significant and excites the group's projective identification of the couple as a mutually gratifying

situation that is unfairly enjoyed when others feel lonely and frightened in the large group. If I ever feel like ducking this issue, I need
only remember the image of the two pregnant rhinos. Without
need of art media, fantasy images are there in the emerging themes
and can be elicited to detect the prevailing projective identifications
about the couples and individuals who represent the teaching and
learning task. Our teaching method at the Washington School now
includes a teaching style that encourages the examination of projective identificatory processes that affect the introjection of the material to be learned and a programmatic design that integrates cognitive and emotional learning in the here and now of the group and
the conference institution.

IN THE COMMUNITY

Working as a community psychiatrist based at the Royal Edinburgh
Hospital in Edinburgh, Scotland, I found that understanding of the
relation among intrapsychic, interpersonal, and intergroup phenomena, conceptualized in terms of a projective identificatory
system penetrating these three dimensions, facilitated the consultation and community development aspects of community psychiatry.

The Endopsychic System

A simplified sketch of the psychodynamics of a young woman may
serve to recall the object relations approach to the individual. Mrs.
Rogers complained of a phobia of her son's mouth. She could not
stand to see him swallowing. This symptom caused her either to
avoid looking at her son and his swallowing mouth, or to yell at him
and nag him about his habit. It soon became apparent that there
was a basic personality disturbance that made relationships difficult for her. Mrs. Rogers had a vicious attitude to her own babyish,
orally needy self. When she looked at her son's urgent swallowing,
she projected this part of herself into his mouth and rejected it

there. Enjoying his power to annoy and control his mother, the son exaggerated his swallowing to assert his anger at her for rejecting him. She had to suppress his anger too, since she was also afraid of her own angry infantile self that had resulted from her frustrated needs as a child. In the transference, sometimes she hated the professional, clinical part of me, which she regarded as cold and hostile to her needy self, and at other times she demanded gratification of her needs from me as a purely good feeding mother and felt angry and disappointed when her demands were not met.

She was split by the trauma of early experiences into an angry self, a needy self, and an attacking controlling self, each of which she projected into other people. In object relations theory, her personality can be viewed as a system of parts, each deriving from inner object relationships established in early life. These operate in a nonintegrated way and relate only to parts of the selves of other people. Through projective identification these internal object relationships recruit corresponding object relationships in such a way as to evoke real relationships now that confirm the pattern of those experienced earlier. This feedback loop created in present interaction preserves and confirms the personality as a closed system of parts in fixed relation to each other. Object relations therapy has to do with breaching this closed system, allowing it to become a more open, flexible, reintegrated system.

The Community System

From this view of the individual organism we can move to a corresponding view of the community organism as a system of parts in dynamic relation; the local community in relation to the city and to the city authorities, the local community in relation to the professional care-givers, the subgroups of care-givers in relation to each other, and so on. Like the individual, the community has its dependent, needy parts that may demand to be gratified, for instance, by the social worker as an indulgent, feeding mother or by the family doctor as a caretaking and discipline-enforcing father.

But the community may then express its resentment at the power of these authorities to supply and refuse satisfaction. The community expresses itself through its angry violent parts that emerge through the youth gangs who, on behalf of the total community, vandalize property and terrorize people in their own or other parts of the city. The community's controlling parts then step in, often just as viciously as does the individual's superego, in the form of practical restraint by police or spiritual censure by religious institutions.

A small community within a large city expresses a part of the whole. As a community psychiatrist in Edinburgh, I worked with a population of 30,000 people living in a peripheral rehousing scheme with few amenities and high rates of medical, social, and psychiatric breakdown. The city renovated its inner city apartment buildings and raised the rents, so the current inhabitants had to be rehoused. In this way, the city split off and projected into that community its rejected objects. The city scapegoated and vilified the community as the embodiment of all that was unacceptable, infantile, inadequate, deprived, and violent. The local press published frequent accounts of unacceptable action in the community. By stamping in the stereotype, the press helped to maintain the relationship between the city and its suburb as a closed system, apparently forgetting that back in the 1920s when this rent-subsidized-housing scheme was conceived, during a period of environmental stress, the city (like the patient's threatened central self) split off from itself all that was undesirable in its population and actively repressed it out into this peripheral rehousing estate where the city fathers hoped "the police could keep an eye on all the troublemakers together." Not surprisingly, the concentration of trouble and poverty and their active repression led to an escalating retaliation from the community against the rest of the city. Applying Fairbairn's description of the endopsychic situation to the society, we might say that the central city ego was then threatened with the return of the repressed bad objects.

As in individual therapy, community psychotherapy has to do with breaching the closed system of parts. This is done by analyzing the projective identificatory system built up between the parts of the community to defend against basic anxieties. With this insight, the community (which means in practice each one of us) recognizes that each part is expressing something on behalf of the whole and can take responsibility for all its parts. Then the different distressed parts that are expressed in relation to the various care-giving parts of the community are together understood as symptomatic of a basic disorder of relationships in the community as a whole.

To make a full assessment of the distress of the community we need to put together the experience of all the care-givers to whom the varied symptoms are brought. In other words, we have to provide a psychological space in which the minister who deals with sexual guilt, the social worker who pays out to stave off the threatened eviction, the policeman who seizes the property of the delinquent drug-taker, and the doctor who prescribes for continuing somatic discomfort, can all talk to each other safely. Only together can we build the total picture. Then together we may learn how to work with the community to understand the underlying tensions in its system of relationships. We can explore how to build in more self-help mechanisms within the system so that it need not rely solely on professional help from outside the system. If care-givers could create a model of collaboration and respect of difference, this would supply a holding environment in which the disadvantaged population may be encouraged to make a continuing commitment to living and learning through stress situations, instead of collapsing under them. Here we are putting a value on growth and flexibility. Of course, there will still be community symptoms in the form of individual and family clients, parishioners and patients that specially trained professionals will serve on behalf of the community.

Such collaborative teamwork offers a model for the community that promotes its integration, while in the absence of such a model the community struggles along in a disintegrated way. A parallel to this is seen in the psychiatric ward where patients produce disturbed behavior that unconsciously expresses tensions in this staff group. Just as attention to staff integration allows more integration in the patients, so collaboration among the care-givers minimizes disintegration in the community. But how do we achieve this collaboration when we care-givers operate so independently? And why do we prefer independence to interdependence?

Here again is the situation of a closed system of parts that are split off from possible central coordination and integration in response to stress. The community, like the individual personality, evolves as a system to contain the tensions within it, and it actively resists attempts to open up, because of the fear of the explosive emergence of overwhelming material. The community resists the community psychiatrist's interventions as actively as the individual resists the individual therapist. As the community psychiatrist in the setting, I undertook the analysis of this resistance. I worked on it in meetings with the various care agencies, at first singly and later together.

Consulting to Trained Social Service Workers

In small weekly seminars where I consulted to a mixed group of professional and trained ancillary social service workers from the same agency, we discussed our work with clients and patients. Perhaps a probation officer might discuss her attempt to relate to unattached youth. A social worker might discuss his frustration with a client who thwarted his efforts to stave off her eviction. The community development worker often spoke about poverty as a social and economic force that destroyed hope. The marriage guidance counselor wanted to explore the dynamics of a difficult couple. The mental health worker sometimes asked for help in planning a hospitalization for a psychotic person who did not want treatment. While addressing the concrete aspects of the issues being raised, I helped the group to develop a shared object relations approach to case problems and to build a common ground from which to grow further. The members of the consultation groups worked well together on understanding discrete problems of the professional–client relationship and on conceptualizing the social and economic pressures facing the community. They were not, however, ready and willing to broaden their understanding and their intervention power base by cooperating with other groups not located in their own buildings. Here I confine my description of the analysis of the resistance against cooperation to that operating in the relation of doctor and social worker and hospital-based psychiatrist.

The psychiatrist, the analyst, and the psychotherapist had stayed too long in the office, building up a professional mystique and colluding with community expectations that they should magically deal with problem individuals. Psychiatrists were anxious about stepping out from behind their soundproof doors to face the real needs of the community for fear that the idolized wise old men would be found to have feet of clay; and certainly if they were shod in the medical model they would soon be plodding. They had to cross not only the physical boundaries between hospital and outside world and the theoretical boundaries between intrapsychic and interpersonal and intergroup work, but also personal emotional boundaries so as to open themselves to respond in new ways and to acquire the appropriate skills.

It is easier to work out of a secure and flexible institution that functions well as a support base because it has overcome its own resistance to change, where there is cooperation between departments, and integration of policy. The institution that has created a system that is cohesive, open, and flexible offers a professional mental health model that transfers in reality to the community. The institutional model must be consonant with the community mental health outreach approach. The outreach team, like a satellite built on the same principles as the institution, reflects and influences the learning and values of the institution. Like the institution, the cohesive multidisciplinary team offers a cooperative model that is able to receive and make sense of the collated varied experiences of the different professional care agents.

Projective Identification in Professional Role Relationships

Having considered some of the resistances in psychiatrists and the institutions they represent, let us look at the relationships between social worker and doctor as I experienced them at the time of the study. In Great Britain in the 1970s, social work was viewed as a relatively young profession that doctors regarded as having as yet extremely uneven standards of training and competence. The social worker was viewed with suspicion by the doctor from what he described as his "centuries-old professional tradition with its clearly defined code of ethics and means for enforcement." He had been everything to whole families of *his* patients in the past. Why should he give up part of his lifelong domain to a succession of short-stay social workers who could detract from his kudos and omnipotence? He was used to making decisions that were unquestionably right and he was used to getting *his* nurses to act on them. He was dismayed when the social worker seemed unable to carry out orders urgently and unquestioningly, frequently preferring to make a considered social assessment for herself before offering an independent professional opinion for discussion with the doctor as a colleague of equal status. The social worker tried to educate the family doctor in this way of working, but when treated as ancillary, she might withdraw. She tended to excuse her understandable retreat on the grounds of the real urgencies of heavy caseloads and overwhelming statutory obligations, while the family doctor complained to his medical colleague in the public health department that the social services had collapsed now that they were no longer under medical control.

Unconscious phenomena complicated their attitudes. The role of the doctor was generally regarded as a male authority role while that of the social worker was a female service role. Family doctors described social workers as disobedient, tardy, permissive, naive girls who were not mature enough to be objective and firm with clients, while social workers saw general practitioners as unreceptive, hurried, rigid, paternalistic, and authoritarian in attitude toward both patients and colleagues. It seemed to me that, in order to protect himself from suffering through introjective identification with patients, the doctor had to reject the receptive, identifying, female part of himself and project it into nurses. But when he was confronted with this in the unfamiliar social worker, his defense was threatened and he had to reject the female parts of himself he saw in her, and so also rejected her as a colleague. The social worker was struggling for an independent professional position. Like all of us, she had been a patient from time to time and tended still to relate to the doctor in the helpless, dependent way learned from childhood illnesses, when the doctor was an omnipotent father who could hurt and heal. This was at variance with her preferred professional attitude as an adult colleague.

Social workers and doctors each had the same difficulty with me compounded and concentrated, because whereas by training I am a doctor, I looked to them like a social worker. In fact I was something else, namely a psychiatrist. My role was complicated not only by these professional identity problems, but also by my ambiguous consultant-in-training status. My consultative position as a psychiatrist, free as I was from a heavy patient caseload, was the object of much envy. Doctors and social workers alike hoped that I would be able to solve all *their* problems. The reality was that I did have some psychodynamic and psychiatric knowledge that I shared with them, while learning from them what they wanted to tell me of their work. But they imagined I could do far more, and were disappointed when I could not. Then their envy of my imagined omnipotence led to their simultaneously experiencing me as impotent. Those care-givers whose skills increased through consultation then excited similar envy in their colleagues. Under the stress of dealing with envy, I sometimes wondered if their evaluation of me as impotent was justified. Perhaps this was my defense against my sense of omnipotence about trying to make a difference to a whole community. Although in a consultative role here, I was at the same time a trainee-in-supervision. I had the same dependent, envious feelings about my supervisor and had projected my wishes for his omnipotence and impotence into him as the care-givers had done into me. At least, the disadvantages of not having full-fledged consultant status for this consultative work were compensated by the advantages of having a valency to identify with the consultees' feelings.

Consultees also expected that I would be secretly, powerfully psychoanalyzing them. I thought that this expectation arose from their fear of the exposure of their infantile incompetent selves and the projection into me of their critical and rejecting objects. I found myself inhibited about making my contribution in case it should confirm their fear. I was also filled with fear about my being incompetent in the consultant/consultee relationship since my skills had been learned in the therapy situation. Would I succeed in focusing on the client, seen through the consultee's eyes when the consultee's eyes were so often in a fixed gaze on himself and the critical part of himself he saw in me? Here I was in a state of introjective identification with the projected infantile parts as a defense against identification with the rejecting object.

My femininity in the consultant role was also a problem. Like the consultees I tended to deny it and took refuge in the unisex cover of my doctor title. I thought that men were uncomfortable with the idea of a woman wedded to the task rather than to one of their kind. I noticed that some of them tried to solve the problem by relating to me as a sexual object instead of as a professional female colleague. I worried that if I mentioned any of this I would face the retaliation of rivalrous women into whom I had projected my own competitive feelings. Fortunately, I realized that this was probably not my problem alone and I raised the issue. With the support of female consultees who had experienced problems in the workplace because of their gender, the group was able to discuss the nature and power of female authority. More cooperation between male and female members of the staff ensued.

Consulting to a Group of Untrained Neighborhood Representatives

These defenses did not, however, operate so powerfully as a source of resistance when I was consulting to a group of local housewives.

This could be partly explained by the fact that they themselves asked for help. They wanted to understand the overwhelming feelings arising in themselves and their families after they began to be involved as untrained workers whose role it was to be available to neighbors who asked for their help. In contrast to this, consultation to the professional care-givers had been initiated at the request of their director, and was not a request from all the workers to whom it was offered—a significant difference in the contract. Uncertain of their director's motives in obtaining consultation for them, they were likely to be more reluctant to explore what I could offer than the neighborhood workers.

These neighborhood workers freely admitted weakness and did not suppose I would be critical. If they did suspect I could divine their problems they said so early on. They dealt with their envy about my education and mixed feelings about my femininity by harnessing both my qualities to their own ends, with the use of humorous fantasies, such as hoping that I would lend them my psychological and educated female power to impress husbands as well as clients. Their receptiveness enabled them to learn quickly what I actually had to offer. Then, with no more resistance, they began to use me to help with individual casework and to understand community phenomena.

All of these neighborhood workers were also members of a local festival society that existed originally and primarily to put on a yearly community drama. That is how they had come together in the first place. As it happens, I had a valency to join them in this shared avocation. My interest in drama as a process important for self-expression and mental health (Savege 1971, 1975) and in theater as art form cemented our relationship on a basis other than the purely consultative. Through their festival, they had developed verbal fluency and administrative expertise, and through their group participation they had developed social awareness and responsibility. The festival society soon extended its primarily cultural activities to include social and political action. Social action included the neighborhood casework I have just described, as well as the running of youth

clubs, preschool play groups, and lunch clubs for the elderly. Their
political action included cooperation with local government representatives and organization of planning workshops and community
conferences. The festival society executive committee was then designated as the administrator of funds allocated to the community by
the government. At their festival society meetings, the community
discussed local government development plans for housing, building,
and education. In consultation with its bank of resource people,
including community workers, planners, architects, social adminis-
trators, and psychiatrists like myself, the community leaders then
drew up alternative proposals more specific to their needs. Then they
entered into dialogue with the relevant local authority committees
and a rudimentary form of liaison government emerged.

In consultation with the social workers in the area, I realized
that they tended to shy away from this organization for good
reason. They were afraid of repercussion from their employing
local government department that might be challenged by the society's activities. This was a projection into their boss of their own
wishes to retaliate against possible attack. When this was pointed
out, they were able to admit that they were also afraid that their
competence might be called into question in direct confrontation
with these representatives of the consumers of their services. They
had projected their incompetent bits into the untrained neighborhood workers and attacked them there by expressing dislike of
these "amateurs" who were messing with their territory. The amateurs were then identified as being like both the clients who could
never be satisfied and the professionals who could not do enough.
Previously unrecognized ambivalent attitudes to their difficult
clients were dealt with by the splitting and projection of the negative feelings into these neighborhood workers. This then led to the
social workers' guilty withdrawal from them. Unsupported by the
professionals, the neighborhood workers became resentful and
demanding. Their introjective identification with the projection
actually provoked the feared attack. When I gained the trust of the
various professional and volunteer groups, I was able to interpret

these defensive projective identifications and demonstrate their repercussions in maintaining splits among the care-givers.

After a year of this preparatory analysis of resistance, it became possible to arrange a meeting of all parts of the care-giving system. This became established as a monthly community care-givers' meeting involving every care-giving agency, including the festival society, to consider the mental health needs of the area. The task continued to involve detoxification and metabolization of projective identifications among groups represented in the meeting, so that the tendency to withdraw under stress to the security of the professional peer group was less necessary. Various defenses appeared from time to time. For instance, rather than continue the complicated and personally demanding task of solving territorial argument and intergroup suspicion by discussion and negotiation, the group hoped to elect one person as a coordinator-go-between. I recognized the plan's defensive functions and the group's disappointment in me for failing to take on such a role. I was trying to find a tactful way to interpret the projection of hope into the new savior. I did not have to speak, however, because one of the social workers who had identified with my point of view interpreted the plan as a fantasy. The group gave up its plan, in favor of the real possibility of each of the group representatives working together and sharing the responsibility of collaborative planning for community mental health.

By making myself available to the various professional groups, to the festival society as a consultant and member of their executive committee, and to the monthly care-givers meeting, I demonstrated my recognition that their conjoint planning for social change was integral to planning for the mental health of their community. Neighborhood planning included some specifically psychiatric issues: a club for parents of the mentally handicapped was begun and a hostel for the area's discharged psychiatric patients was planned with help from the hospital's community psychiatric nursing team. Community representatives and professionals together expressed strong interest in a community health center so that independent family practitioners were encouraged to move slowly toward this concept. Together they began negotiations with the housing department to provide pre-illness hostels for unattached youth. By working together, professionals and community representatives developed a more powerful voice for effecting change. The model of integration among the care-givers was introjectively identified with by the community. The community executive functions gained strength from this, just as in psychotherapy the central ego is enriched by the integration of previously split-off object relations systems.

8

Projective and Introjective Identification in the Arts and the Media

The science of psychoanalysis is credited with introducing the concepts of projective identification and introjective identification to society. If we look beyond science to the arts we will find both precursors to the emergence of projective and introjective identification as psychoanalytic principles and elaborations upon them. Artistic sensibility to human phenomena frequently predates scientific acumen. Freud himself is quoted as saying, "Ach, die Dichter haben alles gekannt!" The remark was made during a conversation with Thornton Wilder who in his semi-autobiographical novel *Theophilus North* translates the line: "The poet-natures have always known everything" (Wilder 1973).

183

One thing that Wilder himself knew was the limitation of Freud's interesting libido theory. He wrote "One can talk all one wants about the libido element in parental and sibling love—yes, but one falls into the danger of overlooking the sheer emotional devotion which is a qualitative difference, and must be continually recognized as such" (Harrison 1983, p. 170). Wilder does not dismiss the sexuality Freud drew attention to in family life but, like an object relations theorist, he emphasizes attention to the emotional attachment and commitment that characterize family relationships. He was teaching this at Harvard one year before the publication of Fairbairn's (1952) book *Psychoanalytic Studies of the Personality*. Not surprisingly, Wilder's plays, including the classic *Our Town* (1960) are replete with family relational themes that show mutual projective and introjective identification in action. These are particularly evident in novels in which he explores the relationship of twins (Glenn 1986). I will return to projective identification revealed in literary explorations of twinning later in this chapter.

Although the term projective identification did not appear until 1946, artists were aware of the phenomenon long before it was reified as a concept. For instance, James (1881) tells us that the novelist Turgenieff was aware of a variety of visions of people in relation to each other in his mind. These provided the inspiration for his writing. I see these visions as one-body projective identifications. Turgenieff was concerned not so much with a story line as with showing these people in their relations with each other. These ghosts of characters, these visions waiting to be given fictional life, can be thought of as personifications of internal objects, their dynamic relation to each other in Turgenieff's mind impelling him to make his story a description of their projective and introjective processes.

A modern dramatization of the same idea can be found in Pirandello's (1921) *Six Characters in Search of an Author*. There the playwright is claimed by his dramatis personae who demand to be revealed in a family constellation as well as in the play in which they are supposed to appear. The play then carries a conscious plot and an unconscious drama based on the family history. The characters represent, for me, the family unconscious, which molds individual development through projective and introjective identification and profoundly shapes the perception of new relationships.

Returning to Turgenieff, this is how James described his creative internal object world in *The Portrait of a Lady*:

> I have always fondly remembered a remark that I heard fall years ago from the lips of Ivan Turgenieff in regard to his own experience of the usual origin of the fictive picture. It began for him almost always with the vision of some person or persons, who hovered before him, soliciting him, as the active or passive figure, interesting him and appealing to him just as they were and by what they were. He saw them, in that fashion, as *disponibles* [usable objects], saw them subject to the changes, the complications of existence, and saw them vividly, but then had to find for them the right relations, those that would most bring them out; to imagine, to invent and select and piece together the situations most useful and favourable to the sense of the creatures themselves, the complications they would be most likely to produce and to feel.

> 'To arrive at these things is to arrive at my "story,"' he said, 'and that's the way I look for it. The result is that I'm often accused of not having "story" enough. I seem to myself to have as much as I need—to show my people, to exhibit their relations with each other; for that is all my measure. If I watch them long enough I see them come together, I see them *placed*, I see them engaged in this or that act and in this or that difficulty. . . . As for the origin of one's wind-blown germs themselves, who shall say, as you ask, where *they* come from? We have to go too far back, too far behind, to say. Isn't it all we can say that they come from every quarter of heaven, that they are *there* at almost any turn of the road? They accumulate, and we are always picking them over, selecting among them. They are the breath of life—by which I mean that life, in its own way, breathes

them upon us. They are so, in a manner prescribed and imposed—
floated into our minds by the current of life. [pp. xxvii–xxviii]

In James's description of Turgenieff's experience, Turgenieff's
visions appeal for his involvement with them as an active or passive
participant. This awareness predates and validates Racker's insight
that projective identification may involve complementary identification with the object or concordant identification with a part of
the self. In describing his visions as *disponible* Turgenieff had to turn
to French, the literary language of his time, for the word to convey
the quality of his object world. *Disponibles* translates as *at one's
disposal, available,* but it also means *unoccupied, disengaged, vacant*:
An exact descriptor for internal objects that are there to be used
and yet need to be invented. *Disponibles* may also mean *realizable
assets,* a translation which captures Turgenieff's awareness of the
potential value of his objects and refers to his ability to make
something of them. Through his creative use of his objects, Turgenieff transcends the personal to offer his culture universally appli-
cable insights about self and object engaged in projective and
introjective identification. He gives us a striking image of projective
identifications as the breath of life, floated *into* us by the course of
life, and then given life *by* us as we modify and develop them
through introjective identification and containment in relation to
others' projective identifications.

A luminous example of projective identification in an aunt's
marriage can be found in Nobel prizewinner Elias Canetti's (1979)
biography *The Tongue Set Free.* The 10-year-old Canetti was quite
aware of his Aunt Bellina's nature and how it related to the character of her husband, Canetti's Uncle Josef. The family relationships
were complex, because Bellina's husband Josef was also her cousin.
Canetti sets the stage by beginning and ending his account with
information about the death of Bellina's father, Señor Padre, who
was Grandfather Arditti to his grandson, Canetti, the author. In
addition to being Bellina's father, Señor Padre was also her husband's uncle, being the younger brother of Josef's late father.

When he died, Grandfather Arditti left all his money to his wife, thereby excluding his nephew and son-in-law Josef, as well as his daughter Bellina, from the inheritance. Josef was enraged by the rejection and deprivation, but Bellina appeared unaffected by it.

Loss has driven the couple's projective identificatory system to a level where each of the spouses is impoverished by the projection of parts of the self and its objects into the other and each is possessed and controlled by it. Describing his beautiful aunt, Canetti writes:

> She lived in a spacious yellow mansion in Turkish style, right across from her father, Grandfather Arditti, who had died during a trip to Vienna two years earlier. She was as kind as she was beautiful; she knew little and was regarded as stupid because she never wanted anything for herself and always gave presents to people. Since everyone so well remembered her avaricious and money-conscious father, Aunt Bellina was anything but a chip off the old block; she was a wonder of generosity, unable to look at a person without reflecting how she could do something special for him. There was nothing else she ever reflected about. When she fell silent and stared into space, heedless of questions from others, somewhat absent, and with an almost strained look on her face—which did not, however, lose its beauty—people knew she was thinking about a present and was dissatisfied with any that had already flashed into her mind. She would give presents in such a way as to overwhelm the recipient, but she was never really glad, for the present always struck her as too meager, and she even managed to excuse herself for it with honest words. . . . She had married her cousin Josef, a choleric man, who made life hard for her, and she suffered more and more from him, without ever giving the least hint of it. . . . People whispered about his fits of rage. I was warned about them, they said he was absolutely horrible when he lost his temper.
>
> I heard this warning so often that I anxiously looked forward to it. But when it did come one day, during a meal, it was so terrible that it became the real memory of that trip. "*Ladrones!*" he suddenly

shouted, "*Ladrones!*" Do you think I don't know that you're all thieves!" The Ladino word *ladrones* sounds much heavier than "thieves," something like "thieves" and "bandits" together. He now accused every single member of the family, first the absent ones, of robbery, and started with my dead grandfather, his father-in-law, who had excluded him from part of the legacy in favor of Grandmother. . . . But then it went on, now it was the turn of the three sisters, even my mother, even Aunt Bellina, his own wife, who was such a kind-hearted person—they were secretly conspiring against him with the family. These scoundrels! These criminals! This riffraff! He would crush them all. Tear their false hearts out of their bodies! Feed their hearts to the dogs! They would remember him! They would beg for mercy! But he was merciless! . . . "You think you're so smart, don't you?" he suddenly turned to my mother. "But your little boy is a thousand times smarter. He's like me! Some day he'll drag you into court! You'll have to cough up your last penny!" . . .—he now turned to me—"you didn't know your mother's a thief! It's better that you know it now, before she robs you, her own son! . . . All of them, they're all thieves! The whole family! The whole town! Nothing but thieves." With that final "*ladrones,*" he broke off.

Most of all, I was amazed at my aunt. She took it as though nothing had happened and was already busy with her presents that very same afternoon. In a conversation between the sisters, whom I eavesdropped on without their knowledge, she told my mother: "He's my husband. He wasn't always like that. He's been this way since Señor Padre died. He can't stand any injustice. He's a good man. You mustn't go away. That might hurt his feelings. He's very sensitive. Why are all good people so sensitive?" Mother said it wouldn't do because of the boy, he mustn't hear such things about the family. She had always been proud of the family, she said. It was the best family in town. Why, Josef himself was part of the family. His own father had been the elder brother of Señor Padre, after all.

"But he's never said anything against his own father! He'll never do that, never! He'd rather bite off his tongue than say anything against his father."

"But then why does he want that money? He's a lot richer than we!"

"He can't stand injustice. He's gotten this way since the death of Señor Padre, he wasn't always like this." [Canetti 1979, pp. 98–101]

In Canetti's piece, the simple way of giving, so characteristic of Aunt Bellina, contrasts with her greedy father. She is not a chip off the old block but its soft-hearted core. She has not introjectively identified with the greedy aspect of her father, but instead projects it into others, including her husband, where she feeds and satisfies her greed. Through projective identification, she identifies a part of herself as if it were a feature of the object. She is immune to introjective identification with the greedy, raging aspect of her husband and cannot contain and transform it for him. So her husband looks desperately for somewhere else to put it. He projects his greed into the family with vehemence and identifies it as arising in the objects of his projection so that he then experiences paranoid anxiety about their wish to thieve from him. His wife explains that this part of him did not emerge from repression until the hurt following the loss of Señor Padre. Clinically, we often find that the trauma of separation and loss triggers the projective identificatory mechanism (Spillius 1991) and drives it down the developmental continuum to a more primitive level (Ravenscroft 1991).

My next example comes from the life and work of Vincent van Gogh. My point is not to show that he used the mental mechanism of projective identification as a product of his insanity. In fact I am not trying to prove anything about him or his state of mind or even his artistic intentions. I simply want to look at four of his vivid paintings, two self-portraits and two portraits of people concerned with his health, for visual images of projective identification relating to the therapeutic relationships in which he found himself. Of course psychotherapy or psychoanalysis as we know it was not offered to van Gogh, but I am assuming that the relationships he established with the caretakers he wished to paint were important to him and evoked transferences to them in him. First some background material to place the paintings in context.

Vincent van Gogh was voluntarily admitted to the asylum in Saint Remy in May 1889, at age 36. In his record of that time in the artist's life Pickvance (1986) tells us that Vincent van Gogh had been suffering from acute mania and epilepsy with visual and auditory hallucinations that had driven him to cut off his right ear. Van Gogh settled down sufficiently to paint the insects and flowers in the asylum garden, but did not have the necessary introspection for figure painting. In mid-July, another attack hit. For five weeks he was not able to paint, partly because he did not have the spirit for it and partly because it was unsafe as long as he might be tempted to poison himself with the paints. By August 30th he had regained his lucidity and resumed work at full speed, beginning with two self-portraits. Writing to his brother Theo (van Gogh 1978) he described these portraits as follows: "One I began the day I got up; I was thin and pale as a ghost. It is dark violet-blue and the head whitish with yellow hair, so it has a color effect. [Figure 8-1] But since then I have begun another one, three-quarter length on a light background" (pp. 201–202). [Figure 8-2]

In the same letter he goes on to describe his portrait (probably painted on September 3rd, according to Pickvance 1986) of the chief attendant of the hospital, Trabuc, "a man who has seen an enormous amount of suffering and death," a man of the people and yet with an expression of "contemplative calm" that van Gogh associated with the elite (p. 203). [Figure 8-3] Van Gogh commented: "If it were not a good deal softened—completely softened—by an intelligent look and an expression of kindness, it would be a veritable bird of prey" (van Gogh 1978, p. 206).

Two weeks later, van Gogh described his views against photographic portraiture in a letter to his sister Wil (van Gogh 1978), asserting that "the painted portrait is a thing which is felt, done with love or respect for the human being that is portrayed" (p. 458). According to Pickvance (1986, p. 124), van Gogh's "no-

Figure 8–1. Vincent van Gogh. Self-portrait. Oil on canvas, 22½ × 17¼ in. (57 × 43.5 cm.) Unsigned. Collection of Mrs. John Hay Whitney.

Figure 8–2. Vincent van Gogh. Self-portrait. Oil on canvas, 25½ × 21¼ in. (65 ×54 cm.) Musée d'Orsay, Paris.

Figure 8–3. Vincent van Gogh. Portrait of Trabuc. Oil on canvas, 24 × 18¼ in. (61 × 46 cm.) Unsigned. Kunstmuseum, Solothurn, Switzerland.

tion of the painted portrait as antiphotographic, as a re-created image, as a "felt" experience is reaffirmed, also to Wil, when he describes his *Portrait of Dr. Gachet*. In early October 1889, Pissarro had recommended Dr. Gachet as a physician that van Gogh could stay with as an alternative to hospitalization. But van Gogh did not leave the hospital until the following spring.

In May 1890, van Gogh was discharged when he was apparently better, but unable to cope with the noise of Paris. He went to live in Auvers at an inn in the neighborhood of Dr. Gachet, patron of the arts and physician, to whom he could turn for help if an attack occurred. Upon meeting him, van Gogh found him an eccentric, troubled man, "as ill and distraught as you or me" (van Gogh, 1978, p. 276). He speculated that Gachet's knowledge as a physician protected him from the full impact of his own nervous disease. Nevertheless, when he did his portrait, he painted him "with the heartbroken expression of our time" (van Gogh 1978, p. 287).

In the first self-portrait (Figure 8-1) the vivid colors against the ghostly yellow face create a halo effect, suggesting an idealized view of the self as artist. In the second self-portrait (Figure 8-2) the artist appears as a troubled man without the props of his profession, the bluish color and fluid texture of his suit echoed in the background. Turning to the portrait of Trabuc (Figure 8-3), I note a bluish tone and a severe expression with beady eyes that are reminiscent of a bird of prey. Where is the contemplative calm that van Gogh saw in him? Admittedly, it is suggested by the quiet cream of the background, but in Trabuc's face I find an expression of worry and intensity quite like that in the self-portraits. The eyes are especially like van Gogh's own eyes in Figure 8-1. And I wonder about the appearance of Trabuc's right ear. Although it is perfectly drawn, and its color is in keeping with the man's ruddy complexion, a line of red on the edge of the ear gives the suggestion of amputation.

In the portrait of Trabuc, I suggest that van Gogh has identified a projected part of himself. Since van Gogh sees Trabuc's face as softened by his intelligence and kindliness, I suggest that Trabuc also represents the well-functioning mother's face, an image of Trabuc's capacity to detoxify van Gogh's projections into him as a predatory object. Whether Trabuc was actually induced to identify with the original projection or the revised projective identification in the course of the sitting is another matter for conjecture.

How do I justify using these images to illustrate the occurrence of projective identification? Perhaps to some extent every portrait is both about self and other. But in van Gogh's case, since he was painting while under treatment, I speculate that there was an additional factor driving the emergence of projective identificatory processes in the image, namely transference. It is possible that Trabuc was a transference figure for van Gogh, both in his own right as chief attendant of the hospital and also as a substitute for M. Peyron, the hospital director, thus accounting for van Gogh's recognizing in him the dual qualities of being a man of the people yet reminiscent of the elite.

Even allowing for van Gogh's intention to get beyond photographic likeness, I see these three portraits as a progression, each one a permanent image of the artist's projection of his own self-concept and feeling state. They have an established temporal sequence that lends weight to my argument.

The next portrait I include (Figure 8–4), the portrait of Dr. Gachet, was painted the next year. Van Gogh himself recognized in it "the same sentiment as the self-portrait I did when I left for this place" (van Gogh 1978, p. 276). There is a similarity to the other portraits in terms of facial contour. The expression, however, is less tense and more deeply melancholic, although the eyes are similar to those of the artist in Figure 8–2. Like the artist, the doctor has red hair. The color of his coat is deep blue, a color midway between those of the background and the artist's cloak worn by van Gogh in the first self-portrait Figure 8–1. The outline of the back of his chair creates the effect of a cloak for the doctor. From the flat surface of the table and textbooks, foxgloves that symbolize homeopathic medicine point up like the artist's brushes

Figure 8–4. Vincent van Gogh. Portrait of Dr. Gachet. Unsigned. Private collection.

from his palette in the first self-portrait (Figure 8–1). Dr. Gachet must also have been a transference figure for van Gogh. I suggest that as a troubled person, the doctor had a valency for being viewed as a troubled part of the artist. As a physician, he may have been projecting the mad part of himself into the patient. As a painter and etcher himself, Dr. Gachet may have been identifying cherished but frustrated parts of himself, projected into and enjoyed in the outstandingly talented artist. As an inspired portrait painter, van Gogh may even have unconsciously resonated with Dr. Gachet's projective and introjective identificatory processes and sought to establish the connection that I now discover!

What I have tried to show in this discussion is the evidence of projective identification in spectacularly vivid images of faces of self and other. The artist projects parts of his self or objects into the external object before him (including his own face in the case of self-portraits). And he misidentifies the object as if it were a part of himself. In the case of the Trabuc portrait, the projective identifications are returned to the artist in a modified form. I also suggest that a portrait artist who is not in need of treatment also produces images that derive from projective and introjective identificatory processes, but in the case of the healthy artist these will be based more securely on countertransference responses to the other, rather than on transferences to object and self as I see in van Gogh's paintings during the period of his illness.

In the popular culture of the late twentieth century, I find projective identification inferred in the lyrics of a hit song by Oliver Lieber performed by Paula Abdul. In the song "Opposites Attract," two lovers are discussing their relationship:

Baby seems we never ever agree
You like the movies
And I like TV
I take things serious
And you take 'em light

I go to bed early
And I party all night
Our friends are sayin'
We ain't gonna last
Cuz I move slowly
And baby I'm fast
I like it quiet
And I love to shout
But when we get together
It just all works out
I take—two steps forward
I take—two steps back
We come together
Cuz opposites attract
And you know—it ain't fiction
Just a natural fact
We come together
Cuz opposites attract
Who'd a thought we could be lovers
She makes the bed
And he steals the covers
She likes it neat
And he makes a mess
I take it easy
Baby I get obsessed
She's got the money
And he's always broke
I don't like cigarettes
And I like to smoke
Things in common
Just ain't one
But when we get together
We have nothin' but fun—
Baby ain't it somethin'
How we lasted this long

> You and me
> Provin' everyone wrong
> Don't think we'll ever
> Get our differences patched
> Don't really matter
> Cuz we're perfectly matched
> *(Courtesy of Virgin Records)*

The voice of the song speaks for a number of characters, the girl, the guy she loves (and vice versa), the two of them as a couple. Now, when we read "I party all night" we think it should be "you," not "I." The point is that even sung as a duet, the libretto indicates confusion about who is who. The voice of the song even changes from "I" to "She" and "He" when it represents the people who observe the relationship. The blurring of boundaries between self and other, characteristic of projective identification, is well illustrated. We also see the loving couple as an object of fascination for the group. In the music video of the song, one of the lovers is represented by a light-brown-and-cream-colored furry cat that walks upright and sings the contrary refrain. To me, this cat is the transitional object that carries hope for love to exist between the different personalities of the lovers. I also think of the cat as an embodiment of the repressed internal object that is seen to exist outside the self and inhabits the beloved. Its cream and brown color reminds me that totally opposite unconscious elements coexist in the object that is split off and projected into the beloved and there find their corresponding matches in the beloved's unconscious.

I find more images of projective identification, this time on greeting cards made in the 1980s by Sandy Gullikson. The concept is even closer to penetrating the art form. In the first card, the artist portrays two coyotes in a state of immediate intimacy (Figure 8–5). The communication lines between them suggest that what seems to be the background is really the layering of conscious and unconscious levels in their shared internal space.

Figure 8–5. Sandy Gullikson 1985. Two coyotes experiencing non-verbal communication. Drawing and words copyright © Sandy Gullikson.

Figure 8-6. Sandy Gullikson 1988. Love at first sight. Drawings and words copyright © Sandy Gullikson.

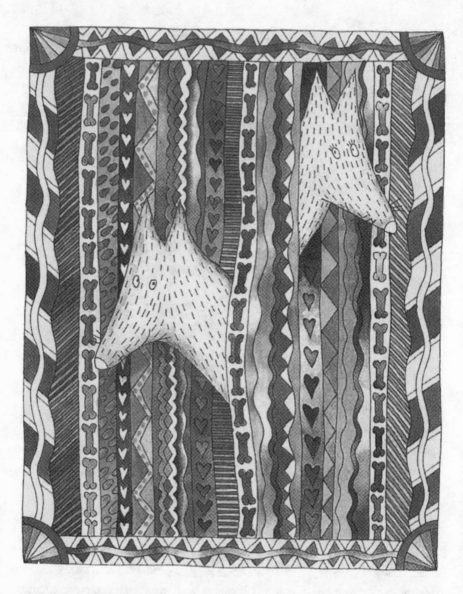

Figure 8-7. Sandy Gullikson 1989. Two coyotes surrounded by and lost in mutually overlapping thoughts and feelings. Drawings and words copyright © Sandy Gullikson.

The second card (Gullikson 1988) depicts love at first sight (Figure 8–6). In this visual version of the attraction of opposites, the unlikely lovers are a small fluffy rabbit and a monstrous cactus. Yet they do seem to be a pair, because the artist gives us clues about the underlying mutual projective identification. Round spots on the rabbit correlate with the cactus segments while the cactus spines echo the stray hairs on the rabbit's ears. Maybe her ears remind him of his mother's finest segments. We can imagine how she values his strength, self-sufficiency, and longevity, how he adores her warmth, gregariousness, and accessibility. We can see her long for his protection; we can feel his love of her boundless energy. Nevertheless, I do not think that the unconscious fit is sufficient to overcome the problems. To quote from an earlier book, "The short-term intimacy of early courtship consists of a rapid interpenetration, a sudden recognition of similarities and complementarities, often emphasizing one shared aspect of internal objects which does not, and cannot, take into account the total balance of internal economies" (Scharff and Scharff 1991). That fluffy, white bobtail just does not match up: it seems to me to pull the rabbit ultimately away from the cactus.

The third card (Figure 8–7) provides a summary image of projective identification. It is a colorful picture of two coyotes peeping out of an enfolding patchwork quilt that is decorated with hearts for love, bones to chew on, and dog biscuits for food. The caption speaks poetically of projective identification.

Returning to literature we find further evidence. Many examples from Shakespeare suggest themselves. In The Merchant of Venice we learn that Portia, a beautiful young woman, has inherited a fortune and a grand estate. She is independently wealthy, yet she is still controlled by her father, even from the grave. He has decreed that she may marry only the man who solves the riddle he has devised. The puzzle facing the suitor is to choose among three caskets of gold, silver, and lead. Only in the correctly chosen casket will he find Portia's picture and thus earn her hand in marriage. Portia is annoyed about this and says:

I may neither choose whom I would nor refuse whom I dislike. So is the will of a living daughter curbed by the will of a dead father.

[1.2. 24–27]

We do not yet know her father's motives, although we might guess he is trying to protect her assets. Our projective identification is with the young woman. Through her eyes we see the father as a man who has to control his loved object. We might speculate that he has projected his own sexual and aggressive feelings for his daughter and identified them in her potential suitors from whom he then needs to protect her. But her companion, Nerissa, who is not in the grip of Portia's dead father, reassures her:

Your father was ever virtuous, and holy men at their death have good inspirations; therefore, the lottery that he hath devised in these three chests of gold, silver, and lead, whereof who chooses his meaning chooses you, will, no doubt, never be chosen by any rightly than one whom you shall rightly love.

[1.2. 30–36]

Even if his intentions were good, he is confident that the best choice for his child is a love object that is identified with him. And perhaps he is right. Portia's opening line, which appears to be about her discontent with her lack of choice, may also refer to her longing to join her father in the next world.

By my troth, Nerissa, my little body is aweary of this great world.

[1.2. 1–2]

Unlike Shylock's daughter Jessica who has to trick her father in order to marry the man she wants, Portia respects her father's will and finds that Bassanio, the man she wants to marry, is the one her father would have chosen. Bassanio's values propel him to choose the lead casket that her father believed a suitable husband would prefer. Before this happy resolution is reached, Portia dresses in male attire as Bassanio's attorney to plead his case so that his debt of a pound of flesh owed to Shylock cannot be collected. As a man, Portia has as much power over another's destiny as her father had over hers. She rescues her loved one from certain death. Metaphorically, as a man, introjectively identified with her father, she gives herself a live husband from the dead, one who is a suitable object for receiving her father's projective identifications.

Dressing in male attire was a theatrical convention of English theater in Shakespeare's time, not simply to capitalize on or disguise the fact that all the actors were male, since educated women did not work. Instead, Shakespeare used the convention to challenge assumptions about the matchmaking authority of the older generation and gender constraints upon the individual, and especially to explore the possibility of wider choice for women. By dressing as a boy the heroine could project herself into the male element in her own personality; an element whose expression was not encouraged by society at that time. Lowenstein (1982) says that Shakespeare gave the woman the chance to be like a man, which meant that she could move around in society and get to know men in the intimacy of single sex partnership without the pressures of romantic attraction, requited love, and matrimonial property pursuits. She could exercise her own will, and therefore, upon return to female form, choose her own husband. Most important to me, she could find a form of self-discovery through projective identification into the male and then by introjective identification with the male element, become a fulfilled, self-actualizing woman. Lowenstein points to a prime example of this in *Twelfth Night*. The heroine, Viola, an orphan is shipwrecked on an island governed by Duke Orsino, an eligible bachelor she had heard of from her late father. Now, however, Orsino is in love with a rejecting woman. Because her twin brother was not rescued from the storm with her, Viola has no family to turn to. She disguises herself as a boy called Cesario in order to gain access as a page to the unavailable Duke Orsino, whom she secretly loves. As Cesario, Viola becomes Orsino's loved confidant and messenger. One day, she hints about her secret love:

> My father had a daughter lov'd a man
> As it might be perhaps, were I a woman,
> I should your lordship.
>
> [2.4. 107–109]
>
> She pin'd in thought
> And with a green and yellow melancholy,
> She sat like Patience on a monument
> Smiling at grief.
>
> [2.4. 113–115]

We can read this as an oblique description of herself as Viola might have become had she been locked in feminine passivity and silence, had she accepted by introjective identification the culture's projective identification of her as a woman of her time. Lowenstein (1982) writes: "There is much melancholy here, but there is also the breathless curiosity of seeing yourself in the third person, as someone with an open future, seeing yourself at a distance, as if your life were on stage" (p. 4). Projecting herself into the male element of her own personality allows the woman distance from her feminine self. She can then invoke the observing capacities of the central self to appraise her feminine self. Ultimately, the central self can integrate both male and female elements within the personality, which is enriched by the recovery of parts of the self that had only been experienced through projective identification into an external object of the opposite sex. When marriage takes place, the woman of Shakespeare's plays then fully inhabits her traditional feminine role, and leaves the masculine role to her husband. She does this with a confidence that stems from the successful introjective identification by her feminine self of her central self and the male element now contained within it.

In Viola's history there is an intriguing complicating factor. She is a twin. She has not seen her brother Sebastian since they were separated by the storm from which she was rescued by the captain who told her that Sebastian was last seen clinging to a mast. She maintains a shred of hope that he may have reached the shore, but we tend to assume that he perished. So when the Duke asks her as Cesario:

> But died thy sister of her love, my boy?
> [2.4. 120]

Viola replies:

> I am all the daughters of my father's house
> And all the brothers too; and yet I know not.
> [2.4. 121–122]

Eventually the twins are reunited, but because Viola is still dressed as Cesario, Sebastian does not recognize her. He is merely astonished by coming face to face with his double. Of course as fraternal twins, they would not have been identical really, which as the father of opposite-sex twins, Shakespeare certainly knew. The theatrical license taken is, nevertheless, true to the sense of shared identity commonly felt by fraternal twins, regardless of any dissimilarity of appearance or sex, since even fraternal "twins raised close to each other have difficulty separating self representation from object representation" (Glenn 1966, p. 737). The onlookers are confused by the sight of two identical young men and the Duke says:

> One face, one voice, one habit, and two persons,
> A natural perspective, that is and is not.
> [5.2. 215–216]

> Sebastian: Do I stand there? I never had a brother;
> [5.2. 225]

Viola, of course, recognizes her brother and persuades him of her identity by sharing facts about their family history. The point of conviction is reached when each remembers their father.

> Viola: My father had a mole upon his brow.
> Sebastian: And so did mine.
> Viola: And died that day when Viola from her birth
>   Had numb'red thirteen years.
> Sebastian: O, that record is lively in my soul!
>
> [5.2. 241–244]

Lowenstein emphasizes that they find themselves in the physiognomy of the father, male authority being most important in Shakespeare's time. An apparently surface characteristic, what one might term a birthmark, is linked with the dating of the father's death, remembered in terms of their own lives. The twins shared the loss of a father at the pubertal age of 13. They recognize each other, ultimately, through their shared introjective identification with their lost male object, possibly a shared defense against the pain of the loss of their mother, rather than a culture-bound elevation of the male to a position of greater importance.

I want to address another aspect of Viola's dressing like her twin. Apart from the already-mentioned motives for dressing like a man, Viola had the additional reason of achieving in fantasy a reunion with her lost male twin. Freud (1917a) showed that identification with the deceased is a defense mechanism for dealing with mourning and that it is the basis for the state of melancholy. Viola is aware of her melancholy, but she attributes it to her pining for Duke Orsino. I suggest that she was in a state of grief about losing her brother and that it recalled the trauma of losing her father at 13 years of age. (A similar correlation between loss of twin and parent has been described by Engel 1975). Viola consciously dealt with her situation by trying to find a husband, one that her father had thought well of. To reach him, she had to dress as a page. Unconsciously, she was reaching her lost brother by projective identification into his attire and then by introjective identification with him.

Twinning is used as a metaphor in a Turkish novel by O. Pamuk. In *The White Castle*, Pamuk describes the relational processes between two scholars who look amazingly like twins. Pamuk makes a fiction of identity and personal boundaries when he explores the master–slave partnership between the two scholars. When Hoja, the master, learns all that his slave knows, he will free him. For his part, the slave, in the course of their personal exploration of truth and reality, will absorb his master's manner and his life story as if it were his own. Anxious to gain favor with their sovereign, both men compete and yet cooperate to impress him. The slave, who is the narrator, reports:

> I began to believe that my personality had split itself off from me and united with Hoja's, and vice versa, without our perceiving it, and that the sultan, by evaluating this imaginary creature, had come to know us better than we knew ourselves. . . . The sovereign would stop suddenly and turning to one of us, say, "No, this is his thought, not yours. . . . Now you are glancing around just as he does. Be yourself!" When I laughed in surprise, he'd continue, "That's better, bravo. Have you two never looked at yourselves in the mirror together?" He'd ask which of us could stand to be himself when he did look in the mirror. [p. 115]

Like a marital therapist making observations, their sultan drew to the scholars' awareness the state of flux between their two personalities. A laugh of surprise indicates a moment of insight on the part of the narrator. No interpretation here. Just observation and brutal confrontation enabling a degree of separation, which, however, may have been illusory. Parini quotes the above extract in his review (1991) and asks: "Hoja—or his slave? Were they, perhaps, always one person — the bicameral mind reified as two separate people for the sake of the story? The more one tries to figure this out, the less certain one becomes."

This is precisely the feeling I have when I struggle with projective identification. This novel seems at first glance to be about projective identification processes, but equally it is an exploration of introjective identification and extractive introjection.

The processes of projective and introjective identification in the special situation of twinning are further illustrated in the life and work of Thornton Wilder, the quintessential American playwright and novelist. Glenn (1986) noted a preoccupation with twinning in Wilder's work and described how the author's twinship affected his choice of material. As evidence, Glenn mentions many plays and novels, but focuses especially on the novel *The Bridge of San Luis Rey* (1986). There Wilder explores the lives of the victims of the collapse of a bridge. Among them is Esteban who, grieving for his dead twin Manuel, had undertaken a long journey in the course of which he crossed the bridge on the fateful day. The date originally assigned to the collapse of the bridge was the birth date of Wilder and his twin before Wilder changed it prior to publication (Glenn 1986). So, in the story, the twins are reunited in death on a date associated with the birth of the author and his twin. In this story, as in much of his writing, Wilder uses death to examine the meaning of life. Glenn (1986) also refers to the semi-autobiographical novel *Theophilus North* (1973), a study of love and virtue set in the Newport of the twenties (A. Wilder 1980). The protagonist, Theophilus North, a bustling, do-gooding, adventurous, quixotic character, rescues people from a series of nine settings. Glenn suggests that this theme reflects Thornton's wish to rescue himself and his twin from the unhappy result of the nine months of pregnancy. And Glenn reminds us that *Our Town* (1960), a play about family and community relationships that celebrates the marvelousness of the commonplace, begins with the joyful announcement of the birth of twins.

Amos Wilder (Thornton Wilder's older brother) translates and paraphrases Oppel's (1977) emphasis on the death theme in Thornton Wilder's work, "a recurrent *topos* in the writings, that of descent into the underworld or converse with the dead" (A.

Wilder 1980, p. 18). Taking the two themes of death and twinning, we can see that they derive from the impact on Thornton Wilder of the loss of his twin at birth. Amos Wilder writes of Thornton, who survived his twin Theophilus, as follows:

> As himself a twin who lost a brother at birth, he was predisposed to fascination with this relationship. Indeed one could hazard that he was haunted all his life by this missing alter ego. Thus he plays with the after life of this twin in the dual *persona* suggested by the title of his last novel, *Theophilus North*, "North," of course, representing an anagram for Thornton. In this way he was able to tease both himself and the reader as to the borderlands between autobiography and fable. [p. 10]

In other words, Thornton Wilder was creating an examinable projective identificatory system between his life and his art. In *Theophilus North*, Theophilus is everything that Thornton was—and was not. Glenn (1986) develops a hypothesis that Thornton's survivor guilt and longing for reunion with his twin, motivated him to bring Theophilus to life in the form of a character with which he could then identify. This identification yielded both togetherness and the pain of suffering the character's tribulations. I suggest that another motivation was simply to create the missing living opportunity for projective identification into the twin.

Thornton was the unlikely survivor of the twinship, being a sickly, underweight baby who had to be coddled. His brother was a well-formed infant who was, however, stillborn. It must have seemed as though the wrong twin died. Apparently, the family story was that the delicate Thornton was carried around on a pillow for the first year of his life (Harrison 1983). This story brings to my mind the image of Cinderella's discarded glass slipper being borne on a display pillow by a footman, until the appropriate foot could be found to fit into it. After a delicate childhood, Thornton eventually did become robust enough to fill his twin's shoes. As an adult he was a successful long-distance runner. He was able to withstand the effects of heavy smoking and social drinking, but he remained psychologically preoccupied with death and survivorship. Although firmly in favor of marriage and the family, he did not take the step of marrying himself; his most significant relationships in adulthood were those with his siblings, particularly his business-manager sister Isabel.

The brother–sister relationship is shown in *Our Town*, featuring the everyday lives of the families of Mr. Webb and Dr. Gibb, which run in parallel, as if the families were twins. Each family has a boy and a girl. George Webb grows up to marry Emily Gibb. Emily bears one child successfully but dies in unsuccessful labor with the second. Again there is the theme of death and survival in a sibship. Emily, the dead sibling, returns to her family of origin as it had been on her 12th birthday. She discovers how much she had missed by being unreceptive to the pleasures of ordinary human existence. Finding the noncommunication too painful to bear, especially because it reminds her of her living experience in her family with her busy parents, Emily returns to her grave. The conscious message is one of regret at failing to appreciate the marvelousness of the ordinary. The underlying message here is that family life is unbearable and that the attempt to recreate a family will send one to one's grave or kill an unborn child.

Thornton chose the family bond rather than the marital relationship for himself. I suggest that this represents an identification with his parents' marital adjustment. His parents, each a person of character, remained committed to their marriage, yet chose to live apart on different continents for much of Thornton's life. Each was devoted to the children. I think that Thornton introjectively identified with each of his parents separately. We can see in him the qualities of his mother—her literary and artistic interests, her gregariousness and musical sensibility—and his father's austerity, morality and intellectual drive, his writing ability, ebullience, and wit. According to Thornton's mother, his father was dictatorial, not tender with her. He was unable to recover from the loss of an earlier love and thought of himself as a widower at heart. She thought that she and he could have "rubbed along comfortably enough" but there was not enough understanding between them to contain the strain of their long separations (Harrison 1983, p. 14).

My hypothesis is that Wilder was unable to take in his parents as a loving couple, except perhaps when he was a very young child and his father was at home. From experiencing a father who thought of himself as the survivor of a dead couple, the actual death of his twin, and the psychic death of his parents' marital union as a daily reality for the growing child, Thornton's inheritance was that of a dead internal couple (see Chapter 6). Despite his immense creativity, which allowed him to explore and illuminate this issue for all of us, Thornton Wilder was personally unable or uninterested in bringing the couple to life for himself in the married state that is celebrated in his plays.

As I write I am exercising my own capacity for projective identification in order to speculate as I do about the life of the author. I do not base my speculation only on the factual texts about his life (Gallup 1985, Harrison 1983)—especially the one written by his own brother (A. Wilder 1980)—because Wilder's own creative works are just as illuminating. The plays and novels are themselves the sublimated products of the author's capacity for projective identification into his characters, breathing life into them, and his ability for introjective identification with them so that he can be guided by the drama that they compel him to create for them. The whole projective and introjective identificatory process is then repeated, as the actor studies for his role.

So much for indirect expression of projective identification in the arts and the artist. Leaving inference behind, I began to look for direct references to projective identification and introjective identification in trade publications. I found none in therapist Harville Hendrix's (1991) best-selling text on the couple relationship, *Getting the Love You Want*, even though he describes the effects and interaction of unconscious object relations in marriage. He does not use projective and introjective identification as the technical terms of his explanatory principles, although he refers to their action. To my surprise, I found Zinner's (1976) application of Dicks's (1967) concept of mutual projective identification methodically explained, translated into everyday language, and illustrated with full deference to its complexity in another best-seller, *Intimate Partners* by well-known author Maggie Scarf (1987). She writes:

> In order, however, to fully understand the ways in which partners come together to construct their intimate relationships, the reader will have to become familiar with the manner in which a certain mental process (its technical name is projective identification) operates. Some familiarity with this process is, in my view, essential. The term itself, which derives from a certain form of psychoanalytic thinking, cannot be explained in a moment. Once it *is* understood, however, something vitally important about the nature of intimate attachments will have been learned. . . .
>
> But here let me just say, by way of a very preliminary explanation, that projective identification has to do with one person—say, me—seeing my own denied and suppressed wishes, needs, emotions, etc., in my intimate partner and not experiencing those wishes and feelings as anything coming from my own self. If, for instance, I were a "never angry" person, I might see anger as coming *only* from my husband and actually get him to collude in this by forcing him to lose his temper and *express my anger for me.*
>
> Or if, to take another instance, my mate could not accept his vulnerabilities and distresses, I could do the work of getting upset and distressed *for him* every time he began giving me the cues that this was necessary. But because the process occurs at an unconscious level, he might become extremely critical of my constant complaining—might see in me, and dislike and *fight* in me, the feelings that he cannot perceive within himself.
>
> Intimate partners often perform this function for one another: experience and express what are actually the spouse's unacknowledged and repudiated emotions. When one person is always angry and the other is never angry, it can be presumed that the always

angry spouse is carrying anger for the pair of them. And similarly, when one partner is very competent and the other is nonfunctional (depressed, for example), there is usually an unconscious deal in effect, a collusion about who will take ownership of which particular feelings. [pp. 22–23]

Projective identification is mentioned again many times throughout the book and earns forty entries in the index. When Scarf's book was excerpted in the *Atlantic Monthly* (November and December 1986) with a guaranteed circulation of 450,000, and a pass-around readership besides, the concept of mutual projective identification reached a lay audience of at least 450,000 people. Her book sold 530,000 copies in the United States edition. It has also appeared in British and Canadian editions and has been translated into Hebrew, German, Dutch, Swedish, Italian, and Portuguese. By my conservative estimate, at least a million members of the lay-reading public have heard of projective identification. Introjective identification still awaits its audience.

PART IV

The Use of the Therapist's Self through Projective and Introjective Identification

9

Theory and Technique of Countertransference in Individual Psychoanalysis and Psychotherapy

COUNTERTRANSFERENCE BEFORE
OBJECT RELATIONS THEORY

Freud (1910) described countertransference as a reaction to the patient's influence on the analyst's unconscious feelings. He thought that it arose from the analyst's avoidance of the emergence of unconscious infantile complexes stirred in him by the patient's transference. Thus he saw it as a threat, a regressive temptation, evidence of the need for analysis. He did not go further to give examples of problems and their working through, perhaps because, as Strachey (1958) suggested, he did not want to reveal his technique. Too much reporting of subjective responses would have undermined his attempts to present psychoanalysis as an objective science and could also have wrecked the ideal of the analyst as a blank screen. Tower (1956) and Greenson (1967) also viewed countertransference as the analyst's difficulty in managing his own unanalyzed conflicts evoked by the patient. They saw a constructive purpose to countertransference, nevertheless, provided it was subject to self-analysis. In Gitelson's (1952) opinion, countertransference is transference to the patient.

These views of countertransference correspond to Freud's (1895) concept of transference as a resistance to therapeutic action, in terms of his topographic theory. Transference is, then, a repetition of unremembered feelings separated from the thought that went with them—feelings so painful or difficult that they had to be repressed. Similarly, in classical views of countertransference, the analyst is seen as repeating instead of remembering. Classical views of countertransference also fit with Freud's growing appreciation for transference (1905) as a revised edition of the original forbidden impulses, wishes, and fears directed to a new object. In classical countertransference, the analyst, because of repression of his own insufficiently analyzed infantile complexes, cannot analyze those of his patient. If he does analyze his own complexes, then therapeutic action can proceed.

Tracing the development of Freud's concept of transference, we can see that he moved from awareness of transference as manifestations of resistance that must be undone to a view of transference as the re-creation of the infantile situation in relation to the analyst as a replacement object to gratify or forbid the expression of the drives. No longer a series of fleeting manifestations, transference became an intense crystallization of the conflict underlying the neurotic symptom or character, now focused in relation to the analyst. So the transference neurosis was born and has remained a central concept in psychoanalysis.

Although Freud (1905) moved on to think of transference as

"the most powerful ally" of psychoanalysis (pp. 116–117), he certainly did not progress toward seeing countertransference in such a constructive light. Instead, he stayed with his definition of countertransference as interference with the analyst's responses and understanding.

I propose applying this conceptual trajectory of the development of Freud's thinking on transference (from resistance to manifestation to crystallized neurosis) to the development of the concept of countertransference. Countertransference appears early in the development of psychoanalytic theory, as it does in the early phase of the treatment process. At that time in the 1900s, it was viewed as an occasional problematic interference that could be removed by de-repression of the infantile complexes stirred in the analyst. Later in the twentieth century, as in the mid-phase of analysis, countertransference is seen as a response specific to the patient and indicative of the patient's unique transference. I suggest that the next stage in the development of the concept, reflecting what I have experienced by the late mid-phase of an analysis, is to gather the countertransference and view it as a deepening coalescence of feelings on the part of the analyst—a countertransference neurosis in response to the transference neurosis. I think that we are now in a position to use countertransference as the most powerful ally of analysis.

Others have noted a shift in the prevailing attitudes about countertransference in the literature. Tansey and Burke (1989) report that the classical view has given way to first a totalist and then a specialist perspective. In the 1970s and 1980s, they note, in the totalist view, countertransference had become an all-inclusive term applied to the continuum of therapist responses from the neurotically based to the unique objective response induced by that patient, all of them regarded as helpful in understanding the patient. They also detect a "specifist" trend in which writers try to distinguish between types of countertransference responses and to locate them specifically along the continuum.

PROJECTIVE IDENTIFICATION
IN COUNTERTRANSFERENCE

Many theorists in the Freudian tradition have emphasized the constructive aspects of using countertransference defined as the analyst's subjective responses and reactions to the patient for the benefit of the analysand (Jacobs 1991, Sandler 1976). Before countertransference could be found as helpful in analysis as Freud had found transference to be, I suggest, we needed the concept of projective identification, contributed by Klein (1946), elaborated by the British School of Object Relations, and applied from the mother–infant relationship to the treatment situation.

Object relations theory was fully discussed in Chapter 2, where I tried to do justice to the distinctions between Kleinian and Fairbairnian object relations theories in relation to projective identification. Here I offer a potted version of a composite British object relations theory of personality development and projective identification as follows: The patient's personality is built of a complicated structure, determined by the early experience with the caretaker and by the infant's unique style of perceiving it. The structure is added to and refined as the infant moves from primitive mental sorting of experience into good and bad, to more discriminating cognitive categorizations. Mental structure becomes more complex as the child becomes capable of relating in a three-person system. Those experiences that were satisfying can be held in consciousness where they color expectations of future relationships as potentially enjoyable. Those that were too frightening, painful, or exciting have to be repressed. In dynamic equilibrium as the unconscious object relationships that comprise psychic structure, they affect perception of the other and operate to seek repetition in the here-and-now of present relationships. This happens through the mechanism of projective identification.

The mental structure at the conscious and unconscious levels contains not just the infant's perception of experience and feelings about it, but also a representation of the "object"—namely the caretaker—and of the part of the self in relation to the object. Self and object representations are in active relation to each other in object relationships where they are integrated as composite structures. In Fairbairn's view of endopsychic structure, these object relationships are of two main types, the exciting and the rejecting as described in Chapter 3, while in Klein's view the basic division is into good and bad, colored by oral, anal, phallic, and oedipal fantasies that are relevant to the different developmental stages. Integration of the good and bad aspects of the object improves as maturation proceeds. Each object relationship is in dynamic relation to the other split-off and repressed object relationship system (Fairbairn) or systems (Klein) in unconsciousness and also to the unrepressed conscious central ego and ideal object system.

A part of the self or of the object may be projected out toward a new external object, seeking to find a similar self or a familiar object in the other. This new object can be a lover, a baby, a boss, or a therapist—anyone of importance. Obviously, the other party has a mental structure too, and is subject to the same conscious and unconscious strivings in relationships. This is true of the patient-analyst relationship too. But it is as yet not widely accepted that the therapist's reciprocal set of projective identifications is anything other than a pathological interference. Klein herself, who contributed the concept of projective identification that is so useful in understanding countertransference, did not approve of its being taken as evidence of the patient's transference. She saw countertransference in the classical way Freud did—as evidence of the analyst's difficulty (Spillius 1991).

In my view, all the therapist's responses are evidence about the interaction with that patient. All of them must be subject to the therapist's process and review. The neurotic ones will require further work for reasons independent of the therapy at issue, but they warrant study in the light of the patient's issues, too. The therapist is likely to learn as much or more from the patient's resonance with her own vulnerability than from the so-called "objective," that is, "patient-induced," responses alone. I hope to make the case for such use of countertransference as the most powerful ally of psychoanalysis, the major tool of therapy, fully reflective of and reciprocal to the transference and to the transference neurosis.

Heimann (1950), in an influential paper, objected to the prevailing view of countertransference as "nothing but a source of trouble." Instead, she saw "the analyst's emotional response" as "one of the most important tools—an instrument of research into the patient's unconscious" (p. 81). She hoped that the analyst's analysis could be viewed as something that did not sanitize his intellect from emotional interference, but rather that left him able to have and bear feelings aroused by the analysis of a patient. She wanted the analyst to be free to operate with a "freely roused emotional sensitivity" that was "extensive, differentiating and mobile" and therefore in the most open condition to receive unconscious communication from the patient in the form of personal impact out of which understanding in the shape of interpretation would emerge (p. 82). Countertransference, though part and parcel of the analyst–patient relationship, was always "the patient's creation, . . . part of the patient's personality" (p. 83). Heimann valued countertransference highly, and recognized that it often brought the analyst "nearer to the heart of the matter than his reasoning" (p. 83). Yet, she advocated that it remain the analyst's private affair. He should not communicate his feelings to his patient. He should merely use countertransference as one more source of insight into his patient's unconscious conflicts and defenses.

Little (1951) challenged Heimann's insistence that countertransference never be communicated to the patient. Despite her enormous contribution in raising the value of countertransference, Heimann was nevertheless to some degree maintaining the prevalent attitude about countertransference as something for the privacy of one's own analysis. Little's contribution was to blow the whistle on this "paranoid or phobic attitude towards the analyst's own feelings which constitutes the greatest danger and difficulty in counter-transference" (p. 38). She agreed with Heimann's view that confessions were inappropriate, but she thought that there were times when it was appropriate to acknowledge her counter-transference—her subjective experience, her thoughts, feelings, and impulses to action—as on something she was working to explore with the patient. In reaching this position she was guided by a respect for the patient's capacity to respond to and recognize the analyst's countertransference. At a certain point in the analysis, she said, the time would come when "it is essential for the patient to recognize the existence not only of the analyst's objective or justi-fied feelings, but also of the analyst's subjective feelings; that is, that the analyst must and does develop an unconscious counter-transference, which he is nevertheless able to deal with in such a way that it does not interfere to any serious extent with the pa-tient's interests, specially the progress of cure" (p. 37). In this I find a challenge to the idea of the objective scientist. Little's femi-nine, humanizing attitude is consistent with a deeply ingrained commitment to the therapeutic relationship as the primary re-source of the analysis, and with her belief that "growth depends on an alternating rhythm of identification and separation brought about in this way by having experiences and knowing them for one's own, in a suitable setting" (p. 35).

According to Money-Kyrle (1956), the expanded view of countertransference as having its causes and effects in the patient when used in the way described by Heimann (1950) offered an important technical advance. He saw countertransference as a "nor-mal" (by which he meant ideal) phenomenon in which the analyst in a state of benign neutrality and concern stays in tune with the patient through a series of oscillations between introjective and projective processes that operate between the unconscious child in the patient and in the analyst. This normal empathic state is charac-terized by continuous understanding that generates effective inter-pretations followed by further understandable associations. But this happy state is frequently interfered with and the analyst feels the material is obscure, loses the thread, and becomes anxious. This compounds the process. Of course, this can happen because the analyst is disturbed by the material for reasons of personal pathology that requires further analysis, but even so, the patient has unconsciously contributed to this state of affairs, according to Money-Kyrle. The analyst may react to the strain of not having an interpretation through which to re-project the patient's experience by offering reassurance or love instead, or by becoming depressed about or angry with the patient. The careful discrimination of the patient's contribution from one's own is essential before an effective countertransference interpretation can be made to restore the flow of the analysis.

Countertransference as a function of the patient's personality is not a universally accepted view, according to Segal (1981). Personally committed to it, Segal describes countertransference as an unconscious "nonverbal constant interaction in which the patient acts on the analyst's mind. This nonverbal activity takes many forms. It may be underlying and integrated with other forms of communication and give them depth and emotional resonance. It may be the predominant form of communication, coming from preverbal experiences which can only be communicated in that way. Or it may be meant as an attack on communication; though when understood, even this can be converted into communication" (p. 82). Countertransference represents an interference in the analyst's capacity to open his mind freely to his impressions while at the same time maintaining distance from his own feelings and reactions to the patient. These interferences may disrupt the analytic containing function by "invasion of the analyst's mind in a seductive or aggressive way, creating confusion and anxiety, and attacking links in the analyst's mind" (p. 83).

Racker (1968), whose work was referred to in Chapter 2, described countertransference as a fundamental condition of receiving the patient's projections and tolerating them inside him as projective identifications. His reception of the projections was unconscious, out of his awareness until he subjected his experience to process and review. Only in this way could the patient be truly understood. In Racker's view, countertransference is a fundamental means of understanding the patient's internal world. Racker went further to point out that the therapist might identify with parts either of the patient's self or objects. Identification with the patient's self he called concordant identification. Identification with the object was called complementary identification.

Writing in the United States, Stone (1961), referring to Racker's work, recorded "the growing appreciation of the countertransference as an affirmative instrument facilitating perception, whereby a sensitive awareness of one's incipient reactions to the patient, fully controlled, and appropriately analyzed in an immediate sense, leads to a richer and more subtle understanding of the patient's transference striving." Schafer (1990) has noted that analysts nowadays are moving away from the conventional view of the structural concept and its energic underpinnings to one in which structure is the relatively stable repetition of themes. Interested in object relationships and self experience, analysts are now better equipped to explore transference and countertransference, and thus to extend and deepen Freud's clinical wisdom. In the clinical situation, psychoanalytic deconstruction of the history of the patient's conditions for loving, hating, or feeling dead and empty leads to the patient's construction of a more fully comprehended, more fulfilling narrative, as the analyst retells the story empathically. For Schafer, analysis is a dialogic process—never, however, limited to two people. Instead, it contains a multitude of inner world voices located in others through projection. According to Schafer, the task of analysis is to relocate these voices so that they are no longer misidentified.

The significance of the advances has been grasped but a suspicious attitude toward the countertransference persists among many analysts in the United States to date. Two recent, striking exceptions to this point of view come to mind. Jacobs (1991) takes the unusual step of revealing his self-analysis of his countertransference difficulties. He contends that the analyst must get access to his repressed countertransference before its extraordinary resonance with secrets of the patient's life can be turned to therapeutic advantage. Welles and Wrye (1991) describe and illustrate in detail the woman analyst's maternal erotic countertransference as a defense against loving and hateful, archaic, perverse, and magical erotic wishes toward her actual body parts, as well as to their symbolic counterparts. They call for awareness of these overlooked issues and self-analysis so that the woman therapist can become able to participate as an object to be used in these ways, but they refer only briefly to the processes of projection and introjection and do not yet address the working through of the maternal erotic transference and countertransference.

So far this literature helps us to view the therapeutic task as the reception and clarification of the patient's projections, followed by analysis of the interpersonal conditions under which these occur. How is this worked with in practice? There are times when the situation is simply thrust upon us by the evocative power of the patient's projective identification. At these times we feel taken over by a feeling state that does not seem to be our own. Then we get to work on figuring out what this represents of the patient's experience. Are we being given to feel like a part of the patient's self or one of his objects in relation to him as himself? At other times we have to monitor the transference by deliberately exploring the countertransference, even when it is not causing trouble. Casement (1991) describes his technique of using trial identifications (Fleiss 1942) in a number of ways. He says, "I may, for example, think or feel myself into whatever experience is being described by the patient. I may also put myself into the shoes of the other person being referred to. . . . I also try to put myself into the patient's shoes in his or her relationships to me. I try to listen (as the patient might) to what it crosses my mind to say. . . . With practice it becomes possible to use these two viewpoints simultaneously, the patient's and one's own, rather like following the different voices in polyphonic music" (p. 35). Casement refers to this technique as the synthesis of apparently paradoxical ego states. His technique calls for the analyst's evenly hovering attention to the figure and ground of the analytic narrative, on ego and object, and on internal object relations of patient and analyst, individually and together in the therapeutic relationship. Casement is describing a technique that is not new, but his contribution lies in his simple articulation of the fundamentals of empathy, intuition, and countertransference technique.

Bollas (1989) advocates including "the analyst's personality as an object of use" (p. 106) and relates analytic skill to the analyst's ability to present himself authentically as the various necessary objects. Concerned with the analytic task of converting the 'unthought known' into ideation, Bollas recognizes many ways in which this can be accomplished, for example, through the representation of dream, daydream, or phantasy. He says, "Most frequently, however, it is through the interlocking logics of the patient's transference and the psychoanalyst's countertransference, when both persons psychologically enact a process, that this knowledge is first thought about by the patient" (p. 14). Furthermore, he views each transference–countertransference exchange as a "paradigm which can become part of the unconscious ego structure of the analysand in his subsequent processing of self and other" (p. 106). So Bollas holds that the necessary transformation of the unthought known into mental representations owes much to the analysis of the living process of the transference–countertransference.

Bollas (1989) also values projective identification as the source of understanding the patient in the countertransference. He writes, "Psychoanalysts, receiving patient projective identifications, come to know something, and psychoanalysis of the countertransference becomes the effort to think this knowledge" (p. 214). Of great interest to me, he views each transference-countertransference exchange as a "paradigm which can become part of the unconscious ego structure of the analysand in his subsequent processing of self and other" (p. 106). Here he is describing the action of introjective processes on the part of the patient without actually calling it that.

However modern, these views fall short. They recognize the analyst's necessary involvement in projective identification, but they do not take into account her valency for introjective identification. They do not address the interplay between the two, except insofar as introjective identification is a subphase of projective identification. Bollas's concept of extractive introjection (1987) pushes us to credit introjective identification on the part of the analyst—even the well-analyzed one—with an active independent status. To omit the possibility of the introjective identification with the patient by the analyst is to ignore the creative potential for the analyst to be cured by the patient, an aspect of the psychoanalytic relationship that Searles (1979) regards as crucial. This topic is explored in Chapter 12.

COUNTERTRANSFERENCE IN INTENSIVE, INDIVIDUAL, ANALYTIC THERAPY AND ANALYSIS

The following example illustrates countertransference in the opening phase of analysis as a response to transference as resistance to therapeutic action. It illustrates countertransference as a defense against the undoing of repression during transference, and later countertransference coalescing as a response to the transference neurosis. I hope to show that countertransference has two functions. In the first place, it enables us to detect the problem. Secondly, it is the medium for its resolution.

Countertransference to Transference as Resistance in the Opening Phase of Analysis

Dr. R. was an adult male psychiatry resident, an intense, intellectually gifted, tall, dark, and handsome man. He complained of physical stress induced by a compulsively overactive life-style that left him little time to sleep, relax, play, or eat. He knew that his sexual and aggressive feelings were severely inhibited, that he could not experience the usual range of feelings, and that he tended to compartmentalize, temporally and spatially, his social, work, and sexual roles. He regretted that he felt too caught up in hostile and protective feelings about his parents. He also described maintaining a socially charming facade, using method acting to portray feelings that he lacked.

Despite his good looks, I did not feel any physical attraction to him because of his softness, his subservient manner, and his self-preoccupation. I was not surprised to learn that he felt unsure of his identity as a male. He may have had little physical appeal for me, but I had apparently no impact on him whatever. My vacations and absences meant nothing to him. I felt of as much importance as a speck on the wall. Dr. R. talked in such an intellectually convoluted way, I often felt quite shut out and unnecessary. As his analyst, I was always working extra hard, like he did, struggling to understand his mysterious construction of reality. Despite my efforts to comprehend, I felt that I had no idea what he was talking about. Yet he assumed that I always knew exactly what he meant.

I inferred that my countertransference experience of over-functioning was an introjective identification with his self. My feeling like a speck on the wall reflected my introjective identification with his projective identification of me as an object that did not matter a speck. Later I saw that this was a defense against recognizing how much I mattered. It served to disguise a hidden introjective identification with me in which he was taking me for granted and assuming that I was perfectly in tune with him.

I asked myself what it could mean that I found myself frowning and straining to catch every word and to comprehend his abstruse language. Why did I feel anxious and over-involved in trying to understand him? Why did I feel shut out by his obsessing over his physical exhaustion? My answer was that I thought he related to himself as if he were his own mother, very solicitous of his well-being. No wonder he did not need me.

Here was an example of inhibiting the projective identification of me with his caretaking object, so that I had no access to his internal object world. I could not be in relationship to him. But it was not quite so simple. How could I understand the over-concerned feeling when basically I felt so shut out? Perhaps I felt shut out as a father excluded from an intense mother–son romance. Perhaps, when I felt so invested in understanding him, I was being held on to as a child might have held onto his mother.

Dr. R. arranged his own vacation without reference to my schedule and with no regard for its impact on his analysis. Some months later, he dealt with my impending vacation in his usual cavalier style. I said that he was using method acting to create feelings in place of his own. Suddenly, he was surprised to find himself filled with melancholy triggered, he thought, by my impending departure. He related this to his lifelong awareness of his mother's sorrow by which he always felt both mystified and preoccupied. He had not wanted to burden me with his or her sad feelings in case they would upset me and overwhelm me. He said that he did not want me to expect him to have feelings, either.

> As he gave each meticulous detail of his mother's feeling states, I felt invoked in me her grief, her remoteness, and her dependency on him. He recreated his intense involvement with her in the transference. I felt as if I were his mother, about to expect too much of him, too liable to upset him, and too easily affected by him. At these times I felt that I must exert myself to remain in a neutral position or even to remain alive as myself.

From this countertransference I infer that I experienced alternately a complementary indentification with his smothering object (when I felt over-involved in trying to understand him) and a concordant identification with his self as a nonentity when not involved with the smothering object (when I felt shut out or fighting to stay alive as myself). This application of Racker's (1968) theory of countertransference gives a cybernetic view of the patient's internal object constellations repeated in the transference. To me, this is more interesting and helpful than simply observing his transference as a defense against the threat of dependency, for instance. In the opening phase of treatment, I viewed these simultaneous transferences, experienced in my alternating countertransference responses, as a resistance to expressing his transference to me as a whole object, about which he felt ambivalence and conflict.

Countertransference As a Response to the Transference Neurosis

Over time, repeated experiences of this sort coalesced from an alternating pattern to a persisting simultaneous expression of both types of transferences to me as a rejected or smothering object. I experienced corresponding, simultaneous, countertransference responses that no longer felt contradictory.

Dr. R. developed a habit of talking about "this work" in such a way that I did not know whether he was talking about his work as a doctor, of which I was not a part, or his work as a patient in analysis with me. He tended to say "we felt this" or "as we said" without saying who "we" referred to. I did not know if it meant all the parts of himself, his mother and him, or him and me. He continued to assume that I understood, and I continued to feel over-involved in trying to understand him. Once I saw this clearly as his pattern of relating, his transference neurosis, I felt free of my countertransference response. I was no longer trying to find out what he meant. I assumed I would know sooner or later and let myself drift without knowing. Now I was able to interpret what had been happening.

From my countertransference experience I got access to his transference neurosis. I interpreted the projective identificatory process as follows: I said, "Your assumptions about my understanding and your including me as the "we" in your mind have re-created with me the sense of at-oneness with your mother, which you have felt and enjoyed but which has killed off the separate person with sexual and aggressive feelings that is you."

In the laboratory of the analytic situation, we had experienced this profound unconscious communication. The internalized object relationship of fusion with the object and annihilation of the self had been actualized.

When I interpreted the projective identificatory process to Dr. R., he recognized it immediately and felt relieved and powerfully affected. He said, "This is my core fantasy, the basis of my transference neurosis." (He was familiar with these terms, from his training as a psychiatric resident.) "My neurosis," he went on, "has taken the form of an inability to define my true sense of self as a person and a male." As he further explored his relationship to his mother, he said, "It's always been too intertwined, and so I had to create my own space and stay in it. It wasn't possible to impose reality on the space I shared with my mother. It's troubling to realize how my intellectual and emotional development has been tied up by this and how I've more or less gone on despite it." A few sessions later, he expanded on his relationship with his mother. "What's disturbing is we had been seeing ourselves in each other or at best in terms of each other. I thought of myself in those terms and it didn't suit me. The facade was a way of ensuring the constancy of that relationship."

At this point, the essence of the "fantasy" had become clear in the transference, had been experienced in the countertransference, had been interpreted by me and responded to with insight by him. He no longer lived in its grip. After several months of this sort of work on projective identification, the patient resolved his ambivalence about his mother in the transference. Now free to shift his object cathexis to non-incestuous objects, he became able to define himself psychologically as an attractive, loving male. He began to lift weights, gained in muscular development and lost his corpse-like color. In my countertransference, I now became aware of his masculine appeal. I felt that he had finally inhabited his male body.

Dr. R. became successful at work, involved himself in sports activities, and later on started dating. Looking back on this phase, he said, "I used to let my pesentation of myself be determined by other people's expectations. Now, my sense of self, *I* am defining it. There, you have it." I was interested in the change from active to passive, from false-self to true-self functioning, and most of all in his referring to me as "you," indicating that he perceived me as a separate person who was there to relate to. He would soon go on to explore his fear of having sexual and aggressive feelings about me in the paternal as well as the maternal transference.

Countertransference to Issues of Narcissistic Vulnerability

In a female patient's third year of analysis. I began to wonder whether analysis was really any good. Then I started to fret that maybe I was not any good. I felt helpless, unable to anticipate her lapses to former behavior or analyze them thoroughly enough. Whether I asked more about the feelings or silently encouraged their expression, she felt that I did not want to hear them. When the patient was at her best, being freely associative and directly expressive of her angry and disappointed feelings about me, I thought the analysis was going better, but I felt worse. I knew from experience that, at these times, active interpretation of her underlying unconscious envy and murderous rage at me because of all I have that I do not give her tended to promote relief and return to a higher level of functioning. This progress was important to her and her family, but it interrupted the regression that seemed to me to be necessary for therapeutic effect. I was always given to feel that I hadn't got it quite right, that I hadn't met the needs of the analytic work, but at least I always got another chance at it. It also helped to know that I had been in this place before with a similar female patient who had a good result from analysis. But of most support to me, as usual, was the concept of projective identification, which gave me a way of using my experience to understand the patient's.

A sample session from Mrs. Collins's analysis illustrates my point. She was first mentioned in Chapter 3 where her experience of goodness in the analytic relationship was described.

Mrs. Collins, married to Bob, is a full-time mother with two children, a daughter Mindy age 8, and Luke, her 3-year-old son. Mrs. Collins was an eldest daughter herself and had felt special to her mother in some rather exciting ways until the unexpected arrival of her brother, born when she was 3. Mrs. Collins hated his being the baby and felt that he was her mother's favorite because he was a boy. But such anger or jealousy was never tolerated by her parents. She suppressed her feelings and tried to be like her brother, but better than he. As the session opens, Mrs. Collins moves from talking about her disappointment in analysis to describing a difficult time she had with her daughter Mindy. Referring to an intense session the day before in which I had worked on the transference on her fury at being kept out of her parents' bedroom she began:

"It's just so difficult to leave off in one place and try to pick up again. I'm so disgusted with this process. It's just not meeting my needs at all. I can't recreate what was happening yesterday and I don't feel like doing it. What I need is practical help about how to deal with Mindy. She just picks up on everything. Everybody's on edge, everybody's fighting. Last night Bob didn't get home 'til 8:30; everybody was screaming as he walked in. Then he goes 'How was the analysis? I can tell as soon as I hear your voice that you've had a bad session and it's going to be an awful night.' I tell you it's your fault." In a typical move, she turned her aggression on herself. "But it's really my fault," she corrected herself. "It's my shit getting stirred up in every interaction and they just get poisoned. And the words that come out of Mindy's mouth are exactly what I feel; that nobody sees any of the good things she does, that she's stupid. Even Bob got mad at her. And I got mad at that. I wanted to be allowed to feel as awful as I did about me and her, and have him stay objective and not get into it: so, I ended up feeling crazy. And I know how she feels: she just feels helpless.

"And I feel *you* don't care about this and you don't care about me. And there's never enough time and it's always interrupted. And that's when Mindy screams the loudest and Luke interrupts."

I suddenly remembered an occasion a month earlier with my own children. I left the office after enjoying an art project with a 6-year-old boy in analysis, thinking that I'd like to do something like this with my own 6-year-old daughter. My 4-year-old was watching

Sesame Street and the baby was eating in his high chair. "I should do this more often," I said to myself. It seemed a good time to spread paper and markers on the kitchen counter. She and I eagerly set to work. She wanted to map out a village and I should color in the grass. Within three minutes, the 4-year-old was scribbling furiously on the village and the baby climbed from his high chair onto the counter where he was stomping all over the picture, which had to be abandoned. The 4-year-old was crying because her sister had pushed her too hard, the baby was screaming because he was now restrained in his high chair, and the 6-year-old was yelling that I never did anything with her. Everybody needed me and I remembered why I didn't do this more often with only one child.

Here is an example of the use of projective identification in my empathic response to the patient's material. I could well imagine her shame and her husband's irritation at the scene greeting him. I could feel her pain and helplessness at the frustration of her mothering intentions.

"When our session ended you felt interrupted, as when a brother calls on Mommy or her husband takes her attention," I suggested, responding to my countertransference association.

But the patient was not looking for empathy or interpretation.

"You're not gonna do anything about it," she accused. "What is there to do about it? Bob hates me, my kids hate me, and you probably hate me. I can't believe a week ago everything was so good."

"You enjoyed how good it was," I agreed. "And I don't think you spoiled it because it made you anxious, as happened before. What happened is that, feeling good, you felt good about considering giving up your session to do something important for Mindy at a time that might not be negotiable with me. When you called me in the evening to confirm that you would have to cancel, you still felt good about the decision but you felt bad when my husband answered and passed the phone to me." I reminded her, "It took you into the depths of your fury at being excluded from your parents' room when you were frightened at night. You lost your feeling of being a good mother and the wife in the loving couple and felt taken over by the feelings of the excluded child." Mrs. Collins was nodding slowly, as if following me. I finished up my rather lengthy comment, saying "Meanwhile, it feels hopeless to get back to your place in the loving couple."

Mrs. Collins was silent, pondering this comprehensive interpretation, I thought. Suddenly, she took the deepest breath and screamed, "All I care about is: I wanna be first! I want you to pay attention to me and nobody else and I can't think about anything else." Sobbing loudly, she continued, "And I will never have that. I hate you 'cause you can't do that for me. All I'm left with is these horrible feelings about everybody, everybody else. Nobody cares. They just wanna take things from me: they want me to do things for them. Then they criticize me and tell me I'm not giving them what they want." Crying sorely, she concluded, "I feel sad and alone and I feel nobody is ever gonna love me and make me the best." She lay there quietly, seemingly all cried out.

I responded, "Being so mad about that makes it hard to love yourself enough to make yourself the best. You're so mad that I can't do it for you that it's difficult for you to take what I do for you in our work and make it into what you need, make something good of it. I think that is what makes you feel so rotten."

"So, what's wrong with me that I can't do that?" she demanded. "If I could do that for myself, I would never have had to be here in the first place. I look at my own child and I see her struggling with exactly the same things. Is she gonna end up as dysfunctional as I am, with such a rotten feeling about herself? Is this how all families are? Does everybody get screwed up? Mindy's screaming about it already."

"Yes," I said. "Mindy is screaming at you, but she is doing it now and you are finding it painful. You couldn't scream as a child, because you felt your Mother didn't want to deal with that kind of pain, and you're screaming about it now."

Mrs. Collins did not feel understood. She snapped back, "You're saying 'You have to do this. I'm not gonna do it for you. I can't help you. You have to figure out how to get over this rage and love yourself.' And I'm saying, 'I don't know how to do that.' I scream and I cry and I talk about how I feel and it doesn't make a bit of difference."

I was feeling that she had a point. Maybe my earlier comment about finding it hard to love herself had sounded like I was blaming her. Perhaps it was premature. I had thought she had fully expressed her rage from the depths of her being, but perhaps I had moved too quickly to comment. Had I pushed her on and away from her angry longing for me? I felt paired with by her in an angry, envious, demanding way that controlled me and made me feel bad and guilty for not being more help. I thought I was quite accepting of these feelings, but now I began to wonder if I had grown tired of that kind of angry way of relating to me and had prematurely turned the transference back to the original pair.

Substitution of pairs was on her mind, too. She was thinking of her tendency to feel close alternately to me, at which times her husband was on the outs, or to him, in which case I got the cold shoulder. We had been over this again the week before. This time she confirmed her need to create a couple with either him or me, while ensuring that he and I could not be held together in her mind.

I suggested, "Your rage and longing to be cared for and loved prevent the idea of a couple developing, because you would feel excluded by it and then would feel even more rage and longing."

Mrs. Collins continued, "I realized last night that this same business of pairing goes on between me and my children. Mindy was reading something to me and Luke couldn't tolerate it so he picked a fight with the cat. I got furious. I don't know how to be with both children at once. I must be communicating that it's no good unless you're in the one-to-one. Then, I have to calm the cat and Luke's screaming on the floor, 'Nobody loves me. I don't have anyone to play with.' When Bob's there, it just doesn't happen 'cause he's there to be with one of them.

"What good does it do to get upset about all this? I'm as angry and blaming of Mindy as before I started analysis. I may understand more about it, but when I'm feeling bad, that's the way I behave. When I'm feeling better, I don't act that way. But that was true before analysis also. I suppose the only difference is that now

when I'm angry at you and I won't let you help me, this type of
thing happens predictably with my children and my husband. And
when I feel good about what's happening in here and am letting
you help me, then it doesn't happen."

In Freudian language, one might say that Mrs. Collins was
experiencing feelings about her mother and father in a new edition in relation to the physician (Freud 1912) and that her transference to the physician was displaced onto the children. In the
oedipal phase, she must have felt enormous anxiety about her
murderous feelings toward her mother for being possessed by her
father and toward her father for having the phallic power to
interest her mother more than she did. In defense against recognizing her wish to kill her mother to get the father to herself and
enacting her expectation of retaliation, she had turned her aggression against herself and felt bad, depressed, and defeated. She had
not resolved this oedipal complex. Narcissistic wishes and infantile feelings kept her thinking of herself as the excluded child and
prevented her from fully enjoying her adult role as wife and
mother.

In object relations terms, using projective identification, the
formulation includes the pre-oedipal domain. As a baby, Mrs.
Collins felt very special to her mother. But her mother was responsive only to behavior that reflected well on her. I gathered this
from the history and from reports of current interactions. I also
experienced it in the transference, registered in my countertransference wish for her to let me feel better about my work as an
analyst. The opening phase of analysis had been a wonderful
time for Mrs. Collins, when she had felt listened to and cared for,
a time that reflected a gratifying—possibly over-gratifying—infancy.

In the mid-phase she was in a state of letdown and rage that I
could not help her and that I did not want to hear such complaints. From this, I guessed that in childhood, when she became

more separate and more murderous toward her mother, who had broken the closeness of their bond by having another child, Mrs. Collins felt that her mother could not reliably contain her child's anxiety and frustration. She suppressed this rageful, hurt part of herself in order to be a good, compliant girl who would gratify her mother and who could be loved for that, at least. Now this angry part of her was returning from repression and requiring to be experienced by me. It had to be borne and contained in a way that would ultimately allow its modification and integration with the rest of her personality.

My countertransference of feeling no good, with which I have a valency to introjectively identify because of some lingering self-doubt, enabled me to detect the problem of Mrs. Collins's own feeling of worthlessness. She projected into me the part of herself that feels no good in relation to her original object, the successful, sexual, fertile mother. She also projects this part of herself into her child in hopes that she can control it there. Sadly for the child, she, for her own reasons, tends to identify with the projection. Mrs. Collins also projected into me her internal rejecting object, derived from accumulated perceptions of her experience with her mother and with her father who could not relate to his daughter as well as to his son. She was creating intense pairs—with her daughter, with her son, with her husband, with me—and preventing the formation of enriching triangles, because she could not bear to come second to someone more loved than herself and to feel excluded by the couple. The infantile feeling of exclusion from the parental dyad was excited when she called and talked to me and my husband in quick succession at night when she imagined we might have been in bed. Her exclusion of me when she was happy with her husband, and my discomfort with his being rejected when she felt glad to be in analysis with me, led me to see how defended she was against the pain of linking the two of us. My analysis of my countertransference detected her projective identificatory system and gave me a way of talking to her about it.

Countertransference-based interpretation does not magically cure the pathological way of perceiving objects and using them, but it provides a way of working toward its modification so that projective identificatory processes no longer distort or reinvent external reality to fit the expectations of the internal object relations set of the individual.

10

Transference and Countertransference in Couple and Family Therapy

TRANSFERENCE, CONTEXTUAL AND FOCUSED

In family or couple therapy, family members or marital partners enter the therapeutic space with preformed, intense transferences to each other. We observe these expressions of individual internal object relationships, shown externally as family members relate to each other. But our therapeutic focus is on the system-wide family or couple transference to us as therapists. At the moment of crossing the boundary into therapy, or even diagnostic consultation, the family is pushed by its anxiety about what therapy offers to reveal its usual ways of defending itself from the unknown. Some families are unable to work together as a group, and some couples cannot cooperate to give a coherent account of their difficulties. To defend against chaos, the couple or family substitutes an individual to deal with the therapist. If our training has been in individual therapy this may be an attractive offer. To avoid colluding with the defense of producing an index patient, we prefer to take a group interpretive approach. We look at how the family as a group, or the couple as a small group of two, approaches and uses the first interview as an indicator of the group's defensive functioning and strengths.

We find that there are two types of transferences to the therapist (Scharff and Scharff 1987). The first is called the *contextual transference* and it refers to the group's reaction to the therapist's provision of the holding environment. The second is the *focused transference*, which refers to the group's experience of the therapist as an object available for intense, individual object-relating with one of its members. When individual transferences substitute for the contextual transference, the therapist experiences a deviation from involved impartiality (Stierlin 1977). Recovering her balance from a series of these pulls away from the neutral position, the therapist can put them together to give an image of the denied contextual transference. When she can speak of the group's experience in using her, she is providing for them the contextual holding that the family or couple is not yet providing for its members. But how does she detect these transference responses? She receives the communication in the cognitive realm by registering patterns of interaction and comparing them with past clinical experience, and in the psychological realm by recognizing and working with her own responses.

Her responses are not organized at first. They emerge out of the therapist's attempt to empathize with and understand the family or couple's experience. Their struggle with their internal world, their external world, and their coming together at the boundary of the therapeutic space gets mixed up with the therapist's own life issues. Through processes of projective and introjective identification, the therapist sorts out the fit between her own internal object relations and those that are being projected into her. She allows her own object relations set to resonate with that of the couple or family and so becomes available to them as an object to be used and learned from. Through personal analysis and supervision, she gains confidence in the value of her vulnerabilities as exquisitely sensitive receptor sites for understanding the couple or family pathology. By examining her countertransference, she learns what is troubling to the family or couple and can interpret their defenses and anxieties from inside her own experience with them. This way of working uses the principles of countertransference elaborated in Chapter 9 on individual therapy, except that the family or couple therapist tunes her unconscious transference-receiving apparatus to a living, breathing group in the interpersonal dimension rather than to an individual's object relations in the intrapsychic dimension revealed in relationship to the therapist.

CONTEXTUAL AND FOCUSED COUNTERTRANSFERENCE

The therapist's experience with a couple or family gives rise to feelings, thoughts, and sometimes behaviors that are unique and specific to each case: this is what I mean by countertransference in general. The family therapist is likely to experience countertransference to the family as a group and also to its individuals and interactive pairs of family members. To be more specific, these countertransference experiences tend to cluster in relation to the contextual and focused transferences, which give rise to the *contextual* and *focused countertransferences* respectively (Scharff and Scharff 1987).

The *contextual countertransference* refers to the therapist's reaction to the patient's contextual transference, namely the patient's response to the therapeutic environment, shown in attitudes about the frame of treatment, unconscious resistance in general, specific conscious feelings, and behavior toward the therapist as an object for providing a holding situation. The *focused countertransference* occurs in response to the focused transference, namely feelings the patient transfers to the therapist as an object for intimate relating in hateful and loving ways.

Early in individual therapy, a focused transference response is a transference manifestation that qualifies as a resistance. Except for these focused, sporadic transference manifestations, we find that contextual transference and countertransference predominate in the opening and closing phases of individual treatment, and that focused transference and countertransference are phenomena more typical of the deepening therapeutic relationship in the middle phase. Focused transferences become more prominent until they crystallize into the transference neurosis, yielding a countertransference neurosis through which the transference neurosis is related to, worked with, worked through, and finally resolved.

In family therapy the contextual transference and corresponding countertransference are found throughout the course of family therapy. In family therapy we are not surprised to find ourselves with a focused countertransference response to an individual family member or to an interacting pair of family members. We realize that this indicates the emergence of a focused transference that the treatment alliance has been insufficient to contain or which the family group has substituted for its wider concerns. We compile the focused transferences to generate a hypothesis about the group transference and we work to expand the field of participation to the group-wide level. In family therapy, the contextual transference-countertransference dimension predominates.

In couple therapy there is rapid oscillation between focused transference–countertransference and contextual transference-countertransference.

Clinical examples of the therapist's work with countertransference in couple therapy and in family consultation illustrate the types of countertransference encountered.

Countertransference in Couple Therapy

The Clarks (in Scharff and Scharff 1991) consulted me about their marriage, which was close to divorce. Mrs. Clark was the one who called to make the arrangements and persuaded her busy husband to take time off his orthopedic practice to discuss their need for treatment. Yet when they entered my office, Mrs. Clark swept past me with a hostile glare and said nothing. Her husband explained that she was upset as usual. Mrs. Clark launched into a tirade against her husband, whom she furiously referred to as "Mr. Doctor God," because he thought he was so wonderful while putting her down as a total lunatic. Mrs. Clark kept interrupting me and dominating the conversation. This along with her swearing and contemptuous facial gestures left me feeling turned away from her. I found myself sympathizing with Dr. Clark who seemed so reasonable and undemanding, and I felt ashamed of my denigrating view of Mrs. Clark and of losing my neutrality. Although she was not actively berating me, Mrs. Clark looked at me accusingly. Pointedly addressing me as Doctor Scharff, she challenged me to prove the usefulness of therapy.

In my countertransference I experienced a deviation from "involved impartiality" (Stierlin 1977). I realized that Mrs. Clark was expressing anxiety and envy in a focused transference toward me as a doctor (the same profession as her husband). I asked myself why her husband was not able to reassure her. Perhaps in his own way he too had doubts about me and therapy.

Dr. Clark denied that he had doubts but admitted that he had some questions about my level of training. He was relieved to learn that I was a board-certified psychiatrist with more years of experience than he had guessed from my appearance. Learning this, I was then able to show that he too had anxieties about starting treatment with me.

When Mrs. Clark was anxious, she became angry, domineering, and contemptuous. When Dr. Clark became anxious he controlled it with intellectual defenses and retreat, which left Mrs. Clark all the more anxious and angry. In the countertransference, I, as a doctor, was identified with the hated and envied object that had been idealized before it became rejecting and that was usually projected into Dr. Clark. Thus, through their projective identifications of those objects into me (the couple transference) and my introjective identification with those objects (the countertransference), I was able to understand the couple dynamics from my experience of the couple unconscious in relation to my own. In feeling ashamed of my thoughts and my technique, I was identified with the denigrated object usually projected into Mrs. Clark. Through mutual projective identification, the outspoken Mrs. Clark carried rage and envy for the couple, while the reasonable and apparently confident Dr. Clark was insufficiently assertive, like his inwardly quite insecure wife. Mrs. Clark's focused transference was a cover for the couple's shared transference to the context of their proposed treatment.

After months of therapy in which good sessions were followed by claims that therapy was no use, I often felt that the anger between them killed off any goodness in my work, and yet it survived. Then I learned of a deeper level of projection of anger and anxiety into Mrs. Clark. Dr. Clark got up the courage to talk about his predominant sexual fantasy, a sadistic and murderous one in which he tormented hated women and then killed and chopped them up during orgasm. Mrs. Clark was somewhat frightened by this revelation, but mainly she felt enormous relief at his taking back the rageful projections. She expressed her gratitude to him for taking responsibility for his feelings, which allowed her to become much less angry and to show a degree of compassion I had not seen before in her. Mrs. Clark became capable of a more mature level of functioning and Dr. Clark sublimated his regained aggression into a new assertiveness about his career.

THE ART OF NEGATIVE CAPABILITY

In training we aim to develop a capacity for non-anxious containment of projections. A quote from John Keats captures the essence of this quality. He referred to *negative capability*, a capacity for "being in uncertainties, Mysteries, doubts, without any irritable reaching after fact & reason" (Murray 1955, p. 261). Thus the state of not knowing is valued, is aspired to, so that the meaning of the experience can emerge from inside the experience itself. How does this translate into clinical action? The therapist allows herself to take in the projections, to be affected by them without trying to explain them, to become aware of them, and then get to work on understanding her experience and what it means for the family. Through this process, she models the creation of psychological space (Box 1981) in which the projections can be reworked in the light of current experience.

In writing about this state of mind we attempt to communicate the ideal; yet it always begs the question "How?" Fortunately, we get some help from Keats's line, which evokes clearer meaning than any amount of technical description. The following example from the therapist's state of not knowing the facts illustrates the use of a bizarre countertransference association that usefully emerged from the experience of meeting with a family in a consultation session.

COUNTERTRANSFERENCE
IN FAMILY CONSULTATION

Sometimes a countertransference experience seems to come out of the blue. You take a chance and use it. If it does not work, you can appear rather crazy. This happened to me once when I joined a family-therapy student to do a consultation interview of a family, observed through a one-way screen by a group of eight family-therapy students and videotaped for future teaching purposes. When I am subject to feeling crazy following a comment that seems out of touch, I accept my fate and wait to see what happens next. In this case it was rather interesting.

Countertransference and Expressions
of Anger and Mourning

The Perry family consisted of a single-parent mother and her four daughters, each born of different fathers with whom they were not in regular contact. But only the three younger daughters, Sherri, Sharone, and Lilla, were present. After initial discussion of their feelings about being observed and filmed, the family began to talk about the absent 17-year-old daughter, Matsui, who ran away from her mother's home, supposedly with telephoned permission from her father in whose custody she was. She was now living with an older boyfriend in a group house and not going to school. Mrs. Perry disapproved of and distrusted the arrangement, saying that a 17-year-old should be home under the control of a parent, even though she herself had first been married at the age of 15. These facts did not come out sequentially, however. The picture gradually emerged out of a fog of hinting, lying, cheating, manipulating, backbiting, and name-calling.

I found myself interrupting to get the record straight. I tried to defend us all against feeling lost, but every time I asked for clarification, I was buried in an avalanche of contradictory information, accusations, stories of eavesdropping, knowing looks, and nods.

Mrs. Perry tried to establish herself as a concerned mother, while the children shot down her attempts to look good by reminding her of her past difficulties when she left them in the care of their abusive fathers and their second and third wives. Now that she was in a good job and was able to provide for them, she hoped to give them the stability and knowledge of a good life that they had missed. But Matsui had rejected her wish to care for her and the other children doubted the sincerity of their mother's supposedly good intentions.

I rather liked the children's spunk. They were not afraid to confront their mother. I admired Mrs. Perry for improving her position to where she could support four children. But I felt anxious being with them. The usual rules did not apply. There was not an adequate generational boundary. There was no trust between them. I didn't feel much support from the family therapy student who had been their therapist for a year, and who must know the story and must be keeping me in the dark. There were so many interjections, I could hardly get in a word without interrupting. As for a neat interpretation to teach the students, forget it. And all this was being preserved on tape by a crew of three on cameras and mikes. I wanted to run away. I could really understand Matsui's decision.

Mrs. Perry and the girls were heavily into an argument about whether the girls were at the mall last night, as they said, or whether they were visiting their errant sister and the unsavory group she lives with, as Mrs. Perry suspected. Apparently, they had kept it secret that Matsui's boyfriend was 27 years old, so Mrs. Perry was suspicious about what else they knew and were keeping from her. On the other hand, they had let slip that Matsui had been to hospital to get psychiatric help and was supposedly dying because of her birth control (a cause of death I did not understand but there was no room to ask). Now Mrs. Perry was worried that the girls would let slip to Matsui that she had filed papers to get custody of her so that she could legally get her medical care and control her whereabouts.

Mrs. Perry went on: "So what it boils down to, she is 17 years old. She is living with or off a boyfriend who is 27. She is living with a group of people who have what I consider to be an unfavorable background. They have problems with drugs. Actually, there is a question who she is living with because they keep moving out and moving in. None of it looks stable and because of that she doesn't need to be out there. Because she is at a point in her life when she can either forge forward and have goals and things, or she can screw up everything she ever wants to be. It all spells trouble."

The children protested and corrected her impressions about the ages of the people at the group house.

"So how about this wonderful new group's background?" she countered.

"Your background," said Sherri darkly.

"No, it's not my background," Mrs. Perry corrected her.

Lilla insisted, "You have a background. You used drugs."

"But I don't have a drug and alcohol arrest background. No one's serving a subpoena on me. I don't have 'contributing to minor charges' filed on me," Mrs. Perry replied. "But this is the supposedly wonderful group she's moving in with to get a supposedly healthy environment."

"I would rather live there than be constantly yelled at, I mean God!" said Sharone. "Mom an' Matsui. They hate each other. Why does she want to get her back?"

"It's like trying to kill your daughter and then making her come home so you can kill her again," Lilla thought.

Mrs. Perry wasn't having any of it. She retorted, "After all the crap she feeds them, they come home acting sassy and flip and think they can throw the same abuse at me she did."

Maybe this was a useful discussion, but I had stopped listening to the content. It felt to me like a cover for something else, as the effect of drugs or alcohol often is. Was I upset by the talk of killing? Who else had died? I was suddenly overwhelmed by the number of females in the room, it was all I could think about. I had a desperate longing for a man somewhere, any man would do.

I said, "I am sitting here noticing that here I am in a group that is all female, four of you, two therapists, and even the camera crew is female. If you had Matsui here that would be another female. She's gone to be with a man. I guess the trouble in getting along together is because of there being so many females in the family and no man here to give his authority to the situation."

The student family therapist in the room with me looked puzzled. The family looked at me as if I were out of order. I am told that the class behind the screen groaned in disbelief. They could not see where I got that interpretation, even though I spelled out the countertransference. It seemed off the wall. When Sharone said to my student co-therapist that she wanted to see her alone, I knew I had caused trouble. To my surprise Mrs. Perry encouraged Sharone to talk in the meeting, but Sharone felt too much in the middle to do so.

"Is it about me?" asked Lilla. "Just tell me."

"No," said Sharone. "But I don't want you to know. I can't say it because it'll blow it."

"Say it," said Sherri.

"Don't say it," Lilla countered.

The three girls discussed what dreadful thing would happen if the secret was told. Gradually it became obvious that all three of them knew what it was. Something about Mom's past that Matsui planned to tell the judge in hopes of getting Mom fired from her job. Lilla got so anxious she left to go to the bathroom.

Sherri took over. "You know, Mom."

The family was still hovering around the topic when Lilla returned. Mrs. Perry finally figured it out. "It's not that big a deal to me," she said. "Many years ago at a certain time in my life . . ."

"Mom, don't," cautioned Sharone, the one who raised the topic in the first place. "I will have to leave the room."

"I'll have to leave, too" said Sherri. "You guys can get it over while I'm gone."

Mrs. Perry continued, "During a certain time in my life, I decided that relationships with men were probably not real helpful. Because of that I ended up involved with a female relationship. After all the relationships I had with men, this was the only stable relationship I ever had. To me, it was a learning experience, it was comforting. To me, I don't think it is that much of a shameful thing. Yes it did affect them, mainly because they saw the goodness of the relationship, but they couldn't get past the female thing. So it was a pull-tug on them because they were pretty comfortable, she was so nurturing and motherly. Am I making sense?"

"Not to me and Sharone," said Lilla. "We thought Sue was more like a father."

"No," said Sherri, "No one knows how I feel. Having your mother . . ."

"It was more terrible for me," interrupted Sharone.

Sharone and Sherri now talked at once, each telling her own story of coming home with a friend and going upstairs. "It was so embarrassing because I had a friend with me and I found my Mom and . . ." Sharone trailed off. "And . . . I don't want to talk about it," concluded Sherri.

"You don't want to talk about the sexual aspect of the relationship. You didn't want your friend to be aware of that," I suggested.
"*We* didn't want to be aware of it," Sherri said, speaking for
them all. "We just didn't like it. Sharone and I were at school one
day, and me and my friend Andrea, we got in a fight. So Andrea
goes and says to all our friends about my Mom being a les. We just
don't like people knowing about it."

The therapist who had been working with them for a year had
not known of the mother's lesbian relationship. It took a lot of
work to get to this sharing of their discomfort and anger at their
mother. It would take much more before they could reach a state of
compassion and acceptance of her right of choice. A single interpretation, based on my countertransference feeling of longing for a
man, did not accomplish so much. Nevertheless, without it, I do
not think that the girls would have felt drawn to speak of their
feelings about their mother not having a man because they could
not have recognized their own longings for a man to care about
them. The discussion led, not surprisingly, to the topic of the
absent fathers, a subject about which they usually joked. Arriving
at it from their feelings about their mother's lesbian solution to the
problem of unreliable men, they were able to share the sadness they
all felt about their missing, inconsistent fathers.

The primary method for teaching about countertransference
has to be through sharing case material and personal reactions. This
can be done in a number of ways other than in discussion after
observed clinical work. Countertransference responses can be seen
on videotape, but the therapist still has to be willing to report the
feelings relevant to the moment. It has to be described laboriously,
tracing its development within a session or over a few weeks.
Perhaps the best way to learn about it is through discussion of
process notes, presented by a therapist who is willing to track and
report personal emotions, behaviors, and fantasies in relation to
the patient. Obviously, this risky task requires a collaborative
group of trusted and respected colleagues who are equally commit-

ted to process and review. Thus we prepare ourselves for working in the countertransference.

Further help comes from our own personal analysis or therapy. Only with thorough therapy can we reach the state of self-knowledge and of automatic checking of responses that allows us to calibrate our own transferential vulnerabilities against those stimulated by interaction with a certain family or family member. In this way we learn to remain neutral, to not import pathology into the patient–therapist system. We may have our independent transferences, but we will recognize and work with them. They may at times cause countertransference interference with therapy, but we will work to contain them so as to secure a freely responsive countertransference. In the next chapter, I will elaborate on models of teaching the use of countertransference.

11

Models for Teaching Projective and Introjective Identification through the Use of Countertransference

A MODEL FOR TEACHING ABOUT COUNTERTRANSFERENCE IN FAMILY ASSESSMENT

Describing to a colleague or student, or writing in a book, about my countertransference and how it informs my subsequent intervention is of limited use. I find that my teaching is more effective when the student's own countertransference is elicited and worked from. I work this way in regular supervision, using the student's own therapy cases, a technique that I will describe later in this chapter. But how can we teach a larger one-time-only group using the students' countertransference to our presented clinical material from assessment interviews? My colleague Robert Winer suggested the use of a short, nonverbal portion of videotape of a family interview to be followed by discussion of the students' emotional responses to the videotape. We found that the absence of verbal information heightened the awareness of personal emotional responsiveness. In just two minutes of soundless videotape from a first assessment session, the group had learned a great deal about the family dynamics.

Since then, teaching larger groups of mental health professionals, David Scharff and I have developed the model as follows:

1. Show two minutes of tape without sound, edited from the opening moments of the diagnostic consultation interview.

2. Discuss reactions.

3. Show another two minutes without sound, edited from later in the interview.

4. Discuss reactions and compare to the earlier ones.

5. Then show longer video segments with sound.

6. Discuss reactions after each segment and monitor the flow of the group's countertransference to the family in relation to verbal and nonverbal material.

We find that people have very different reactions. One therapist gains access to the family through an early identification with a child, another feels more in touch with the mother, yet another feels oppresed by the father and so on in endless combinations. Our own countertransference is clearly based on our valency to respond to the family in terms of our own past experience with our family of origin, our personal nuclear family now, and other families whose transferences have been worked with in prior therapy. No single countertransference is regarded as healthier or more accurate than any other. Each one is regarded simply as that individual's point of entry to understanding the family dynamics. The compiled group-wide responses yield an emerging countertransference image of the family transference, far richer than any one author or therapist could provide from personal process and review.

Countertransference in a Family Assessment

The Denvers were nice, responsible people. As soon as their gifted son began to have trouble performing in school and getting along with his friends, they brought him for consultation. They readily agreed to a family interview in the television studio. Not inhibited by the setting, they expected to find the session helpful. They spoke easily and coherently about their son's current problem and family life factors relevant to its emergence. In short, they had a positive contextual transference.

The Earlier Nonverbal Segment

A nonverbal segment from the opening third of the interview showed the following:

Morgan, age 12 is looking rather grave. Mrs. Denver is talking, her head bent toward her husband or glancing at her children on the other side of her. Morgan and his sister Susie are wearing brightly colored clothing, while the parents are both wearing gray. Mrs. Denver is in a subtly checked jacket, white blouse, and plain grey skirt. Mr. Denver's argyll sweater is a bolder version of the same shades and emphasizes the squareness of his face and upper body. While Mrs. Denver speaks, Morgan and Susie listen gravely. Susie brushes her hair away from her face. Mr. Denver sits with his arms crossed. He is frowning. Susie deliberately curls and uncurls the fingers of one hand. Morgan sneers and then smiles self-consciously. He shrugs, talks and looks down. Mr. Denver smiles and nods while Morgan speaks. Then he frowns. The children are twisting their chairs from side to side. Susie extends her arms in a circling gesture and a second later Morgan follows with the same gesture. The others listen intently while the father talks seriously. Mrs. Denver looks down when her husband addresses himself to Morgan. Mr. Denver uses hand gestures that indicate an imaginary box in front of him. Now Mr. Denver uses only his right hand, jabbing the air as if emphasizing a point. Morgan looks downcast. Mr. Denver straightens his cuffs. Susie smoothes the hair back from her forehead.

The ensuing group discussion included the following responses:

"This has to be a military family. That father! Smiling or frowning at what his son says. He has to have that boy just the way he wants. And the way the mother bent to the father's wishes reminded me of my own mother who was raised in the South."

"The little girl showed a great deal of tension in her fingers."

"The little girl is coy. She gives her Daddy just what he wants."

"I felt so sorry for the boy. He looked so browbeaten by the father. I think the boy is the identified patient."

"I thought the mother was the identified patient."

"I thought the mother was concerned with appearances. She is the boss."

"I felt so tight watching them. I felt like I was in a box."

"I felt shut out."

"I felt sad."

"I liked them. I thought they cared for each other and listened to
what the others had to say."

As we elicited comments from the group, we drew together
themes and compiled the disparate focused countertransferences
experienced by individuals into a comprehensive picture. Without
sound, the group had identified the family's strength and good
holding capacity in just two minutes. A projective identification
between father and son had been evident. The defensive aspects of
their well-meaning attitude had been uncovered. A countertransference to the constriction of affect left the group feeling shut out,
as I myself had felt in the session. Another countertransference
feeling of sadness suggested what the repressed affect might be.

The Later Nonverbal Segment

We then presented a nonverbal extract from later in the session.
Here is what the group saw:

Dr. David Scharff is talking. As he does so, the son is pulling on his
shoelaces. The daughter puts her finger in her mouth and looks
away. The mother rolls her tongue in her mouth. The father anxiously checks on the children. Dr. Scharff finishes. The father
relaxes and the mother laughs. Both parents listen thoughtfully
while the boy talks. Then both children listen while the father talks
with a serious expression. While he is still talking, the daughter
signals to her mother and the mother nods in agreement. The
daughter picks up the pad of paper and the markers, rubs her
nose, and starts to draw.
   She continues to draw while the mother talks in brief spurts,
as if answering questions. Suddenly, the mother gets upset and
holds her head in her hand. The father comforts the mother by
patting her palm with his fingers. She cries. The son looks concerned for his mother. The daughter cries and then smiles in an
embarrassed way. The mother holds her husband's hand. The
mother holds her husband's hand in both her hands now and his

hand is still. The children are looking down. The girl wipes the tears from her eyes. The mother talks and smiles through her tears, looking more relaxed and prettier. The father looks on gravely. The son, who is fiddling with a pen looks annoyed when his sister pokes him. They argue briefly and her father hands her a handkerchief. The daughter wipes her eyes and laughs nervously. She cries and blots both eyes. As her father talks, she shrugs, nods, and shakes her head. The son looks down, looks deeply moved, and shifts in his chair.

Discussion of this later nonverbal segment included the following:

"They still seemed constricted at the beginning, but when the mother cried I felt so relieved."

"I felt sad for the mother. I thought that she was grieving."

"I noticed Jill looked withdrawn and I wanted to see her say something."

"I hated the way her husband patted her hand as if to tell her to shut up."

"The father is so controlling. He's just like my father."

"I didn't realize this before, but in the earlier session my chest felt so tight. I thought I was having indigestion from the doughnut I ate. But in this segment, as soon as the mother cried, I felt my chest return to normal."

"I felt sad for the little girl. She was obviously upset to see her Mom cry and didn't know what to do about it."

"The boy looked concerned and so grown up. I think that they have big expectations of him."

"Dr. Scharff, can you describe the nature of the projective identification between the mother and daughter?"

As usual we got a mixture of countertransference responses
—emotional, physical, and intellectual. The last mentioned response masqueraded as a question to the presenter in violation of
the task. Instead of answering, I said that the idea of a technical
question was a countertransference wish to move into the cognitive
realm to escape from the painful affects of what may well have been
a projective identification between mother and daughter. The
group realized that the previous sense of constriction had given way
to a more workable feeling about the family. They detected a
countertransference affecting me. And the inexplicable sadness felt
by one group member earlier was now being attributed to grief.

Watching the expanded version of the *first* segment now with
sound, the group heard Mrs. Denver present the problem.

"What brought us here was that we've recently had a very traumatic move, returning from Guam after just a year. Not only is it
halfway across the world but it's a drastically different culture from
the United States. And we've returned to an area in the United
States very different from the one we left."

As she talked, Mr. Denver held his arms stiffly crossed and
frowned.

"So when we got back," she continued, "we put the children in
local schools, and a month later we transferred Morgan to a
magnet school for the gifted. But the teachers there are complaining that he is having trouble getting his work done properly or
handing it in on time."

Susie expressed tension in her fingers. Did she feel like making a fist?

"We've known for some time that he was gifted," Mrs. Denver
went on.

Morgan sneered.

"What does that look mean?" Dr. David Scharff asked Morgan.
"How do you feel being gifted?"

"Well," he replied, smiling and shrugging it off, "I just try to
not let it go over my head, go to my head, excuse me. I just try to
act normal instead of acting overly smart."

Mr. Denver who had been frowning now nodded approvingly.

"How does your giftedness show up?" I asked, not impressed so far.

"I'm not sure," he mumbled uncomfortably, shrugging again.

"Speak up," said Mrs. Denver.

I got the impression that Morgan was either struggling because he was at the low end of the gifted stream or that he was inhibited from fulfilling his talent. A good showing seemed important to his mother but perhaps he feared retaliation from his father and sister.

"It's not just his work," added Mr. Denver. "Morgan has trouble with the kids at school. He does not read people well." This is where Mr. Denver made his box-like gestures. "He is oblivious to all that's going on outside himself."

"Personal interactions," Mrs. Denver edited his comments.

Undeterred by her impatience, he proceeded, "He's dedicated to what's in close—like, an assignment he'll do well—and shuts out what's outside. So, when something happens around him, he's not prepared to cope with it and whammo!" Now Mr. Denver was jabbing the air to get the point home to his son. The children began to spin their chairs and to make the similar circling gestures of helplessness.

"You miscue with the bigger picture," he continued talking directly to Morgan, who looked downcast. Indicating Susie, he went on, "She reads them a lot better. Maybe she doesn't pay attention to what she's doing but she sees what's going on around her. She reads people better than he does and she gives them what they want." As he finished, he straightened his cuffs.

Morgan looked down and Susie smiled and brushed the hair from her forehead.

In discussion the group confirmed their earlier impression of a well-intentioned family with a positive attitude to intervention. The father was less haranguing than some had thought. Nevertheless, being in control of the environment was clearly an issue for him. The boy had a problem accepting his giftedness, perhaps because the father had competitive feelings about it and because the mother was so invested in it. Some women therapists were sensitive to the parents' settling for less with Susie because she was

a girl. They thought that my not talking meant that I had identified
with the wife as a military dependent. I may say I had a valency for
this, since my husband was the employee at the military institution
where the film was made and I was the invited consultant, an arrangement that had produced a similar dynamic with another family we
had seen there together (J. S. Scharff 1989). They experienced the
family as willing to talk and engage, but only superficially in order to
keep up appearances. The group felt somewhat frustrated and shut
out. In general, there was remarkable correspondence between what
had been surmised from personal reaction to nonverbal material and
what was communicated when sound was included.

We continued to show the videotape with sound. So far the
interview was moving along without tension in the co-therapy
relationship. We were working well together. Like the group, I was
feeling some frustration at getting past the polite front. Similarly, in
the teaching setting, we were working well, sharing the task of
processing the group's comments.

We continued to show the *second* full-length section of videotape with sound.

"He's right," said Mrs. Denver. "Susie always does enough to
please. She does enough at home or school to meet the standards.
But Morgan, he's super at home, anything you ask him to do, fine,
but at school he's not handing in his work or he's turning in sloppy
work that's been done in a great hurry."

"What was school like for the two of you?" asked David.

The children were surprised to realize that he was asking this
not of them but of the parents. Here he was reaching for the object
relations history of the symptom.

"You first," Mrs. Denver prodded.

Mr. Denver obliged. "My interests were in school. We didn't
use the term gifted in those days."

Susie distracted her mother to get permission to use our
drawing materials. I noticed that this was the second time that
Susie had reacted with physical activity to the word "gifted."

"I was always in, if not special classes, classes that were one
step up from what was considered routine. There are similarities,"

Mr. Denver recognized. "I was never comfortable in school. The other kids would try to feel me out. Someone would be standing in line and jab me. I'd turn around and want to know who did that. Then the teacher would come over and she'd focus on me. And I'd think 'Oh no, got it again!' Whether it's a comment or a dig or a practical joke, I overreacted."

Mrs. Denver responded, "I think this still applies. Small comments hurt his feelings. He'll tell me about it and I'll think 'Why would that hurt your feelings?' He's sensitive to it."

"How about sensitivities between the two of you?" Mrs. Denver was asked.

"Oh, I think there always are between a married couple," Mrs. Denver confirmed, but in a rather dismissive way. "If we ever have anything like that we just tell the other. We don't scream or shout. It's not a problem."

I said, "There is quite a contrast between the secure group of two and the unsafe outer world—the gang of guys, the new school situations and cultures that you meet when relocated by the military. Is there an extended family group intermediate between the safety of the twosome and the outside world that we might learn from?"

"Oh, yes!" enthused Mrs. Denver. "We think of family as all the aunts and uncles, cousins, grandparents—and it even extends to great-aunts. I'm from a much larger family than he is. He had only one sister, but I was the second of five. Our house was always chaotic, kids and animals everywhere. School was a haven for me.

"I had an older brother killed in a car accident when he was 23," she said a bit too matter-of-factly. "So now I am the oldest of the living children. But he went away in the summer to work on relatives' farms for spending money. He didn't want to be stuck home with us guys. From the age of 10, I took care of the younger children in the summers and I have some resentment about that, because I lost a part of my childhood.

"What was really hard was that my father would walk in and say 'We're moving' and we would move in 48 hours. He would lose his temper and quit his job. Or he'd have a fight with someone and get fired. I don't think my children know this. They know their grandfather as a semi-inavlid. (He was medically retired when I was 22.) So they only know their grandfather as a person who's sick, who sits and talks to them and has lots of time for them."

"Going back to how he was fighting and impulsive when you were a child," said David, "Did he drink?"

"That was a great part of it," she confirmed.

The wide-eyed children shared a surprised and privileged look and listened in amazement.

"Was he difficult at home?" continued David.

"Yes," she answered curtly.

"Did he and your mother fight a lot?" he persisted.

"Yes," came another monosyllabic reply.

I imagined Mrs. Denver's pain in sharing these memories, but she was defending herself from it by cutting off her questioner. David, however, kept pressing on. I found him intrusive and insistent. I felt uncomfortable. I felt shut out by him as much as he should have been feeling shut out by her. Oddly enough, I did not feel shut out by her. Although she was not addressing herself to me, I felt myself to be in deep, sustained, nonverbal communication with her. At this point the videotape shows me leaning toward her with an intent expression.

"So, the picture I am getting—" began David.

"Yes," Mrs. Denver cut him off, and went on spontaneously, "That pattern stopped after he learned that he had rheumatoid arthritis, and he is one of the worst cases. Because of the illness, the drinking and the fighting stopped, but I wasn't home to see that. My brothers and sisters think that life was not so bad as I thought it was. Although they were there for the illness and that is a very bad thing, they were not there for the screaming through the night."

"Was there physical abuse?" interrupted David.

"Not for us children," Mrs. Denver replied.

"How did you get along with both of your parents?" he asked next.

I was wondering why on earth he was asking so many questions, instead of letting the story unfold. The more active he became, the more I felt that he was being abusive of the material, and the more helpless I felt to say anything myself. I felt invisible. We were no longer working together. And I was still caught up in an intense involvement with Mrs. Denver and trying to find a way to understand that.

"With my mother I got along extremely well. With my father, I stayed out of the way," she answered. "You didn't want to bring down the wrath of Dad."

I experienced a moment of insight and relief. I realized that she was recreating these relationships in the transference, split between David and me. Through projective identification, an abusive, constantly moving figure was created in him, while in me, a silently empathic one. As Mrs. Denver continued I learned more specifically about this countertransference.

"When Dad was around, you disappear if you can," she said. "Better not to draw his attention. You just withdraw."

Looking at this section of the tape, I see myself bent over, hiding my face in my hand. I noticed that she said "you disappear" rather than "I disappear." I imagined that as a child she told this to her younger siblings and that I had identified with it. But before I could make use of this understanding of the countertransference, I was annoyed to find that my co-therapist was on the move again with another question.

"How old were you when you met and got married?" David wanted to know.

I tried to take a positive view of his questioning. Here he was taking the history of their marriage, a reasonable question during an assessment interview. But I felt that he was caught up in the transference to the maternal grandfather, both as a nice man who was making every effort to talk to them, and as a moving bad object, ready to land on whoever or whatever. As we processed the impact on our cotherapy relationship in review after the session, he said that he was unaware of being intrusive. He only knew that he was desperately trying to find a way to be helpful, given how shut out he felt by the silent family, the mother's one-word answers and his disappearing co-therapist. Our different countertransference responses to the split focused transferences had been mutually reinforcing. Without knowing this in the session, I was now able to confront my resentment of my co-therapist and my countertransference of silent empathy.

I said, "I'd like to interrupt and go back to your life with your family. You are answering questions frankly, even though the children haven't heard this before. I see them making big eyes as if to say 'Fancy that about Grandpa.'"

Mrs. Denver laughed and nodded.

I continued, "But I would think that these memories would be painful, if you let yourself have the feelings about what you are saying."

"We've made a point all their lives not to go into this," she said firmly. "For my father it was past. For my son, his grandfather is very special. He's never yelled at him. He's never seen his grandfather lose his temper. He's truly different now than he was when I . . ." Mrs. Denver stopped and her mouth tightened.

"Do you sometimes feel sad that he wasn't like that when you were a child?" asked David, now back in touch.

"Yes," Mrs. Denver conceded, and quickly went on to defend her parents and put the lid on her feelings. A change had occurred, however. Now she was talking to both of us. "Except he was like that then too. When he was a good father, he was the best. And my mother. Being the oldest daughter, and because our family was separated from the extended family by all the moves, I became my mother's listener. So I was privy to some things I probably should not have been, nothing specific. I knew when she was the most unhappy. I was the person she told her problems to, which put me in a strange position in the household."

"An insider to her?" suggested David, staying with her.

"Yes, and an outsider to the other children," she concluded. "I was always trying to herd them away from him." Her face clouded over and she stiffened again.

"You are upset by this," he observed, still taking the lead, but not now to my exclusion. "What do you find hard?" he asked kindly.

"It's not something I like to talk about," she cried. "I'm sorry." She buried her head in one hand and her husband patted the other one. Therapists who watch the tape find his movement an awkward restraining gesture, but Mrs. Denver took comfort from it.

"It's okay," said David. "I think your feelings are important."

Morgan looked gravely at his mother in her distress, while Susie kept her head down.

Still holding her husband's hand, Mrs. Denver now spoke freely and regretfully of her role as a child. "My older brother and I were always trying to protect the younger ones from the scenes and the fighting."

"You and he were united like parents to take care of the younger children," David said, aware of the intensification of her feelings for her brother as a father and as a partner.

"I still miss him so much," she sobbed.

Now Morgan looked down and Susie started to cry uncomfortably.

"What kind of a man was he?" I asked.

"He was killed when he was 23," Mrs. Denver replied. "So it's hard to say what kind of a man he was. I remember him growing up and at college. After he was out of college a year, he was commissioned in the Green Berets. He'd come to visit me and take me and any of my friends who wanted to come out to dinner. He'd tell me who I should go out with and say I shouldn't give these guys such a hard time," she laughed fondly. "I'd call him anytime, tell him anything and he was always there."

Mrs. Denver, talking freely through her tears, looked relaxed and as pretty as a young girl. She was holding Mr. Denver's hand, now lying quietly in both her hands. Morgan's expression was moved with compassion for his mother, and Susie was crying, wiping the tears with the back of her hand, and spinning anxiously in her chair again. Susie asked Morgan for something to help with her distress and he seemed to get angry with her request. Together they created a diversion from the painful topic and a re-creation of the other brother-sister pair that no longer was alive to love, support, bicker, and tease each other.

Asked what the matter was, Susie said, "I just don't like her to cry."

Mr. Denver explained, in contradiction to the family's earlier presentation, "We're an emotional family. We cry with the best of them and we laugh with them too. Here, Sis, here's a handkerchief."

He did not seem to be damping down her feelings. He seemed to be giving his support to the work.

We gave the family our working hypothesis that swift military relocation had recalled the trauma of Mrs. Denver's childhood disruptions. Morgan's anxiety about being landed on by teachers and kids at school, as his father had been, was not yet manageable because it represented the return of anxiety about being landed on by an angry male, namely Mrs. Denver's father. This issue, which was Mrs. Denver's inner struggle, and for which Mr. Denver had a valency that we did not yet know enough about, had been silently transferred to the next generation. Despite, or rather because of, their success at ensuring no repetition of the maternal family pattern, the issue had been displaced to outside the family, where it haunted the son, whose vulnerability was particularly feared because of their need for him to survive attack, remain gifted, and stay alive, unlike the lost brother. The family accepted our recommendation for family therapy.

The group now understood the transformation that they had welcomed on the nonverbal videotape. They sensibly wondered if the mother's history, compelling though it was and deserving of intervention in its own right, may have been masking a similar problem of denial of affect in the father. All agreed that this was a workable family that they would expect to do well in family treatment. Someone expressed envy that they were easier to deal with than the clients she had to treat. Most of the group was convinced of the usefulness of examining their countertransference responses. All were interested to learn of difficulty in the co-therapy relationship and relieved to see the healing effect of confrontation, though some would not expect such a positive response on the part of their own co-therapists.

A final wrinkle, advantageous to the teaching effort, further illustrated the use of countertransference to comprehend the family's dynamics through the examination of one's own valencies. An interesting here-and-now parallel process occurred when we were sharing the task of small group discussion. The same dynamic was recreated between David and me as had been observed with the family. The group addressed their comments preferentially to David who responded and collated them with increasing intellectual vigor. I pointed out that he was over-functioning. He laughed with the group in recognition of his valency to deal with pressure that way. For my own part, I fell victim to my valency to make way for someone else. As before, when these dynamics were revealed, we recovered in time to make use of them.

WORKING WITH COUNTERTRANSFERENCE IN SUPERVISION

As a supervisor, I find that I am best understood when I work with my own feelings as I listen to the process report. Basing my comments on my experience, I model the process of using therapist experience to inform my interpretation of dynamics. Then supervisees feel encouraged to tell me their feelings about patients or clients. The following three examples demonstrate this way of working and illustrate different degrees of depth that can be achieved in the supervisor–supervisee relationship. Taken from work with supervisees of differing professional backgrounds and levels of experience, the examples come from the early, middle and late phase, respectively, of three separate year-long supervisions. Thus they give an impression of the development of the capacity to work in the countertransference.

Opening Phase Supervision of Family Therapy

Mrs. E., primarily an individual therapist, had recently begun to work with families and was consulting me for the second time

about a family case of a father and mother with an unruly teenage
boy. Her most recent family therapy session had been with only the
father and son. Mrs. E. did not work with this as an aberration, a
break in the frame. In fact, she did not deal with the mother's absence
at all. When I inquired about this, Mrs. E. explained that the wife had
not come because she had been working all the previous night. I
asked if she had discussed this with Mrs. E. the week before or had
telephoned. Mrs. E. said, "No, she hadn't intended to tell me. I only
know because I had called her to change the time from 9:30 A.M. to
11:00 A.M. and she said she couldn't come anyway."

I asked Mrs. E., "Do you have any thoughts about her suddenly not coming?"

"Perhaps it was because of all she said about her husband
when he wasn't there last week," Mrs. E. replied.

I was impressed with that idea, but it wasn't addressing the
transference. I said, "Might she have been angry at you for switch-
ing the time?"

Mrs. E. replied, "I didn't ask that. I thought I'd wait till the
next session when I would see her."

I thought that was fair enough, but I persisted, "Did you have
any thoughts about her not being there or did it seem okay to you?"

"Well," she replied, "I'd seen Tim and her the week before so
it seemed fine to see Tim and his Dad this week."

Mrs. E. then hurried on to give a detailed account of the
session in which Father and son "really got into it." Father had
reported that he had thought a lot about his tendency to fix things
and now felt it was not as helpful as he had thought. His father had
always been "the fix-it parent" for him, while his mother was "the
sympathetic ear." Tim and Mom were as close as he and his
mother, perhaps more so. Anytime Dad and Tim went fishing, Dad
resented it that Mom wanted to come along and make Tim a
mama's boy. Tim said that both parents were holding him back,
especially from having girlfriends; Dad said that Tim was totally
irresponsible. Father and son discussed this heatedly and returned

to the subject of Dad having to fix things. Mrs. E. reported making useful comments to facilitate the discussion.

> *I was feeling vaguely excluded or unnecessary. I had been waiting to hear something about the family's reaction or Mrs. E.'s response to Tim's mother's not being present on this "fishing trip" happening now in the therapy session. But I forgot about it as I joined Mrs. E. in following the father-son dialogue. I came to when Mrs. E. referred to me.*

She said, "I thought about what you said last week, that I should try to remember my comments. I remember that I said that it was strange that Dad had gone on for years fixing things instead of being there to help others take care of themselves and that no one had objected all these years."

It was a nice comment, edging up on an interpretation of the whole family's projection of competence into Dad and dependency into the others.

> *The part of it that empowered me was that Mrs. E. included me again. When she remembered my comment, I remembered that what I had been waiting for was mention of mother's absence. Until then I had been drifting along, lulled by Mrs. E.'s competent report. I felt uncomfortable to have let the issue of absence go to near the end of the session.*

Using my countertransference, I said, "I feel uncomfortable that I've gone along with the father-son pairing and have left the mother out in my work with your material."

"I mentioned it at the beginning," she interrupted, "but I guess it was not really addressed."

"We both noted it, but neither of us pursued it. When our beginning question about the meaning of an absence is not answered in words, we look for the answer in the process. 'Father and son really got into it,' you said to me, and you could have pointed out then that mother was being excluded. Then came another chance to make an interpretation based on your countertransference when you, yourself, were left out as the mother was. You missed that chance because I gather you weren't aware of being left out, but I believe that that is what you conveyed to me so that I felt left out by you and the family."

Mrs. E. did not address that directly. She said, "I had just given them a big bill for 800 dollars and I was nervous about that. It made me feel I should hurry up with the treatment." Apparently, she thought she should jump over obstacles of absence, allow the treatment frame to be bent, and work, blinkered, with only some of the family members before her, in the name of giving value for money. In fact, she was feeling guilty about her importance to them and its mounting cost. I guessed Mrs. E. might also be afraid of the family's anger at her if the whole group got together and expressed feelings about her charges and their indebtedness.

What made it difficult for Mrs. E. to face this was that I had not confronted her about her payment to me being late. I am quite observant about patients' actions around payment, and used to be with supervisees too. But previous students had been offended by my strict billing policies and I was trying to be more flexible with supervisees, who, after all, were not there to work on veiled expressions of their transference to me. This example of parallel process convinced me to return to a model of dealing with supervisees' payments with as much care as I would give to patients, exploring their feelings about their supervision without analyzing their infantile complexes. This provides a model consistent with that of careful attention to the patient's reactions to the frame that we are trying to teach.

Early Mid-phase Supervision

Dr. B., an experienced psychologist, had been in family therapy supervision with me for three months. Now she was doing a careful

child psychiatric diagnostic evaluation of a boy with elective mut-
ism. She had felt encouraged to include a family assessment interview as part of her evaluation and talked about her first session
with the whole family in her next supervision session with me.

Dr. B. began to describe the scene: "Mom and Dad just sat
there. Charlie, the mute index patient, and his older brother
Johnny shrank silently into the corner and the baby was asleep with
her coat on. I said, 'I'm glad everyone could come,' and I introduced myself and then I pointed out the toys. The kids just stood
and looked at them." Dr. B. looked at me pointedly as if to say,
"What are you going to do about it?"

> In my countertransference to Dr. B.'s countertransference, I
> was feeling I should do something.

I did speak, but only to ask about her experience. Thus I was
modeling what she might have done with the family. I asked Dr. B.
to tell me how she had felt at that moment. She said she felt she had
to coax them into life. She said she had to be very gentle and tactful
with this family because they had a "frozen, frightened-to-be-
attacked feeling."

I said to Dr. B., "That's great, you know what you felt. The
problem is that you tried to get over it and get them over it instead
of staying with it."

"Okay," said Dr. B. "I could have said 'I wonder what you
guys are expecting today?'"

"Right," I replied. "And later if they remained frozen, you
could have simply commented on what you observed in your
countertransference. You could say, 'I see the baby asleep and the
boys shrinking away and nobody speaking. I wonder if you see
something here to be frightened of?'" Dr. B. nodded and I suggested we go on.

Dr. B. said that Johnny, the older boy, started to play dominoes, while Charlie, the silent younger boy, watched, before picking up on whatever his brother did. The children played, the

mother talked with the doctor, and the father watched. When the
play got more enthusiastic, the mother told the boys not to be
noisy or they would wake the baby.

I suggested to Dr. B. that she might have interpreted that they
were afraid to make noise and mess because that would "waken the
baby," would bring up other issues and feelings that could otherwise remain silent.

Dr. B. then remembered that she had said, "Something makes
it hard to talk with the kids here." Then the mother had said,
"Well, they're listening now, but in the car journey we can talk
because they're playing." Dr. B. then asked the children what the
parents argued about. Johnny replied that he did not know. This
and other questions got her nowhere and she felt she was pumping
for information. The children's play got louder to drown her out.
She thought that the oldest boy was mad at her, but she did not say
so. As we talked, Dr. B. realized that the something that made it
harder to talk with the kids here was Dr. B. herself. She could have
said, "Perhaps you have some feelings about my being here. It
changes things because I am seriously trying to help everyone to
hear and respond to each other and to work together as a group." A
beginning therapist has still to learn to use her own discomfort.

Dr. B. went on, "I felt stalled. So I said, 'Draw something for
me.' But Father did not draw and neither did Johnny. As before,
they both watched. Mother drew five well-made heads and Charlie
drew one pair of feet."

Dr. B. showed me the drawings. She said, "I felt bad about
Charlie's drawing and so I wanted to improve it. I went ahead and
completed his picture."

Again she was acting upon her countertransference rather than
putting it to use. I gave her three options as examples of levels of
intervention that she could have used. She could have said to the
group, "Can anyone help Charlie out?" or better, "Charlie has
drawn feet. Do you have any ideas about that?" or, "In facing this
drawing task, the group divided up into those who drew and those

who didn't and then divided up the bodies into some with heads and one with feet. I think there's a worry about completing the family picture."

I asked Dr. B. to return to her process report. She said that the mother explained that she felt like Charlie, discouraged and inhibited about drawing because her father was a commercial artist. The father of her present family, her husband, chose this moment to criticize her, saying that her drawing made Charlie look like a girl. Mrs. Allen was silent. Charlie got mad and went back to playing dominoes. Johnny knocked them over and Charlie growled. Dr. B. said, "It seems to be hard to come up with the words for being hurt and angry." After this, Charlie drew and Johnny spoke of scary stuff like Dracula and skeletons.

As we discussed it, Dr. B. realized that this play was an answer to why it was hard to come up with the words. Speaking out was difficult because of anxiety about killing, stripping to the bone, and biting and sucking the life blood out of a victim. It would have been premature to spell that out right then, but still the family could have benefited from a simple comment such as "The skeleton and the Dracula are telling me of dangers and death worries that lie beneath the words."

Supervisors lead the way through sharing a broader vision of the issues so that supervisees can find their own way of understanding. But this requires tact and careful timing. We do not want to "complete the picture" for the supervisee. When Dr. B. did that for Charlie, she lost the opportunity to deal with the lack he was presenting for the family. Sometimes we find ourselves criticizing a student or showing off our skills and experience. A watchful eye has to be kept on our own countertransference—especially the one of enjoying being idealized—and also on the student's countertransference to our teaching. If we think of it as a countertransference, at least we will not be in the pitfall of seeing the student as having transferences to us, transferences that then imply the problem is the student's rather than a product of the student–teacher relationship. An example illustrating what happens when supervisors are not sympathetic to working with the countertransference may emphasize this point:

A student reported his experience of describing analytic material to a supervisor. The student trustingly discussed an extraordinary surge of sexual attraction he had been surprised to feel toward his female patient, because he was puzzled as to what this might mean. Sounding alarmed, the supervisor interrupted, "You wouldn't do anything like that, would you?" "Of course not," he replied—and didn't do anything like discussing his fantasies with his supervisor, either. He felt that this was the correct self-preservative move for him, but he regretted the constraint it put on his learning.

We want our students to be free to discuss their feelings about their families, their work, and about us, without fear of overreaction, censure, or inappropriate interpretation. We have to monitor the student–teacher relationship as we would the therapeutic alliance to be sure it is secure enough to support the emergence of difficult feelings and anxieties about accepting challenges. We want to create an environment of respect and trust with challenge and confrontation but without intrusiveness or patronizing.

Late Mid-phase Supervision

Dr. G., a well-trained child psychiatrist and psychotherapist, had moved into family therapy work about a year before. She had been consulting me for nine months and was now comfortable working with her reactions to the family she was presenting. She began her session with me by stating, "I have been practicing for ten years and never in all that time have I had such a reaction. I have never felt so horrible. I was made to feel totally incompetent—like nothing I'd say made sense. I was furious! And—I was amazed at this—I was nauseous, completely nauseous. Okay, now let me tell you what happened—" She then described a complex session that sounded ordinary enough, which only goes to show that the experience cannot always be conveyed by a report of the words spoken. The experience exists inside the therapist.

Mrs. B., the mother of the family, had called earlier that day to say that her daughter Maggie did not want to come because she was sick of being seen as a problem child. She also said that Maggie and her Dad had had a horrible fight during which he slapped her. Dr. G. felt upset by the call and said, "Let's talk about it in the session," to which the mother agreed. Dr. G., however, did not explore why the mother called ahead and did not use her own feeling of being disturbed by the call. Nor did she link the child's reluctance to the father's wish to stop coming, which he had expressed the previous session. Dr. G. went on to tell me of another event that took place outside the session: "When Father joined the others in the waiting room, he gave a big hug and kiss to the younger girl, Katie," said Dr. G. Her jaw dropped as she continued, "And nothing for Maggie." Dr. G. told me that she felt desperately sorry for the rejected child. Again, she had not brought this experience into the therapy session. All this is not to point out her mistakes, but to show how an experienced therapist can get taken over by a family's preference for ejecting meaningful patterns to outside the session. My ears pricked up when Dr. G. went on to say she had felt just devastated by the father's way of expressing his wish to send his problem daughter off to boarding school. She said, "The family is like a body with a sore on it. Get rid of the sore, cut it off, and the body is healthy again."

Although identifying with Maggie's pain, Dr. G. was also able to identify with the father's rage. She herself felt outraged at Maggie who was unremittingly horrible and nasty to her sister throughout this session and she herself strongly wished to evict her from the office. I showed Dr. G. how she could have used both identifications to help her say something about the object relations of the family, here enacted between Father and Maggie. For example, she could have said, "The family naturally wants rid of such a sore but every sore is also a scab. The sore indicates that there has been a problem and the scab is an attempt at healing. When everyone is understandably mad at Maggie, it's hard to give attention to what she might be trying to express for the family."

I also told Dr. G. that in my countertransference, the image of the waiting room scene had popped into my mind. Perhaps she could have used her experience of that scene to illustrate Dad's rage, Maggie's rejection, and to wonder whether a feeling of displacement by a cute little sister was what was troubling Maggie.

Dr. G. continued describing the session. Father had got Maggie to tell about their fight. Maggie spoke teasingly and smilingly of how Dad threw her on the bed and hit her face because he was so mad. Dr. G. felt uncomfortable about Maggie's apparent pleasure. Then Maggie and Katie got in a fight about the issue over the dog that led Dad to get so mad at Maggie. Katie, who was supposed to walk the dog for a full half-hour, returned after only five minutes. Maggie refused to answer the doorbell that Katie rang repeatedly. Dad was disturbed by the noise and asked Maggie to open the door. Maggie refused because she felt that Katie was in the wrong for not carrying out her responsibility in full. Everyone else thought that Maggie should have opened the door, so Dad sent Maggie to her room. When she stubbornly refused, he had to force her and that was how they got in a fight. Dr. G. paused.

I began to speculate about the dynamics of the interaction Dr. G. described. I suggested that at home Maggie and Dad gave vent to a struggle that also existed between Maggie and Katie but could not be addressed between them. In Dr. G.'s office, attention returned to the real source of conflict. Perhaps both the troubled dyads (Maggie/Dad and Maggie/Katie) were representing unexpressed conflict in the marital couple. Here we remain loosely open to various possibilities. Dr. G. explained that she could not make any such hypotheses because she felt convinced the father would annihilate whatever she thought. She was still stinging from his saying in the previous session that he hated to spend all his money on therapy just to fight, which they could do at home. She told me again that she felt horrible, totally incompetent, devastated, and nauseous. Now it was time to deal with her countertransference by addressing to her my own countertransference.

> *I began with what was on my mind. I associated to a family I have in treatment in which the father has the effect on me of breaking my linkages so that I frequently cannot remember what I have just said.*

I told Dr. G. how I had used that experience to understand why his daughter could not study. Dr. G., thinking that I was describing my own father, enthused about her father. "Oh, my father was nothing like that! He was the most wonderful, warm, supportive man!" As if I had been misrepresenting my own father's way of dealing with me, I immediately defended my father who, though not adoring of me, had never been as destructive as the father of the patient family I had been describing.

> *The main point of interest, however, was that I felt a twinge of jealousy about her adored father.*

I would not have invaded Dr. G.'s privacy to ask about her own father, but when she offered it, I found the information useful. I could guess that at the simplest level her distress might be due to being unfamiliar with a rejecting father. And I wondered silently if she had a sister that her father did not like or a mother who was an oedipal loser. Such questions might need to be asked at a later date if the supervisory process alone could not deal with her countertransference. At that point we would be dealing with Dr. G.'s transference. But for now we were still in the realm of workable countertransference, where I had registered my jealous response for future consideration.

What I did ask was whether Dr. G. had any associations to nausea.

"Oh, yes!" she replied, "As a child I'd get nauseous going to parties and I'd have to stay home."

As she spoke I recalled Dr. G.'s distress at the excitement in Maggie's description of her father's sadism and at the rejection of her during his hug with Katie. I said to Dr. G. that her association had helped me to see her countertransference as a response to repressed and denied excitement between daughter and father. If she could get to this, then later she might get to underlying problems between daughter and mother and eventually to the nature of the marital relationship.

"Yes, I should," Dr. G. replied, "because the kids said to their parents, 'Well, you guys fight, too.' Then the parents objected, 'When have you ever seen us fight?' 'We've heard you,' the kids really insisted. 'We've heard you yelling at each other when we're in bed.'" Dr. G. was now able to make all the connections she needed.

From here we went on to the theme of jealousy, led to it by my response to Dr. G.'s relationship with her father. We talked about Maggie and Katie's fight at the door as a struggle over who should be left out of Dad's affections, who should be left out of the family to keep it intact, and ultimately who would help with feelings of exclusion from a parental dyad that seemed insecure. Dr. G. noted that Maggie had provoked a hateful scene with her Dad to achieve physical closeness with him, a poor substitute for the warm embrace her sister got. Now Dr. G. began to work on how she could have used her feelings of rejection upon observing that scene in the waiting room to help her address this issue empathically.

As often happens late in a supervision session, a crucial piece of information could now be brought into the discussion. Dr. G. now happened to mention that Mr. B. had been out of town the previous week. Mrs. B. had asked if she could come with the girls to the appointment. Dr. G. had said that she could work only with the whole family—a position that is justifiable but arguable. Whether or not she made the right decision is not the point. The point is that now Dr. G. had brought into our session this information about the family being rejected by her. Where were their feelings about this? Now we could see the girls' fight over the locked door as a metaphor for family-wide feelings upon being excluded by the therapist. The family's unexpressed rage and longing, provoked by Dr. G.'s limit, was being picked up by her as a vulnerability to sensing other people's feelings of being left out, as a tendency to want to eject difficulty, and as an annihilated feeling so painful that she felt like vomiting it away.

It bears repeating that the point is not to examine the nature of the therapist's transference to her father or the origins of her childhood symptomatology. If these became permanent blocks to working with the family, then, of course, her infantile complexes would require therapeutic work—but definitely not with her supervisor. The aim is to help the therapist learn from her experience with the patients or clients and then to use that experience in communicating her understanding to the family. Referral for treatment is needed only when the countertransference is inflexible, incapable of modification in interaction with the supervisor and the patient or family and so constitutes a learning block.

Countertransference is not simply a technique for the therapist to invoke when stuck. It refers to a constant process of reviewing how the patient is giving one to feel. Mutual projective and introjective identification between patient (individual, couple, or family) and therapist occurs all the time. When things are going along smoothly, countertransference functions unconsciously as an automatic process of empathy. We have to stop and deliberately review it to monitor the transference. At times of greater difficulty, the countertransference obtrudes and calls for urgent attention. These times are easier to describe. We can be more convincing about the occurrence of projective identification because it has approached the more vivid, pathological end of the continuum. Nevertheless, at any time we could stop the therapeutic action in a freeze-frame and examine the countertransference. There in our own experience we find what we need to know to understand and to work with the projective identifications that characterize the transference to the therapist in individual psychoanalysis, couple, and family therapy, and in supervision.

12

The Therapeutic Action of Projective and Introjective Processes in Psychoanalysis

THE INHERITANCE FROM CLASSICAL THEORY

Freud (1917a) borrowed the term introjection from Ferenczi (1909) to apply to the taking in of an object of pleasure in an oral incorporative sense. Freud (1917a) noticed this introjective process was characteristic of people in states of mourning and melancholia. When the object is lost by death or disappearance, the ego invents a substitute object inside the self by identifying with and introjecting the lost object. This form of introjection was thought to enhance the ego (1921). Freud also applied his insight to the taking in of parts of the parents with which the child's ego selectively identified. When the

284

identification was in the area of the parental ideals, then what was introjected contributed to superego development. He did not, however, extend the concepts of introjection and identification to apply to the analysand's experience of the analyst. The analyst was to remain a mirror who faithfully reflected the patient's images and corrected distortions. Through disconnections between thought and feeling and internal conflicts, and between conscious and unconscious agencies of the personality revealed in the transference, the analyst like a good detective could come up with the good interpretation that the patient might resist but would ultimately accept. Freud did not write about the patient's identification with the analyst as an aspect of therapeutic process.

The psychoanalytic literature had focused on organizing data about the human mind into generalized hypotheses or scientific laws but the findings had not been applied to the therapeutic process (Strachey 1934). At first, therapeutic action was thought to derive from the analyst's determination and skill in demolishing the resistance against making conscious the unconscious source of the symptom. Following this, analysts realized that an important part of the unconscious to be made conscious was the area of repressed erotic feeling that operates as a resistance. In the next phase, it was realized that this infantile feeling attached itself to the analyst as a new object for its gratification or prohibition and that the transference consumed more and more of the analysis until the therapeutic task became that of analyzing the transference neurosis, while educating or encouraging the ego to be more tolerant of libidinal trends.

Searching for the elements of therapeutic efficacy, Strachey (1934) highlights interpretation as the remarkably effective weapon of psychoanalysis. He cautions against too many extra-transference interpretations. Instead, he emphasizes the importance of specific, detailed, and concrete transference interpretations of id-impulses given at the point of urgency. Because of their power to create change, he calls these *mutative interpretations*. This is what is usually remembered and quoted from Strachey's classic paper.

Without minimizing the mutative effect of interpretation on psychic structure, or the paper's mutative effect on interpretive technique, I want to focus on a relatively overlooked earlier part of the paper in which Strachey refers to the *context* for making the interpretations. He emphasizes the therapeutic action of the analytic relationship, getting to it from a consideration of the mother–infant relationship in Kleinian terms. He integrates Klein's views on introjection and projection in the development of the personality with Freud's theory of superego development. Then he proposes his own theory in which the crucial element of therapeutic action is the analysis of the vicious neurotic cycle in which a pre-genitally fixed ego is under pressure from a savage id on the one hand and a savage superego on the other. The analyst's intervention into this cycle is conceptualized as his taking over the functions of the superego and modifying it, but not demolishing it as Alexander (1924) had suggested. The analyst becomes an "auxiliary superego" in relation to the patient's ego (Strachey 1934, p. 139).

In a strikingly Kleinian passage, Strachey applies projection and introjection to explain his model for therapeutic action: "If, for instance, the patient could be made less frightened of his super-ego or introjected object, he would project less terrifying imagos onto the outer object and would therefore have less need to feel hostility towards it; the object which he then introjected would in turn be less savage in its pressure upon the id-impulses, which would be able to lose something of their primitive ferocity. In short, a benign circle would be set up instead of a vicious one" (Strachey 1934, p. 138). He then describes how the mutative interpretation has its effect in terms of introjection and projection: "When a neurotic patient meets a new object in ordinary life, according to our underlying hypothesis he will tend to project onto it his introjected archaic objects and the new object will become to that extent a phantasy object" (p. 139). Strachey warns the analyst to refrain from doing or saying anything that would confirm the phantasy expectations. Otherwise, he will lose the advantage of his auxiliary superego position from which to make his mutative interpretation.

Strachey's view is in line with the then current fear of countertransference as an interference with the therapeutic process. Provided the analyst can remain free of that sort of role induction, according to Strachey (1934), the patient can become aware of the distinction between his archaic phantasy object and the real external object. If the analyst is not retaliatory, the patient, being less fearful, is less aggressive. The object that he introjects is less aggressive, and consequently the aggressiveness of his superego is also diminished. As he reexperiences his early objects in relation to the analyst, the patient gains access to his infantile material.

In summary, Strachey conceived of therapeutic action as resulting from a combination of factors: the abreaction of emotions attached to the release of id-energy liberated in interaction with the analyst as an auxiliary superego, projection and introjection between patient and analyst in a repetition and reworking of the neurotic vicious circle, and extra-transference interpretations that build toward the specific mutative interpretation that he advocates, the latter being the most crucial element of therapeutic action—but not the only one. As he wisely notes: "A cake cannot be made of nothing but currants" (Strachey 1934, p. 158).

Loewald (1960) warns that classical analysis, the model of the mirror analyst, and the preference for classically analyzable analysands, have obscured crucial elements of the analytic process, namely the way the analyst works, the content and timing of his interpretations, and the way the patient integrates them. He suggests attending to such integrative processes as introjection, identification, and projection and studying their formation in early life, subsequent modification, and transformation in later stages of life. Loewald himself is convinced of the need for attention to these phenomena. Loewald (1960) writes: "The child, by internalizing aspects of the parent, also internalizes the parent's image of the child—an image which is mediated to the child in the thousand different ways of being handled, bodily and emotionally. . . . In analysis, if it is to be a process leading to structural changes, interactions of a comparable nature have to take place" (p. 20).

These interactions and the patient's integrative experience of them are less noticeable in healthy ego states. When the analysis or therapy is going along smoothly, the process can be easily overlooked, because it has been taken for granted, as it should be.

More recently, Duncan (1989), a British Independent Object Relations theorist, commented on the constraint imposed by allegiance to the old view of the analyst as objective observer and natural scientist. This view has excluded from study a major aspect of the interpretive process, namely the contribution of the analyst's subjectivity. The analyst brings his personality to bear not only in terms of countertransference responses to the patient's material, but in terms of his sensibilities, vulnerabilities, and ideas, including his preferred theory.

A KLEINIAN VIEW

Klein was not afraid to recognize vulnerabilities and was well aware of the influence of the analyst's personality on the progress of treatment. She was more likely to attribute a countertransference to the analyst's pathology than to resonance with the patient's pathology. She adhered to the classical view of countertransference as a problem to be got out of the way, so that the analyst could once more see the patient clearly. Although tuned in to the interaction with the patient, her focus was always on the patient in therapy—or on the infant in her formulations of the infant–mother relationship.

Klein used introjective identification in her own way to describe the taking in of good and bad experience in the early months of life. But somehow, "taking in" has been less thought-provoking to theoreticians than "putting out." Similarly, introjective identification as a defense against badness has been of greater interest than introjective identification with what is good and satisfying. Perhaps this is because in development the introjection of goodness is taken for granted and becomes a background of satisfactory, wholesome psychic structure, whereas conflict occurs around frustration and bad experience then has to be metabolized. In our phallocentric culture, it may be that "putting out" catches the imagination more readily than "taking in," which has oral and vaginal connotations. Just as the phallus requires the vagina to take it in for purposes of pleasure, bonding, and procreation, and the vagina has to have a penis to encompass in spontaneous, automatic rhythms, so do the processes of introjective and projective identification go together. The analyst's empathy depends on the spontaneous, unconscious operation of introjective and projective identificatory processes.

Another Kleinian, Heimann (1954) offers the following clear distinction between the two types of identificatory processes: "In *introjective* identification the subject's ego becomes like that of the object; *projective* identification render's the object's ego like that of the subject" (p. 166, my italics).

Just as introjection and projection lead to identification in development, so do they lead to identification between analyst and analysand (Heimann 1954). Such identification enables the analyst to understand the patient, but only if it is made conscious and controlled. The analyst is introjecting the patient in an empathic, freely responsive, fleeting way with the motive of understanding, uncontaminated by infantile motives of dominating the patient. Otherwise, unrecognized identifications by the analyst of the patient as an object of the analyst's parent–child history derail the countertransference. Their origin in defective sublimation of the analyst's oedipal complex requires further analysis, after which the analyst's introjective function is free to operate again. In Heimann's view, as in Strachey's (1934), introjection of the analyst is essential for modifying the patient's superego. The impulses that determine which aspects of the analyst are introjected also determine which of them are ego-syntonic for the patient and which of them—because of indiscriminate introjection without identification or projection—operate like loose cannons within the patient's psyche.

Heimann (1954) thinks that the processes of introjective identification are particularly troublesome between training analyst and

candidate and require careful attention. I think that is simply one
area in which the analyst's valency for identification is particularly
likely to come under scrutiny of analytic colleagues who, having
access to the candidate and to information as to the name of the
candidate's analyst, are in a unique position to observe the extra-
analytic enactments of introjective identificatory processes. The
phenomenon is probably widespread but unexamined in other
situations. Heimann's observation usefully draws attention to the
existence of *mutual introjective identification between analyst and
analysand.*

A BRITISH INDEPENDENT VIEW

Duncan (1981) speaks of the positive aspects of such identification
for the analyst in training. He claims that the analyst's "capacity for
maintaining the analytic act was enhanced by the inner confidence
he gained in mastering an area of his own personality in identification with the working ego of his training analyst" (p. 345). Here
introjective identification provides the structure of the analyst's
sensibility. Duncan mentions three features of therapeutic action:
the analysis of the analytic atmosphere (1990), the collateral interpretive flow prior to the making of a firm interpretation (1989),
and intersubjective knowing (1981) into which the analyst is led by
the transference neurosis. In my view, all of these depend on
processes of introjective and projective identification.

THE ANALYSIS OF THE ANALYTIC ATMOSPHERE

Clues to the projective and introjective processes that determine
the patient's use of the therapist as an object are commonly gained
from the analyst's detection of a feeling, thought, or fantasy arising
in association to the patient's material. Duncan (1990) draws our
attention to another clue—the presence of an atmosphere that is

symptomatic deserves attention and can be analyzed. Duncan (1990) realizes that affects and countertransference contribute to the development of atmosphere. Nevertheless, he contends that atmosphere does exist separable from affect, countertransference, and projection, and so it deserves autonomy as a new concept for understanding therapeutic action.

I have certainly been aware of an atmosphere during sessions. I have thought of it as a coloration of the transitional space in which therapist and patient are at play. At such a time when there is an atmosphere, the transitional space is almost tangible. Certainly it deserves independent status, but I cannot consider it apart from the related concepts of introjection, projection, affect, and most conclusively, countertransference. Atmosphere that becomes intense enough to intrude upon the analyst's consciousness is a reflection of the transference–countertransference. I believe that countertransference may be projected onto things. Such an impersonal thing as atmosphere is given the feature of a feeling state because it has not been possible to experience the feeling inside either patient or analyst. In other words, the countertransference is projected onto the impersonal dimension in response to a transference that is being deflected from the analyst to the space between analyst and patient. There in the gap it may flourish. Attention to it can then lead to its reintegration into the analysis.

INTERSUBJECTIVE KNOWING

The analyst's task is to face the unknown without foreclosure. At the same time, she is willing to know without striving to know what cannot yet be known. What she knows about the patient will depend on what she knows about herself in interaction with other patients and family members, and on what she can learn about herself in relation to the present patient. Understanding of the patient's use of the object and experience of the self comes from the process of being used and related to. Even when the patient's or her own defenses or anxieties make it uncomfortable for her, she holds to the task. The analyst persists, and so does the patient. The patient pushes on through defense and resistance toward the development of the transference neurosis. Bringing her own object relations set with its strengths and weaknesses to interact with the patient's transference neurosis, the analyst comes to know and be known by the patient in a way unique to their relationship. This has been called *intersubjective knowing* (Duncan 1981). This process of projective identification of the analyst as the essential object is accompanied by a corresponding introjective identification by the analyst with the object so that the use of her is a living reality. The introjective identification is, however, temporary, in that it is subject to review and reworking so that the projective identification is modified. Simultaneously, the analyst is projecting parts of her self and objects into each of her patients, motivated to help her patients by finding in them parts that she can understand and help. Duncan (1981) concludes "therapeutic shift varies directly with the extent of intersubjective knowing achieved" (p. 344).

THE COLLATERAL INTERPRETATION

The psychoanalytic literature has given more attention to what is said than to what is not said. Duncan (1989) points out that theoreticians have focused upon interpretations, those highly valued, forceful, and supposedly effective tools of the trade, and have ignored the analyst's associative flow prior to making the interpretation. In correction of this omission, he explores and reports on his own pre-interpretive process. He describes an experience of the ebb and flow of readiness to speak and waiting for something to say. He thinks of this activity as an extension of the usual evenly suspended attention that the analyst brings to the session. Unspoken, unformed tentative interpretations change their shape in response to shifting impressions and guesses. This provisional or trial interpretive flow is called the *collateral interpretation* (p. 699).

It seems to me that Duncan's three concepts of atmosphere, intersubjective knowing, and the collateral interpretation devolve upon the same issue and lead us to the same conclusion: we can learn as much from a study of the background as from the foreground. Introjective and projective identificatory processes occur in the space between people as well as in the intrapsychic realm. Therapeutic action depends upon recognizing and modifying these processes wherever they occur.

CONTRIBUTIONS FROM THE PROCESSES OF MOTHER-INFANT INTERACTION: BION, WINNICOTT, LOEWALD

Therapeutic action may be conceptualized as a refinement of the processes of the mother-infant relationship. Just as there is no such thing as a mother without an infant, there cannot be a doctor without a patient, therapist without a client, or analyst without an analysand. The relationship is the medium for fostering development. Like a devoted mother in a state of primary maternal preoccupation (Winnicott 1956), the therapist or analyst attends to the patient's communications, and remains potentially equally receptive to hateful, friendly, anxious, contented, or erotic content. The therapist then metabolizes this content in an internal process in the realm of thought to which Bion (1962) gave the term *reverie*, "that state of mind which is open to the reception of any 'objects' from the loved object and is therefore capable of reception of the infant's projective identifications whether they are felt by the infant to be good or bad. . . . The mother's capacity for reverie is here considered as inseparable from the content for clearly one depends on the other" (p. 36). Bion refers to an aspect of Klein's theory of projective identification in which the infant projects a part of its psyche, namely its bad feelings into a good breast where they are modified and can then be re-introjected in tolerable form. From this theory, Bion got his idea of the container-contained model of human interaction. He thought of the mother and her breast as the "container" into which are projected objects that he called "the contained" (1962, p. 70). The contained objects are metabolized by the mother's alpha function, a processing property of the state of reverie. The infant identifies with the containing function as well as with the container as an object. Applied to the analytic situation, the container-contained idea offers the analyst a model for dealing with the patient's projections.

A strikingly similar view of therapy is expressed by Loewald (1960) who writes: "The whole complex dynamic constellation is one of mutual responsiveness where nothing is introjected by the infant that is not brought to it by the mother, although brought by her often unconsciously. And a prerequisite for introjection and identification is the gathering mediation of structure and direction by the mother in her caring activities" (p. 24). Analysis provides a similar structuring interaction. The analyst works with the transferences in an evolving relationship to objects experienced in relation to the analyst at progressively higher levels of development and understanding. In the course of this, analyst and patient have "integrative experiences that are the foundation for the internalized version of such experiences" (p. 25).

It seems to me that Bion's idea of container-contained applies just as well to the patient's preoccupation with the analyst and the analytic process. The patient is asked to contain the analyst's projective identificatory attempts at empathy and interpretation and transform them into something good enough to make a difference. Loewald approaches the same conclusion: "We postulate thus internalization of an inter-action process, not simply internalization of 'objects,' as an essential element in ego-development as well as in the resumption of it in analysis (p. 30).

Winnicott (1951) subscribes to a model of therapeutic action that is also derived from the mother–infant relationship. He writes: "Psychologically the infant takes from a breast that is part of the infant, and the mother gives milk to an infant that is part of herself. In psychology, the idea of interchange is based on an illusion"

(p. 239). Winnicott puts this illusion to work in therapy, where therapeutic effect is achieved in the transitional space created by the conjunction of the two personalities of patient and analyst at play. Guntrip (1986) affirms that Winnicott holds that "psychoanalytic interpretation is not therapeutic *per se*, but only as it expresses a personal relationship of genuine understanding" (p. 448).

AN OBJECT RELATIONS VIEW OF PERSONALITY AND THERAPY: FAIRBAIRN

Fairbairn viewed the personality as consisting of a conscious and unconscious system of parts of the self, intimately bound to the relevant objects. He moved away from instinct theory and held that the human infant is motivated not by the need to discharge impulses deriving from instinctual tension, but by the need to be in a relationship. During infantile dependency on the life-imparting and structure-building mother-infant relationship, the personality is split by the trauma of inevitably frustrating early experience, into a conscious central system available to learn, interact, and grow, and into an unconscious system, further split into two parts. The most deeply repressed of these is the "libidinal" or needy part, and the other is the "antilibidinal" or angry part, which attacks the needy part and prevents its expression. Similarities between the object relations approach and Kohut's nonclassical theory of self-psychology are readily apparent. Kohut (1982) regards the personality as consisting of "the not-further-reducible psychological unit of a loving self, a lusting self, an assertive self, a hostile-destructive self" (p. 401). Like Fairbairn, he does not see instincts as primary but regards them as disintegration products of failed attempts at psychic structure building.

These positions on the theory of personality have implications for a theory of therapy. In brief, if the relationship with the caretaking person is critical in the development of personality, then the relationship with the therapist is held to be of equal importance. The examination of the qualities of the new relationship and its similarities to and differences from the original relationship with the caretaker is a significant part of the therapeutic task. Classical theory has not fully addressed this issue, even though some classical analysts have written about the transference and the therapeutic alliance, the real relationship between patient and therapist, and the occurrence of countertransference responses. Loewald (1960) holds that "classical formulations concerning therapeutic action and concerning the role of the analyst in the analytic relationship do not reflect our present understanding of the dynamic organization of the psychic apparatus" (p. 16). Loewald suggests that we stop taking the object relationship between patient and analyst for granted and start focusing more carefully on the object relationship as the drive of therapeutic action.

Whether of classical orientation or not, the analyst's theory guides his technique. Theory itself is an object. The chosen theory is an object capable of carrying the therapist's projective identifications in its abstract matter. The therapist or analyst takes in the theory by introjective identification, and so that theory becomes one of the analyst's internal objects that may or may not fit with and be used well by various patients. My own view is that people are so complicated that no one theory encompasses all types. I do not propose doing away with earlier theories that apply in classically analyzable cases. I simply want to overemphasize introjective and projective identificatory processes appropriate to a well-developed object relations theory of therapy. In the past, these processes have been underemphasized in the name of promoting theories that appear to fit the demands of scientific objectivity and that have, therefore, failed to address the intersubjective field.

Applying his object relations theory to the study of therapeutic action, Fairbairn (1958) writes: "In terms of the object relations theory of the personality, the disabilities from which the patient suffers represent the effects of unsatisfactory and unsatisfying object-relationships experienced in early life and perpetuated in an exaggerated form in inner reality; and, if this view is correct, the actual relationship existing between the patient and the analyst as persons must be regarded as in itself constituting a therapeutic factor of prime importance (p. 377). He continues: "*The chief aim of psycho-analytical treatment is to promote a maximum 'synthesis' of the structures into which the original ego has been split, in the setting of a therapeutic relationship with the analyst*" (p. 380). "It is necessary for the patient's relationship with the analyst to undergo a process of development in terms of which a relationship based on transference becomes replaced by a realistic relationship between two persons in the outer world" (p. 381). "The actual relationship between the patient and the analyst constitutes the decisive factor in psycho-analytical, no less than in any other form of psychotherapeutic cure" (p. 385).

EXAMPLES FROM PRACTICE

Extending Fairbairn's application of object relations theory to the practice of psychotherapy and psychoanalysis, I find it necessary to look at processes of introjective and projective identification between patient and therapist. I will do this by looking at three related analyses reported in the literature and then by two clinical illustrations from my own therapeutic relationships.

Projective and Introjective Identificatory Processes at Play in Three Related Analyses

Guntrip provides us with a marvelous opportunity to study projective and introjective processes at play in what amounts to a transgenerational view of interdigitating analyses. I refer to Guntrip's (1986) report of his analyses with Fairbairn and Winnicott, now enriched by Hazell's (1991) account of his analysis with Guntrip, the latter part of which was contemporaneous with Guntrip's analysis with Winnicott. Guntrip's views on therapy were in accord with Fairbairn's theoretical approach, which emphasizes breaching the closed system of early object relationships. This suggested to Guntrip that Fairbairn would be in touch with the infant's relation to his mother. Instead, Guntrip, as his patient, found that Fairbairn insisted on exact, oedipal interpretations. Compounding the effects of this, the unexpected formality of Fairbairn's manner attracted from Guntrip a rejecting maternal transference that viewed Fairbairn as a distant yet dominating mother who imposed interpretations upon him. This tended to perpetuate rather than analyze at source and heal the early object relations system that Guntrip had to bear in himself. In contrast, he experienced Fairbairn as a warm and affectionate fatherly colleague after the formal session was over. So the transference was split, either by the force of Guntrip's trauma or, as Guntrip implies, by Fairbairn's difficulty in relating to him. Guntrip concedes that useful work was done in the sessions. He learned from Fairbairn that his main symptom, namely relapsing into exhaustion illness, derived from the trauma of seeing his infant brother, Percy, dead on his mother's lap. It related to his guilt over surviving his brother who died, apparently for no other reason than that his mother could not keep him alive. At the time of the trauma, Guntrip himself, aged 3½, collapsed with grief and had to be sent to the care of an aunt, who had the maternal warmth that his business-woman mother lacked; she recalled him to the land of the living. His own mother lacked the energy for nurturing children, because she had had more than her share of mothering babies as the oldest girl of eleven siblings.

With Fairbairn's help, Guntrip successfully analyzed his maternal transference during the oedipal stage, and he worked on his withdrawn states as a defense against the repressed battles with his mother. These in turn were seen as an attempt to force his mother to mother him and as a defense against the pain of reliving the trauma of his brother's death. This is a more classical formulation of pathology than Fairbairn's object relations theory would have suggested. Guntrip disagreed with Fairbairn that the trauma was the cause of his problems and became convinced that they derived from the problem of fit between himself and his severe mother long before similar problems in fit were thought to have led to his brother's death. Despite their shared convictions and collegiality, Guntrip could not experience a good fit with Fairbairn as an analyst. He was not able to use Fairbairn as a maternal object other than in the transference version. He did not recover the memory of seeing his dead brother and he was unable to heal the part of himself that had been traumatized and damaged in relation to that event and the mother who could not prevent it.

Not satisfied with his outcome and recognizing that Fairbairn by 1960 was no longer fit for the strenuous work of analysis, Guntrip sought analysis with Winnicott, a much more informal, comfortable person than Fairbairn. Guntrip regarded the two analysts as being theoretically on similar ground, but found that Winnicott was more revolutionary in practice than in theory whereas Fairbairn was more orthodox in practice than in theory. Interestingly, Hazell (1991), noting a similar discrepancy between what Guntrip believed and wrote and how he was as Hazell's analyst, writes: "It was difficult at times to reconcile so gifted a writer, whose writings exuded a depth of compassionate understanding, with the noisy and often intrusive personal reality" (p. 149). How interesting that Hazell had a negative experience of Guntrip's restlessness, just as Guntrip had been affected by Fairbairn's reserve. Both analysands report a problem in using the analyst as an object free to respond to early object relations and readily available for introjective identification because of the analyst's defenses against intimacy. In Hazell's case, however, this discrepancy between theory and practice eventually diminished to Hazell's benefit. In his words, "I had become involved, fortuitously, in Guntrip's increasing growth in relation to Winnicott, as my own therapy progressed" (Hazell 1991, p. 149).

This raises the question for me: What accounts for the therapeutic action in treatment with Winnicott? The relationship was felt to be one that fostered growth. Hazell (1991) says more: "It was not until, under Winnicott's influence, this 'strong father-figure' developed a capacity for maternal warmth that I felt radically eased of my internal burden" (p. 153). It seems to me that Guntrip introjected Winnicott as a good maternal object with whom he experienced a degree of fit in contrast to what he had known before. I suggest that he had also introjected the relationship in such a way that he could then offer Hazell a different, more personal therapeutic environment.

Fairbairn had concentrated on the reconstruction of Guntrip's object relations in the period after age 3½. Winnicott no doubt capitalized on the previous analytic work and took it further, even though the sessions were separated by weeks and numbered only 150. What made the difference to the present analysis of Guntrip were Winnicott's stunning and profound insights into the earlier period of life that had not been touched in analysis with Fairbairn. Guntrip was able to reach down to "*an ultimate good mother, and to find her recreated in him in the transference.*" They got to the basic problem "not the actively bad mother of childhood, *but the earlier mother who failed to relate to me at all*" (Guntrip 1986, p. 460). "Winnicott, relating to me in my deep unconscious, enabled me to stand seeing that it was not just the loss of Percy, but being left alone with the mother who could not keep me alive, that caused my collapse into apparent dying" (p. 462). Winnicott had a way of being experienced as a nonrelating mother while, nonetheless, actively relating empathically to that experience. In other words, he could accept a projective identification, contain it, and return it detoxified by his own empathy in modified form suitable for reintrojective identification by the patient.

Winnicott's death triggered a startlingly vivid dream sequence in which Guntrip saw his mother, black, immobilized, and depressed, staring into space, sometimes even without face, arms, or breasts, and ignoring him while he felt frozen into immobility. Guntrip was now able to break his lifelong amnesia for the infant death and see his dead brother in a dream. In this image, he confronted his collapsed infantile self and the immobilizing effect of his depressed, unseeing mother who could not even keep her surviving child alive by her own efforts. That was the deeper trauma. Now Guntrip's overactive lifestyle and manner can be viewed as an extension of the exhaustive effort required to keep the child within from dying.

Guntrip's report emphasizes the modification of this projective identification of Winnicott as the abandoning mother through Winnicott's being able to bear and speak of the void Guntrip experienced in him, yet remain an emotionally available analyst. What does Guntrip have to say of introjective identification? About the abandoning mother, he says that Winnicott had "taken her place and made it possible to remember her in an actual dream-reliving of her paralyzing schizoid aloofness" (pp. 464–465).

I note Guntrip's projective identification of Winnicott as the unresponsive mother and his projective identification of the late Winnicott with his dead Percy. I am interested in Guntrip's introjective identification with his dead brother, and its repetition in his exhaustion illnesses that followed losses over the years. I am struck by his experience of his mother as black, immobile, and depressed. The image reminds me of what Tustin (1981) called "the black-hole Mommy," a desperately terrifying image of destruction and depletion. In Hazell's (1991) summary of her history, Guntrip's mother was a woman who "prematurely *exhausted* (my italics) by overwhelming responsibility in her family of origin, was not up to caring for her own children" (p. 149). Talking of Winnicott's formulation of Guntrip's dynamics, Hazell writes: "He realized that Guntrip's attempted self-cure, of living energetically for others, was achieved at the cost of exclusion of 'self' which collapsed, too *exhausted* (my italics) and too weak to feel alive" (p. 150).

From the repetition in Hazell's use of the word "exhausted" I am fortuitously drawn to another observation of introjective identification. I am referring to Guntrip's introjective identification with his mother's exhaustion, his infantile way of being close to a woman who seemed to have no face, arms, or breasts for him. In turning his schizoid withdrawal into an object of study for helping others, Guntrip thought that he had identified with the life-giving relatives in his aunt's bustling family for whom he stayed alive. I suggest that a further motivation may have been to revive the substitute life-support activities his mother had performed with energy as the oldest daughter of a large family, before her maternal capacities were eroded by overuse before their time. Thus he would not only be bringing to life himself in relation to a life-giving object (his aunt, his patients). He would be bringing to life his dead object (his mother, Percy). And in his article he brings to life the late theorists, Fairbairn and Winnicott, who are not dead for him or for us.

MUTUAL INTROJECTIVE AND PROJECTIVE IDENTIFICATION: HEALING THE OBJECT IN THE TRANSFERENCE

Therapeutic action results from using the object via projective identification in the transference and healing the object or bringing the dead object to life in the analytic relationship. Therapeutic action also involves finding a lost part of the self in the analyst and recovering it through introjective identification. It seems to me unlikely that the internal object or projected part of the self will be healed if the analyst into whom they are projected cannot experience and benefit from the healing process. As Guntrip (1986) put it, analysis is "a process of interaction, a function of two variables, the personalities of two people working together towards free spontaneous growth. The analyst grows as well as the analysand" (p. 465).

One of Winnicott's interpretations to Guntrip attests to this positive effect of the patient on the analyst. Reportedly, Winnicott actively declared himself gratified by the patient, like a mother who finds her child wonderful. Guntrip quotes Winnicott's interpretation to him as follows: "You too have a good breast. You've always been able to give more than take. I'm good for you but you're good for me. Doing your analysis is almost the most reassuring thing that happens to me. The chap before you makes me feel I'm no good at all. You don't have to be good for me. I don't need it and can cope without it, but in fact you are good for me" (Guntrip 1986, p. 462).

Mutual Introjective Identification and Recovery of Parts of the Self

In my own experience, a patient cured me of suppressing my desire to eat a lot, and he recovered from his inhibition against eating enough. This patient, Andy, was first introduced in Chapter 3. The present vignette is taken from later in therapy. After a period of progress and confrontation of conflict over oedipal fantasy, Andy was once more severely troubled by his eating problem. He began to wonder if he was more accurately to be diagnosed as anorexic. I thought not, because he preferred the appearance of his body when it was heavier and he spent no time envying skinny bodies. In one aspect, however, he was like an anorexic, namely in that he had lost the desire for food, a characteristic of eating disorder pointed to by Ogden (1989).

Andy began the session by talking about why he had chosen to work with me. Unable to get late afternoon times to suit his rehearsal schedule, he correctly surmised that I had a part-time practice. "As a woman working part-time," he said, "You offer me an alternative view to my Dad who worked and traveled all the time, my stepfather who spends Saturdays and Sundays at the business, or my Mom who can't think of working. I guess I'm looking for a model of how to work and still be generous with my time."

I heard in this comment a search for an object to introject. Since weight loss was still the dominant threat to holding a job, I chose to explore how he might be taking me as a model of intake. Dehydration being an issue for him, he must have noticed that I have fluids that I drink as I work. I asked, "What ideas do you have about my eating habits?"

"I know you drink plenty," he replied. "And I'm sure what you eat is very healthy, sensible."

As he continued in this vein, eating began to sound like a chore, not the way I experience food at all. To my surprise, he went on to speculate about my breakfast.

"You might have a bran muffin spread with cream cheese, not too much, not gobs of it, but enough, just the right amount. And a glass of grapefruit juice, yuk, no, orange juice if you have a sense of humor. It's sweeter. And some fruit. Not raisins or prunes, they're gross. Yes, a banana! And some decaffeinated tea. And the children probably have cereal or oatmeal, and you might have some oatmeal, too."

My mouth was watering. At my age and in my sedentary occupation, I cannot eat as much as that on a daily basis without gaining weight or having to skip lunch! I could see the oversize muffin on the plate, its sides dripping over the edge of the pan, the kind I usually pass by when I'm at the bakery. It was beckoning to me—250 calories at least. And with cream cheese! Decaf tea is just what I like first thing in the morning, too.

Examining my countertransference, I saw that he had invoked in me a wish for this food. I guessed that there was a projective identification of me with his healthily hungry self that I had taken in by introjective identification.

I said, "Well, you've given me a tasty and nutritious breakfast to enjoy. What keeps you from doing that for yourself?"

"Oh," he replied, "I wasn't thinking of it as tasty. I was thinking of what would be sensible. The kind of thing you'd eat."

I said, "You weren't thinking of the food being delicious and stimulating the appetite. You were just itemizing a menu, as far as you were concerned, but I think that you were designing a delicious meal for me to enjoy, and you gave me different food from the children."

"Oh yes," he interrupted. "Grown-up food for you. And I gave you the banana 'cause I thought that was Freudian. You could really get off on that."

I said, "You gave me a special breakfast for a grown-up—including a piece of fruit that was like a penis for me to enjoy. But *you* weren't thinking of the enjoyment at all. You put all the desire for the food into *me*."

He seemed to relax, laughed and said, "You called it tasty! It probably is, so why can't I eat something like that? Good question.

Maybe I could. I'd forgotten about oatmeal. We always had that as kids, with lots of honey on it. I loved that. Even the cream cheese—I could see trying that on a muffin."

It seemed to me that Andy had projected into me a disavowed pleasure in feeding from the breast and the penis. In the counter-transference I temporarily introjectively identified with his pleasure, based on my valency to enjoy a tasty, nutritious meal. I did not act it out, however, but simply savored it, presumably because it was not so painful that I had to repress it into my unconscious. Then Andy re-introjected his projection after it was valued and cherished as a projective identification in me. Andy also introjected my pleasure in food, communicated through my counter-transference-based interpretation. I was interested to see what effect this might have on his food intake.

Next session, Andy came in shaved and all dressed up, his raggedy jeans and tee shirt replaced by new cords and a colorful plaid shirt. He told me that he intended to get back to normal weight in a month. I was slightly disappointed but not really surprised to learn that his eating habits had not yet changed, or so he led me to believe at first.

"All I ate was half an apple at ten o'clock last night," he began. "I was going to put peanut butter on it but Mom took a great gob of it, so I didn't feel like it."

I thought to myself that his mother had taken away his appetite. Would this qualify for description as an extractive introjection (Bollas 1989) on her part? Had he experienced me as extracting his appetite yesterday? I awaited more information.

He went on, "I took the peanut butter to the dining room table yesterday and left it up to whether I had the desire for it, because I had the desire for the apple and that makes it easy to eat."

Here he was using my word "desire" from the day before. I felt some satisfaction that my interpretation had been heard and taken in, after all.

"So," Andy continued, "Mom took a gob of my peanut butter. I've been trying to convince her that the brand I buy is better than hers. So I go 'Doesn't that taste better?' And she goes 'I don't know.' So she took a taste—a whole tablespoon of my peanut

306 The Use of the Therapist's Self

butter. I just eat a half teaspon at a time. Then she took another! That much! So I just ate half the apple and gave up.

"Now yesterday my stomach was aching all day and I thought 'Maybe that's hunger, but I just don't have any appetite, so I think it's pain. But if it's hunger I should eat.' And I did. I did very well thinking up things to eat all day, well, quite well for a first day. But the ache didn't go away. But I did eat some things.

"Like you said, I went right home and had a muffin, cream cheese even, and a banana, and that was okay. But I had a vanilla milk shake too, and I couldn't finish it. And in the afternoon I had oatmeal, and a hard-boiled egg. And then I ate the regular dinner Mom cooked. I was really happy about the egg, because I've been off eggs. That went very well. I've had more appetite in the last day than I've had all last week. Oh and I even ate a chocolate chip cookie and a whole slice of Swiss cheese."

Mutual Introjective Identification

What had happened between us was a mutual introjective identification and it had had a healing effect. But something different was happening now, something more like a forced introjection in himself and me. I thought this because of how I started to feel.

I noticed that in contrast to how I felt the day before, today I didn't want the food at all. I felt stuffed. As he went on to talk of not eating the peanut butter, I felt momentarily nauseated.

"I only ate half the apple," he repeated. "And the peanut butter went back on the shelf. I didn't eat it because I had no desire for it."

"All desire for it went to your Mom, just as yesterday you put all appetite for the breakfast into me," I suggested.

"She took two tablespoons!" he exclaimed. "And she didn't even use a spoon. Yuk! She did it with her finger."

Using my countertransference experience of nausea, I realized that my interpretation was not quite right. I was not simply identified with Andy feeling full. I must have been experiencing through introjective identification with Andy a feeling of disgust at the mother's taking of food. Perhaps the patient was experiencing an introjective identification with his mother. Now I felt ready to correct my interpretation.

I said, "No, I think it was different from what happened between you and me. Yes, you had no desire for the peanut butter, but in addition I think you felt revolted by your Mom's taking it."

"Yes!" he interjected.

I went on, "As your Mom took it on her finger, it was as if you had done it."

Yes!" he added.

"And so," I concluded, "you couldn't eat your half teaspoon because it was as if you had already eaten two tablespoonsful."

"Exactly!" he confirmed.

With the oral issue understood thus far, the session continued with Andy returning to oedipal themes affecting his family relationships and his ability to play on band jobs. He told me that he hoped to work on these issues intensively as soon as he gained enough weight so that getting upset, which could take the form of being unable to eat and therefore losing a pound or two, would not be critical.

In this example, my countertransference comprised an introjective identification with Andy's self, revolted by his object with which he had introjectively identified. Interpretation arrived at from inside my experience proved more accurate than one developed by cognitive association.

"Here's something I found in a drawer at home," Andy announced as he walked in for his next session. "Since it's about food, I brought it to show you. It's the only photo I have of me and my father. My Mom was so mad about him letting his work kill him that she threw out all the photos of him. But she didn't get this one. It was taken on my seventh birthday which falls on St. Patrick's day. I'd had three boys to sleep over and here we are in the morning at breakfast. Dad is slicing a green bagel and I look really happy. I held the photo to the mirror to see if my lip could be his lip. The nose was familiar and if I pull my chin back a bit, it looks like his. I stared at him in the picture. I thought it would talk.

"It's so bizarre. I have no memory of that party and no memory of my father either, except once I remember he drove me to school and there is that other memory of him going off in a plane. And that's it. I can't believe I have a dead father. My mother is alive and my stepfather is alive and my father whom I don't remember hardly at all is in the ground, his body rotting away. And I could dig it up and see it, which I have fantasies of doing, because I never saw him dead. I wonder what a body looks like after seventeen years? But to me he isn't anything, not even a dead body. He's more like the hole in the ground they put him into."

I said, "Yes, you have felt that he left a hole in you: no memory of him, no way to think of him alive, and no ability to eat food with holes in it, like bagels or pineapple rings or Swiss cheese, or mushy stuff that is not whole, or anything else."

"Well, I may actually have got over that," he responded. "I ate three meals yesterday and felt hungry for snacks. I may go back to being finicky," he allowed, "but yesterday I ate about everything. A voice said, 'I'm hungry. Go get an orange!' Another voice said, 'No you can't handle citrus.' And the first voice said, 'I want it. Go get it!' So I did and I thought 'This is bizarre!' I just went home and started eating like it wasn't a problem."

A few days later, he was still eating much better. "To tell you the truth," he said, "this eating thing is going pretty easy. I'm dying to know how much I weigh. Oh, look at that. There's the idea of dying and eating again. Okay, let me say, I am really looking forward to finding out how much I weigh."

I was impressed by Andy's new found capacity to create an image of his dead father. I realized that he had been unable to experience him in thought so he had distributed the repressed image of his father's rotting body throughout his food. Naturally this would make the food unappetizing and lead to his refusing the act of physical incorporation. His revulsion at the food and at the associated unconscious idea of eating his father's body was designed to protect the object from Andy's cannibalistic urges. At the same time, since avoidance of food made his body waste away, Andy was unconsciously gratifying his wish to incorporate his dead father's body. By this incorporative fantasy, Andy held onto his father in introjective identification with the object, and was thereby fortified to be his mother's new partner. Then even as an adult he could not leave his mother, because if he did he would expect to break her as the loss of his father had done, or to face her eradication of him by the same rage that had destroyed the image of his father.

Andy addressed this in his next session: "Mom had her heart broken by losing Dad. So what has she got now? A husband who works as much as Dad did—and me, a vegetable. And she won't have me forever, either. Which she knows. In fact, if I don't break free, I'll disappoint her. But if I do break free, I'll break her heart. I go from being her best friend to being incredibly angry with her. But if I don't do it, I won't live. I have to reject her. But if I do, what I feel is that *I'm* in my mother's place being thrown away. Maybe in years, I can go on to an idea of dealing with her and not having to feel her to be me. I wouldn't have to rip myself away to not feel totally taken over by her. The way I see it is it's either her or me. But how on earth am I going to do something that my only living parent has not done?"

When I was able to introjectively identify pleasurably with Andy's healthy appetite, and to become conscious of it, he was able to reintroject that aspect of himself. I was neither destroyed by it nor did I cannibalistically incorporate him. He was then able to think about his father and the impact of his death without being taken over by a deadening introjective identification. With more work of this kind Andy could expect to become capable of experiencing the man he had lost, integrating him as both an alive and dead object, and then mourning his loss, and thereby become able to face losing his mother as a person separate from himself.

In terms of Klein's schema, the patient in this example would be seen as moving, at least for now, out of the paranoid–schizoid position and into the depressive position. Processes of introjective and projective identification continue to occur in the depressive position, but they do so at a higher level of development farther along the continuum from pathology to health.

THE ANALYST AS AN OBJECT TO BE USED

We now have a view of analysis or therapy as a process in which the role relationship developing between patient and therapist functions as an experiential laboratory for the study of the internal object relationships that drive the patient to deal with the analyst the way he does. Hazell (1991) says that the point is not to explain the findings but to experience a "sympathetic identification" with the patient, and so to become "the person he needs in order for him to grow a nature of his own" (p. 164).

Loewald (1960) and Bollas (1989) both subscribe to this view. Loewald holds that objective interpretation of transference distortions are the vehicle through which the analyst becomes more and more available to the patient as a reinvented object, not a new object, but one discovered as the patient retraces the paths of the development of early object relations. In these experiences of the therapeutic relationship, the patient finds a "new way of relating to objects and of being himself" (Loewald 1960, p. 20).

Bollas holds that the analysand's destiny is to transform the analyst into a subjective object for internal possession while the analyst's destiny is to be used as the required object. Playing in the gap between the subjective and the actual object, the person of the analysand then finds its own being through its use of the object. Bollas calls for psychoanalysts to work with their subjective experience with integrity and to confront differences and accept challenges from their analysands so as to contribute to and celebrate the unique idiom of each person (Bollas 1989).

The Female Analyst's Biological Sensitivity to Introjective Identification

Johnny Cardozo, a 9-year-old boy, had been wetting and soiling, both at night and during the day, having temper tantrums, bickering, not doing well at his new school, and not making friends. He was the second child of unhappily married young parents. His mother said that she had nursed him for two years, "until the day he asked for lemonade." At that time, her marriage had been deteriorating, until she and her husband finally separated when Johnny was 2 years old. Weaning and loss of father coincided. Mr. Cardozo saw the children only occasionally the following year. Mrs. Cardozo secured a job, working 12 hours a day, and his sister, then aged 5, is said to have potty-trained Johnny. The real loss of both parents at this time traumatized him at the anal stage. Then, when he might have moved on to the phallic and oedipal phases, his father was not there to see him through. Johnny grew to expect object loss to follow developmental progress. He totally denied loss, demonstrated in his ostrich-like attitude to my impending vacations. He was afraid to let go of what he kept inside for fear there would be nothing to replace it. He was even afraid to speak. He coped with loss by retention—of urine, feces, and words.

Playing with me in analysis, Johnny was reluctant to be drawn into conversation, negated my observations, and destroyed everything he made. In general, he maintained a negativistic style of remaining separate while attempting to relate to me. Gradually, as analysis progressed, he became somewhat more talkative. He reworked his anal concerns, reviewed his worries about there not being enough food to replenish his stores, and moved on to phallic themes, concluding with his curiosity about the father's role in conception. When I tried to explore this with him, Johnny balked, promptly rushed out of the room, and refused to acknowledge curiosity. I tied his interest, and also his denial of it, to his conflict over asking questions that might concern me. I had become pregnant, and it was just beginning to show. He became completely silent.

From the level of phallic interest and cooperative, somewhat verbal play, he regressed to solo, nonverbal play at primitive levels. He spent hours reading or grunting in the dark space between the double doors to my office, or hiding behind the couch, or snug in a corner hugging two large cushions. I interpreted this behavior as his retreat from sexual anxiety and fear of retaliation to the safety of being enclosed. He said nothing. One day, when more obviously pregnant, I was wearing a striped sweater similar to a throw rug in the office. He crawled under the rug and burrowed around. As I watched the stripes on the rug heave and flatten, I felt that his turning there was like the fetal movements under my sweater. In reality, my baby was not moving at that moment, so it seemed as if Johnny was moving around inside now. I said, "You do not want to give me your words but nevertheless you want to show me how you long to be perfectly held and cared for and fed effortlessly, as if you were inside my body like the baby growing there."

As usual there was no reply, but he went into the corner nestled between two breastlike cushions, where he thumped and grunted for a few sessions. I said, "You are angry at the baby inside and wish you could be him. Perhaps you wish you could have helped me make him. You must feel that it's hopeless to tell me of this, so you show it to me by actions and noises, like a baby banging on a crib. Your words must feel very unsafe; perhaps you fear they will make me leave you." The pattern continued over the course of the week: Johnny remained quiet while I ventured such occasional, tentative interpretations of the resistance.

As I had told him, I was away for five weeks. After my return, he continued to use the corner, read books, tune me out, and withhold information in an ever more hostile, passive way, while I commented, or rather tried to guess at his experience. Johnny was getting me to do too much for him. I was colluding with his transference to me as the intrusive mother who needed the baby to gratify her by accepting her breast until the age of 2. I had to learn to stay as quiet as he, working inside myself with my reception of his projective identifications without comment. This was difficult for me, because I felt guilty about his lack of progress, but it was essential to let him be autonomous. Even so, this degree of separateness was not sufficient. I had to stop working inside myself altogether: I had to remove my investment in his speaking or producing. For therapeutic efficacy, I had to empty myself. From the depths of this therapeutic regression, he was slowly able to move forward, approaching me more and more effectively, at higher levels of development until the analysis was no longer necessary.

This vignette illustrates the use of projective and introjective identification as the work of analysis. Because the patient was not using words, there is no verbal screen to distract us from the more primitive level of communication. I think that the introjective-projective identificatory process is always operating, but we are less easily aware of it than in this case. Through projective identification with my own fetus and with Johnny, I recognized his fantasy of being inside me. Through introjective identification, I allowed myself the experience of his turning inside me. So when I spoke to him, my meaning came from inside the experience, which gave more conviction of my interpretation. He fended off the anxiety about such a wish by projecting it in the form of anger displaced on to the cushions. I interpreted this behavior as his anger at the child in the womb, because I felt an upheaval inside me. I also felt extremely tentative about saying anything at all so as not to drive him further away. This feeling resulted only partly from my effort at therapeutic tact and timing. I think that I was afraid of my words due to an introjective identification with Johnny, who thought that words drove people away. Here I was identified with his self. Then when I tried to guess more fervently at his experience, I was identified with the projected part of his object, the overzealous feeding mother. Through projective identification, Johnny had evoked this identification in me. Then I recognized it and I extricated myself from enacting that role relationship with him, by emptying myself of desire and therapeutic ambition. I let my thoughts roam and entertained myself, instead of seeking his response or confirmation. Finding gratification inside the self in this way, I think I was in a state of mutual introjective identification with Johnny, out of which we emerged, both of us the better individuated, he because he could now relate without fear of annihilation, and I because he had cured me of having to pursue, to do, and to know.

Analysis, or therapy, proceeds in a cycle of mutual regression and progression. Analyst and analysand experience each other through the processes of introjective and projective identification. These processes are the mechanics of intersubjective knowing. The patient learns and relearns the source and effects of wishes, fears, and conflicts derived from childhood experience and relationships. The characteristic enactments of early object relations are reexperienced and modified. Both patient and therapist grow and eventually unfamiliar ways of relating can be tried out. By that time, a new, more flexible set of object relations is in place in endopsychic structure. Improved relationships in the extra-analytic interpersonal dimension bear witness to the achievement of intrapsychic structural change. The intrapsychic object relations set is expressed in current interaction with significant others in the interpersonal field through the processes of introjective and projective identification now operating more consistently at the healthy end of the continuum.

References

Alexander, F. (1925). A metapsychological description of the process of cure. *International Journal of Psycho-Analysis* 6:13–34.

Alexander F., and French, T. M. (1946). The principle of corrective emotional experience. In *Psychoanalytic Therapy, Principles and Application*, p. 66–70. New York: Ronald Press.

Bannister, K., and Pincus, L. (1965). *Shared Phantasy in Marital Problems: Therapy in a Four Person Relationship*. London: Tavistock Institute of Human Relations.

Bergman, M. (1987). *The Anatomy of Loving*. New York: Columbia University Press.

—— (1990). *Love and hate in the life of a couple*. Paper presented at the Washington (DC) School of Psychiatry Conference on Romantic Love, November.

Bollas, C. (1987). *The Shadow of the Object*. New York: Columbia University Press.

———— (1989). *Forces of Destiny: Psychoanalysis and Human Idiom.* London: Free Association Books.

Bion, W. R. (1959). *Experiences in Groups.* New York: Basic Books.

———— (1962). *Learning from Experience.* New York: Basic Books.

———— (1967). *Second Thoughts.* London: Heinemann.

Box, S. (1981). Introduction: space for thinking in families. In *Psychotherapy with Families,* ed. S. Box et al. London: Routledge and Kegan Paul.

Bristol, C. (1990). *Romantic love, passionate attachments, and the greater achievements in the case of C.D.* Paper presented at the Washington (DC) School of Psychiatry Conference on Romantic Love, November.

Canetti, E. (1979). *The Tongue Set Free.* Trans. Joachim Neugroschel 1983. New York: Farrar Straus & Giroux:

Casement, P. (1991). *On Learning from the Patient.* New York: Guilford.

Crisp, P. (1986). Projective identification: an attempt at clarification. *Journal of the Melanie Klein Society* 1:47-76.

De Varela, Y. (1990). *Response to "Some pathological aspects of introjection" by I. Menzies-Lyth, 1989.* Paper presented at the Washington (DC) School of Psychiatry Object Relations Theory Training Program Conference, October.

Dicks, H. V. (1967). *Marital Tensions: Clinical Studies Towards a Psycho-analytic Theory of Interaction.* London: Routledge and Kegan Paul.

Duncan, D. (1981). A thought on the nature of psychoanalytic theory. *International Journal of Psycho-Analysis* 62:339-349.

———— (1989). The flow of interpretation. *International Journal of Psycho-Analysis* 70:693-700.

———— (1990). The feel of the session. *Psychoanalysis and Contemporary Thought* 13:3-22.

———— (1991). *What analytic therapy does.* Paper presented at the Washington (DC) School of Psychiatry Object Relations Theory Training Program Conference, May.

Engel, G. (1975). The death of a twin: fragments of 10 years of self-analysis. *International Journal of Psycho-Analysis* 56:23-40.

Fairbairn, W. R. D. (1944). Endopsychic structure considered in terms of object relationships. In *Psychoanalytic Studies of the Personality*, pp. 82–135. London: Routledge and Kegan Paul, 1952.

—— (1952). *Psychoanalytic Studies of the Personality*. London: Routledge and Kegan Paul. Also published as *An Object Relations Theory of the Personality*. New York: Basic Books, 1962.

—— (1954). Observations on the nature of hysterical states. *British Journal of Medical Psychology* 27:105–125.

—— (1958). On the nature and aims of psycho-analytical treatment. *International Journal of Psycho-Analysis* 39:374–385.

—— (1963). Synopsis of an object-relations theory of the personality. *International Journal of Psycho-Analysis* 44:224–225.

Ferenczi, S. (1909). Introjektion und Ubertragung (Introjection and transference.) In *First Contributions to Psycho-Analysis*, trans. E. Jones, pp. 35–93. New York: Brunner/Mazel, 1952.

Fleiss, R. (1942). The metapsychology of the analyst. *Psychoanalytic Quarterly* 11:211–27.

Frank, J. (1989). Who are you and what have you done with my wife? In *Foundations of Object Relations Family Therapy*, ed. J. S. Scharff, pp. 155–173. Northvale, NJ: Jason Aronson.

Freud, S. (1895). The psychotherapy of hysteria. *Standard Edition* 2:253–305.

—— (1900). The interpretation of dreams. *Standard Edition* 4:150–151.

—— (1905). Three essays on the theory of sexuality. *Standard Edition* 7:135–243.

—— (1910). The future prospects of psycho-analytic therapy. Five lectures on psychoanalysis. *Standard Edition* 11:141–151.

—— (1911). Formulations on the two principles of mental functioning. *Standard Edition* 12:213–226.

—— (1912). Recommendations to physicians practising psychoanalysis. *Standard Edition* 12:111–120.

—— (1915). Observations on transference love. *Standard Edition* 12:159–171.

—— (1917a). Mourning and melancholia. *Standard Edition* 14:243–258.

—— (1917b). Transference. *Standard Edition* 16:431–447.

—— (1921). Group psychology and the analysis of the ego. *Standard Edition* 18:67–143.

—— (1924). The dissolution of the oedipus complex. *Standard Edition* 19:173–179.

—— (1933). New introductory lectures on psycho-analysis. *Standard Edition* 22:3–182.

Gallup, D. (1985). *The Journals of Thornton Wilder* 1939–1961. New Haven: Yale University Press.

Geddiman, H. (1990). *Love and fatal attraction*. Paper presented at the Washington (DC) School of Psychiatry Conference on Romantic Love, November.

Gitelson, M. (1952). The emotional position of the analyst in the psycho-analytic situation. *International Journal of Psycho-Analysis* 33:1–10.

Glenn, J. (1966). Opposite-sex twins. *Journal of the American Psychoanalytic Association* 14:736–759.

—— (1986). Twinship themes and fantasies in the work of Thornton Wilder. *Psychoanalytic Study of the Child* 41:627–651. New Haven, CT: Yale University Press.

Goldstein, W. N. (1991). Clarification of projective identification. *American Journal of Psychiatry* 148:153–161.

Greenson, R. (1967). *The Technique and Practice of Psychoanalysis*. Vol. 1. New York: International Universities Press.

Grotstein, J. (1982). *Splitting and Projective Identification*. New York: Jason Aronson.

Guntrip, H. (1961). *Personality Structure and Human Interaction: The Developing Synthesis of Psychodynamic Theory*. London: Hogarth Press and the Institute of Psycho-Analysis.

—— (1969). *Schizoid Phenomena. Object Relations and the Self*. New York: International Universities Press.

—— (1986). My experience of analysis with Fairbairn and Winnicott. In *Essential Papers on Object Relations*, ed. P. Buckley, pp. 447–468. New York: New York University Press.

Harrison, G. (1983). *The Enthusiast. A Life of Thornton Wilder*. New York: Ticknor and Fields.

Hazell, J. (1991). Reflections on my experience of psychoanalysis with Guntrip. *Contemporary Psychoanalysis* 27:148–166. New York: William Alanson White Institute.

Heimann, P. (1950). On counter-transference. *International Journal of Psycho-Analysis* 31:81–84.

—— (1954). Problems of the training analysis. *International Journal of Psycho-Analysis* 35:163–168.

—— (1973). Certain functions of introjection and projection in early infancy. In *Developments in Psycho-Analysis*, ed. M. Klein, P. Heimann, S. Isaacs, and J. Riviere, pp. 122–168. London: Hogarth Press and the Institute of Psycho-Analysis.

Hendrix, H. (1991). *Getting the Love You Want*. New York: Harper & Row.

Hinshelwood, R. D. (1991). *A Dictionary of Kleinian Thought*. Northvale, NJ: Jason Aronson.

Jacobs, T. J. (1991). *The Use of the Self*. Madison, CT: International Universities Press.

Jaffe, D. S. (1968). The mechanism of projection: its dual role in object relations. *International Journal of Psycho-Analysis* 49:662–677.

James, H. (1881). *The Portrait of a Lady*. Oxford: Oxford University Press, 1988.

Kernberg, O. F. (1975). *Borderline Conditions and Pathological Narcissism*. New York: Jason Aronson.

—— (1987). Projection and projective identification: developmental and clinical aspects. In *Projection, Identification, Projective Identification*, ed. J. Sandler, pp. 93–115. Madison, CT: International Universities Press.

—— (1991). Aggression and love in the relationship of the couple. *Journal of the American Psychoanalytic Association* 39:45–70.

Klein, M. (1946). Notes on some schizoid mechanisms. *International Journal of Psycho-Analysis* 27:99–100.

—— (1952). Some theoretical conclusions regarding the emotional life of the infant. In *Envy and Gratitude and other Works, 1946–1963*, pp. 61–93. London: Hogarth Press and the Institute of Psycho-Analysis, 1975.

—— (1955). On identification. In *Envy and Gratitude and Other Works 1946–1963*, pp. 141–175. London: Hogarth Press and the Institute of Psycho-Analysis, 1975.

Knight, R. (1940). Introjection, projection and identification. *Psychoanalytic Quarterly* 9:334–341.

Kohut H. (1971). *The Analysis of the Self*. New York: International Universities Press.

—— (1977). *The Restoration of the Self*. New York: International Universities Press.

—— (1982). Introspection, empathy, and the semi-circle of mental health. *International Journal of Psycho-Analysis* 63:395–407.

Lachkar, J. (1989). *The Narcissistic-Borderline Couple*. New York: Brunner/Mazel.

LaLande, A. (1951). *Vocabulaire Technique et Critique de la Philosophie*. Paris: Presses Universitaires de France.

Laplanche, J., and Pontalis, J. B. (1973). *The Language of Psychoanalysis*. New York: Norton.

Little, M. (1951). Counter-transference and the patient's response to it. *International Journal of Psycho-Analysis* 32:32–39.

Loewald, H. W. (1960). On the therapeutic action of psychoanalysis. *International Journal of Psycho-Analysis* 41:16–33.

Lowenstein, J. (1982). Paper presented at Baer-Lowenstein family reunion. Bethesda, MD, June.

Malin, A., and Grotstein, J. (1966). Projective identification in the therapeutic process. *International Journal of Psycho-Analysis* 47:26–31.

Meissner, W. W. (1980). A note on projective identification. *Journal of the American Psychoanalytic Association* 28:43–67.

—— (1987). Projection and projective identification. In *Projection, Identification, Projective Identification*, ed. J. Sandler, pp. 27–49. Madison, CT: International Universities Press.

Meltzer, D. (1966). The relation of anal masturbation to projective identification. *International Journal of Psycho-Analysis* 47:335–342.

—— (1978). A note on introjective processes. In the *Bulletin of the British Psycho-Analytical Society*, 14–21 October (privately circulated).

Menzies-Lyth, I. (1983). *Some pathological aspects of introjection.* Unpublished paper read at the 9th Brazilian Psychoanalytic Congress 1983 and at the Washington (DC) School of Psychiatry Object Relations Theory Training Program Conference, October 1990.
—— (1985). The development of the self in children in institutions. In *Containing Anxiety in Institutions: Selected Essays,* vol. 1, pp. 236–258. London: Free Association Books.
Money-Kyrle, R. (1956). Normal counter-transference and some of its deviations. *International Journal of Psycho-Analysis* 37: 360–366.
Moreno, J. L. (1946). *Psychodrama.* Vol. 1. New York: Beacon House.
Moses, R. (1987). Projection, identification and projective identification: their relation to political process. In *Projection, Identification, Projective Identification,* ed. J. Sandler, pp. 133–150. Madison, CT: International Universities Press.
Moses, R., and Halevi, H. (1972). *A facet analysis of the defense mechanism of projection.* Unpublished manuscript.
Murray, J. M. (1955). *Keats,* p. 261. New York: Noonday Press.
Natterson, J. (1991). *Beyond Countertransference.* Northvale, NJ: Jason Aronson.
Ogden, T. H. (1982). *Projective Identification and Psychotherapeutic Technique.* New York: Jason Aronson.
—— (1986). *The Matrix of the Mind.* Northvale NJ: Jason Aronson.
—— (1989). *The Primitive Edge of Experience.* Northvale, NJ: Jason Aronson.
Oppel, H. (1977). *Thornton Wilder in Deutschland. Wirkung und Wertung im deutschen Sprachraum.* Akademie der Wissenschaft und der Literatur: Abhandlungen der Klasse d. Literatur, Jahrgang 1976/77, Nr. 3. Mainz/Wiesbaden.
Pamuk, O. (1991). *The White Castle.* Trans. V. Holbrook. New York: Braziller.
Parini, J. (1991). Pirates, pashas and the imperial astrologer. Book review of *The White Castle,* by O. Pamuk. *New York Times Book Review,* May 19th.
Person, E. S. (1988). *Dreams of Love and Fateful Encounters.* New York: Norton.

———— (1990). *Romantic love and the cultural unconscious.* Paper presented at the Washington (DC) School of Psychiatry Conference on Romantic Love, November.

Pickvance, R. (1986). *Van Gogh in Saint-Remy and Auvers.* Publ. Harry N. Abrams. New York: Metropolitan Museum of Art.

Pirandello, L. (1922). *Six Characters in Search of an Author.* In *Naked Masks: Five Plays,* ed. E. Bentley. New York: Dutton (1952).

Racker, H. (1968). *Transference and Countertransference.* New York: International Universities Press.

Ravenscroft, K. (1991). *Changes in projective identification during treatment.* Paper presented at the Washington School of Psychiatry Object Relations Couple and Family Therapy Training Program Conference, Bethesda, MD, March.

Rice, A. K. (1965). *Learning for Leadership.* London: Tavistock.

Rioch, M. (1970). The work of Wilfred Bion on groups. *Psychiatry* 3:56–65.

Sandler, J. (1960). On the concept of the superego. *The Psychoanalytic Study of the Child* 15:128–162. New York: International Universities Press.

———— (1976). Actualization and object relationships. *Journal of the Philadelphia Association for Psychoanalysis* 3:59–70.

———— (1987). *Projection, Identification and Projective Identification.* Madison, CT: International Universities Press.

Sandler, J., Dare, C., and Holder, A. (1973). *The Patient and the Analyst.* New York: International Univesities Press.

Sandler, J., and Joffe, W. G. (1967). The tendency to persistence in psychological function and development, with special reference to fixation and regression. *Bulletin of the Menninger Clinic* 31:257–271.

Savege, J. (1971). Drama in relation to mental health. Fellowship thesis, Trinity College, London.

———— (1973). Psychodynamic understanding in community psychiatry. Proceedings of the Ninth International Congress of Psychotherapy, Oslo. Reprinted in *Psychotherapy and Psychosomatics* 25:272–278.

———— (1974a). *Thomaston School pupils group,* doc. CASR 1031. London: Tavistock Institute of Human Relations.

—— (1974b). Tutors' pastoral care consultation group at Thomaston School, doc. CASR 1031. London: Tavistock Institute of Human Relations.

—— (1975). The role and training of the creative therapist. In *Creative Therapy*, ed. S. Jennings, pp. 191–227. London: Pitman.

Scarf, M. (1987). *Intimate Partners*. New York: Random House.

Schafer, R. (1990). *Reading Freud's legacies*. Unpublished paper presented at the 14th annual Edith Weigert lecture, Forum on Psychiatry and the Humanities of the Washington (DC) School of Psychiatry, October.

Scharff, D. E. (1975). The transition from school to work: groups in London high schools. In *When Schools Care*, ed. I. Berkowitz, pp. 323–339. New York: Brunner/Mazel.

—— (1982). *The Sexual Relationship: An Object Relations View of Sex and the Family*. London: Routledge and Kegan Paul.

Scharff, D. E., and Hill, J. M. (1976). *Between Two Worlds: Aspects of the Transition from School to Work*. London: Careers Consultant Publications.

Scharff, D. E., and Scharff, J. S. (1979). Teaching and learning. An experiential conference. *Journal of Personality and Social Systems* 2:53–78.

—— (1987). *Object Relations Family Therapy*. Northvale, NJ: Jason Aronson.

—— (1991). *Object Relations Couple Therapy*. Northvale, NJ: Jason Aronson.

Scharff, J. S., ed. (1989). *Foundations of Object Relations Family Therapy*. Northvale, NJ: Jason Aronson.

Searles, H. (1965). *Collected Papers on Schizophrenia and Related Subjects*. New York: International Universities Press.

—— (1979). *Countertransference and Related Subjects—Selected Subjects*. New York: International Universities Press.

—— (1986). *My Work with Borderline Patients*. Northvale, NJ: Jason Aronson.

Segal, H. (1964). *Introduction to the Work of Melanie Klein*. London: Heinemann.

—— (1981). *The Work of Hanna Segal*. New York: Jason Aronson.

—— (1990). *Melanie Klein then and now*. A discussion at the Washington (DC) School of Psychiatry Object Relations Theory Training Program Conference, May.

Shakespeare, W. (1596). (*The Merchant of Venice*. New Haven, CT: Yale University Press, 1928.

—— *Twelfth Night*. (1598). New Haven, CT: Yale University Press, 1922.

Spillius, E. (1991). Clinical experiences of projective identification. In *Clinical Lectures on Klein and Bion*, ed. R. Anderson. Number 14 in New Library of Psychoanalysis. London: Routledge and Kegan Paul.

Steiner, J. (1989). *Projective identification and the aims of psychoanalytic psychotherapy*. Paper presented at the Washington (DC) School of Psychiatry object relations theory training program conference, November.

Stierlin, H. (1977). *Psychoanalysis and Family Therapy*. New York: Jason Aronson.

Stolorow, R. D., Brandchaft, B., and Atwood, G. (1983). Intersubjectivity in psychoanalytic treatment. *Bulletin of the Menninger Clinic* 47:117–128.

Stone, L. (1961). *The Psychoanalytic Situation*. New York: International Universities Press.

Strachey, J. (1934). The nature of the therapeutic action of psychoanalysis, *International Journal of Psycho-Analysis* 15:127–159.

—— (1958). Editor's introduction to papers on technique. In *Standard Edition of the Complete Psychological Works of Sigmund Freud*, ed. J. Strachey, vol. 12, pp. 85–88. London: Hogarth Press.

Sutherland, J. (1963). Object relations theory and the conceptual model of psychoanalysis. *British Journal of Medical Psychology* 36:109–124.

—— (1980). The British object relations theorists: Balint, Winnicott, Fairbairn, Guntrip. *Journal of the American Psychoanalytic Association* 28:829–860.

—— (1989). *Fairbairn's Journey into the Interior*. London: Free Association Books.

—— (1990). *The object relations approach*. Paper presented at the Washington (DC) School of Psychiatry Object Relations Theory Training Program Conference, April.

Tansey, M., and Burke, W. (1989). *Understanding Countertransference from Projective Identification to Empathy*. Hillsdale, NJ: The Analytic Press.

Tarnopolsky, A. (1987). Discussion of Otto F. Kernberg's paper. In *Projection, Identification, Projective Identification*, ed. J. Sandler, pp. 126–127. Madison, CT: International Universities Press.

Tower, L. (1956). Countertransference. *Journal of the American Psychoanalytic Association* 4:224–255.

Tustin, F. (1981). *Autistic States in Children*. Boston: Routledge and Kegan Paul.

van Gogh, V. (1978). *The Complete Letters of Vincent van Gogh*. 3 vols. Introduction by V. W. van Gogh. Preface and Memoir by J. van Gogh-Bonger. Vol. 3. New York: Little, Brown.

Volkan, V. (1976). *Primitive Internalized Object Relations*. New York: International Universities Press.

Welles, J. K., and Wrye, H. K. (1991). The maternal erotic countertransference. *International Journal of Psycho-Analysis* 72:93–106.

Wells, G. P., ed. (1984). *H. G. Wells in Love: Postscript to an Experiment in Autobiography*. Boston: Little, Brown.

Wilder, A. N. (1980). *Thornton Wilder and His Public*. Philadelphia: Fortress Press.

Wilder, T. N. (1927). *The Bridge of San Luis Rey*. New York: Perennial Library (1986).

—— (1960). *Our Town*. New York: Harper.

—— (1973). *Theophilus North*. New York: Harper & Row.

Williams, A. H. (1981). The micro-environment. In *Psychotherapy with Families*, ed. S. Box, D. Copley, J. Magagna, and E. Moustaki, pp. 105–119. London: Routledge and Kegan Paul.

Winer, R. (1989). The role of transitional experience in development in healthy and incestuous families. In *Foundations of Object Relations Family Therapy*, ed. J. S. Scharff, pp. 357–384. Northvale, NJ: Jason Aronson.

Winnicott, D. W. (1951). Transitional objects and transitional phenomena. In *Collected Papers: Through Paediatrics to Psycho-Analysis*, pp. 229–242. London: Hogarth Press, 1975.

———— (1956). Primary maternal preoccupation. In *The Maturational Processes and the Facilitating Environment*, pp. 300–305. London: Hogarth Press, 1965.

———— (1958). *Collected Papers: Through Paediatrics to Psycho-Analysis*. London: Hogarth Press, 1975.

———— (1965). *The Maturational Processes and the Facilitating Environment*. London: Hogarth Press.

———— (1971). *Playing and Reality*. London: Tavistock.

Zinner, J. (1976). The implications of projective identification for marital interaction. In *Contemporary Marriage: Structure, Dynamics, and Therapy*, ed. H. Grunebaum and J. Christ, pp. 293–308. Boston: Little, Brown.

———— (1989). *The developmental spectrum of projective identification*. Paper presented at Washington (DC) School of Psychiatry Object Relations Family Therapy Conference, Bethesda, MD, March.

Zinner, J., and Shapiro, R. (1972). Projective identification as a mode of perception and behavior in families of adolescents. *International Journal of Psycho-Analysis* 53:523–530.

Index

internalization and, 81–83
introjective identification and, 87
meanings of, 57
Meltzer on, 50
Menzies-Lyth on, 50
mourning and melancholia and,
284
neurotic process as, 53
object relations theory and, 55
oral impulses and, 53
oral pleasure and, 284
origin of term, 53
projection and, 51, 53–54, 286
psychic organization and, 56
Sandler on, 57
Scharff, D. and Scharff, J. on,
57–58
Segal on, 76
splitting and, 73
superego and, 289
superego development and, 55–
59
therapeutic action and, 286
thought process creation and, 75
transposition of objects and, 82
Introjective identification
anal masturbation and, 70–72
arts in, 183–215
community in, 170–174
complementary, 91
concept of, 49–83
concordant, 91
confusion regarding, 85–86
defensive aspects of, 72–73
ego development and, 56
family in, 99–132
groups and, 161–182
Hinshelwood on, 50–51
ideal object and, 59–64
identification and, 87, 90

indiscriminate, 59
the internal couple and, 133–
157
introjection and, 87
Klein on, xiv, 288
lost part of self and, 302
love and, 133–157
media in, 183–215
mutual, 303–310
object relations theories and,
85–86
partnership in, 92–95
pathological view of, 73
projective communities and,
161–182
re-entry of projections and, 64–
72
renunciation and, 63–64
self-psychology theories and, 86
steps characterizing, 87–89
types of, by object, 90–91
valency and, 91
Introjective mechanisms, 51
Introjective processes, therapeutic
action and, 284–314

Jacobs, T., 222, 227–228
Jaffe, D., 23
James, H., 184
Joffe, W., 31

Keats, J., on negative capability,
249
Kernberg, O.
on countertransference, 33
on defense, 32
on emotional intimacy,
projective identification
and, 136–137
on love, 136